TO MOTHER MARKET
whose rewards when we are right,
stern responses when we are careless,
and fickle changes of direction,
have kept daily life fascinating and challenging.

WHEN TO SELL
for the '90s

Inside Strategies for Stock-Market Profits

JUSTIN MAMIS

FRASER PUBLISHING COMPANY
BURLINGTON, VERMONT

Published by Fraser Publishing Company
          a division of Fraser Management Associates, Inc.
          P.O. Box 494
          Burlington, VT 05402

ISBN: 0-87034-116-2

Library of Congress Cataloging in Publication Data
Mamis, Justin, 1929
   When to sell for the '90s: inside strategies for stock market profits.—
updated and rev. / by Justin Mamis.
      p.   cm.
   "From the original When to sell by Justin and Robert Mamis."
   ISBN 0-87034-116-2
   1. Stocks. 2. Speculation. 3. Investments.   I. Mamis, Justin, 1929—
When to sell.   II. Title.
HG6041.M34 1994
332.6'45--dc20   94—22970
                                              CIP

   Acknowledgment is made to the following publishers for their kind permission to reprint their charts once again: Bank Credit Analyst-Monetary Research Limited; Indicator Digest; The Professional Tape Reader; Standard and Poor's Corporation; Securities Research Company; M.C. Horsey & Co.; Daily Graphs (P.O. Box 66919, Los Angeles, California 90066); and R.W. Mansfield Company (2973 Kennedy Blvd., Jersey City, New Jersey 07306).
   We also want to thank Helene Meisler for her help and encouragement, and Al Yee and Kara Kavanagh at Hancock Institutional Equities Service (a joint venture of Tucker Anthony and Sutro) who have helped make this revised edition possible.

Designed and Produced by PostScript, Inc.

Printed in the United States of America

Table of Contents

Foreword

*T*here've been so many changes in the marketplace since the first edition of "When To Sell"—futures, options, computerized program trading and fancy new indicators as well as the demise of old favorites—that the time seemed opportune to revise and rewrite. What was astonishing to me was not how much there was to change, but how very much remains sound stuff. I didn't think I knew so much back then...but what it really means is that there are some "eternal verities" about how the stock market works—and what to do about it, and when.

You'll notice that many of the companies whose charts are discussed have disappeared. I contemplated replacing them with similar, more current, examples. But "a chart's a chart." The discussion is what's pertinent, not the name attached to the market action, so I've reproduced them from the first edition, while adding to the text where something additionally useful was worth pointing out.

In addition to a complete revamping and re-discussion of the major changes in indicators, readers familiar with the original text will find fresh observations based on further experience during entirely different kinds of markets—different, that is, in their details, but similar in their consistent rhythms. Some of these insights are tucked away in odd paragraphs, parenthetical comments, and added analysis that will help in your battle about "When To Sell."

Lastly, for the sake of getting this edition rewritten within a limited time span, much of the prior language has been left untouched—it was simply easier and faster to pound away at the keyboard until something became necessary to change or to add.

This includes the carry-over use of the so-called masculine instead of the more suitable, but awkward, "his or her." In the "old" old days, Wall Street was a male preserve; women have brought to it a fresh approach (successful but burnt-out male salesmen are an industry-wide employment problem), particularly by not being burdened with the macho sports upbringing of a need to win. The conviction that "the game is never over till the last out" prevents many a sensible sale from being made. Winning and losing goes on all the time; that's why it's important to learn "When To Sell."

Chapter One

The Neurotic Investor

*D*ozens of books have been published on how to buy stocks. Perhaps the reason there are so few on the subject of how to sell them—deciding whether, when, and at what price—is that selling techniques are far more complicated, and subject to considerably more emotional pressure, than those of buying.

If you simply throw darts at the stock tables, you can hit any one of the thousands of stocks listed on the exchanges or traded over-the-counter, phone your broker, and tell him to buy it. Should you hesitate for some reason or other, and miss the opportunity, you've lost nothing; your cash, your purchasing power, is still available until another choice appears. To take the same approach to selling is obviously absurd. The situation is no longer casual or random; hesitation can cost. The rest of the 4,990 or so stocks that the dart missed now are not your concern: for better or worse, you're obliged to confront exclusively and continually the stocks you own.

This problem wouldn't be too severe if you could merely turn the buying process upside down and operate on the simple basis that whatever influenced you to spend your money in the first place will, in reverse, indicate the time and price at which to cash in your stock. That, unfortunately, is a quick way to losses. The law of opposites may be a plausible scientific concept, but stock market analysis is only a pseudo-science, dressed in the trappings of rationality while operating under rules which are consistent only in their perversity. Although the chart pattern of a top when turned around and upside down may resemble a bottom pattern, quite different influences are at work both in the marketplace and in your mind. Different decisions about whether to sell and when to sell are required.

Indeed, if the techniques of selling were but the mirror images of buying, one would expect that at least the "professional" managers, who are paid huge sums to buy and sell for mutual funds, pension funds, bank trust departments, and the like, would have learned by now how to execute sales with skill and dispatch. But this is not the case, as the only widely available statistics from this sector (on mutual fund activities, to be discussed in detail later) consistently prove. One erstwhile hot-shot manager of a supposedly venturesome mutual fund admitted that his firm had chalked up substantial paper profits in the wildly speculative period prior to the 1969-70 bear market, but that "we weren't aggressive enough in selling and lost perhaps 90 percent (!) of the gains we had accumulated." Obviously, he was venturesome only on the buy side but didn't know when—or how—to sell. Indeed, he didn't even learn his lesson; after recouping some of those losses during the next bull phase, and vowing not to make the same mistakes again, he made different ones as the 1973-74 bear market unfolded, and sadly acknowledged later that he'd not only lost those profits but some of the underlying capital as well.

By dint of their allegedly superior knowledge and skills, their access to huge funds which enable them to diversify more broadly than the public investor, plus their advantage of getting first call on brokerage firm analysis and research (and being able to be more objective, too, because it isn't their money at stake), money managers ought to do better than the market even in adverse times. Indeed, some do; but many don't. If 1974 was a bad year for the market, it was an abysmal year for mutual funds. Whereas one out of every eight listed stocks was able to close out the year with a gain, only one out of every fifty mutual funds had a positive record. These statistics suggest that at the outset of 1974 you'd have had six times better odds using a dart than entrusting your money to a professional fund manager.

Having subsequently spent over a decade talking directly with such portfolio managers, we know it is not that simple, but we remain convinced that even the experienced and reputable have trouble when it comes to selling. Had the mutual funds, non-profit foundations, college-endowment funds, and other similar institutions known how to sell properly during that great bear market, *and* had they been *willing* to sell (which is the harder, emotional, part), they would have cut their losses early in the decline and held a substantial amount of cash in reserve for a later buying opportunity. Instead, despite full-time concentration, Harvard Business School degrees, Brooks Brothers suits, and carpets on the floor, they rode the devastating 1973-74 bear market down with virtually fully invested positions. How do highly paid professionals succeed in chalking up a record little better than the most amateurish man in the street? The inability to sell when one should, often when one "knows" one should, repeated time and again by amateur and Wall Streeter alike, has all the earmarks of neurotic behavior.

Selling: The Irrational Fear

Stocks are bought not in fear but in hope. No matter what the stock did in the past, it assumes a new life once a purchaser owns it, and he looks forward to a rosy future—after all, that's why he singled it out in the first place. But these simple expectations become complicated by what actually happens. The stock acquires a new past, beginning from the moment of purchase, and with that past come new doubts, new concerns, new conflicts. The purchaser's stock portfolio quickly becomes a portfolio of psychic dilemmas, with ego, id, superego, and reality in a state of constant battle...especially since, in the stock market, one is never quite sure what the reality is.

Consider these nagging questions: If the stock has gone up, will it go up more? or is this the time to sell? Or, if it has gone down, will it slide some more or turn around and go up at last? probably the minute after it is sold. Should I take a small loss now? Could I swallow such a huge loss or should I at least wait for a rebound?

Now that it is finally rebounding, should I hold until I'm even? Now that I'm even, shouldn't I reward my (albeit forced) patience by aiming for a gain? The decision *not* to sell maintains hope, thereby preserving a future. Indeed, the thought of selling a stock and thus abruptly ending the dream is so paralyzing that for every conceivable market situation there are ready-made excuses for holding on at least a little while longer. And these excuses invariably are based on the desire to believe that the future will be better than the present. Any excuse, however, absurd, becomes convenient as long as it postpones the necessity to act. Those in unhappy marriages will understand *that*.

You've probably seen brokerage-house reports that admit "the next few quarters are going to be lower" or "the stock could sell off further over the short term"—appraisals which give absolutely no selling advice in conclusion. Instead, hope is held out for the more distant future—"we are reiterating our long-term buy recommendation"—when these real troubles will be past and everything will be glorious. (How they can be so sure that far out in time, when they couldn't even predict the current trouble is a form of *chutzpa*) But while the advisor is daydreaming of a better tomorrow, the firm's margin clerk remains unconvinced. All he knows is that the customer's paper loss in following that advice is real enough right now to require more cash in the account. And to show how irrational this "it's only a paper loss until I sell" excuse is, the person getting such a margin call will actually shovel out more of his own money, just to prove to the margin clerk that it *is* only a paper loss, that he, and his dream, are still alive. This neurotic optimism is, unfortunately, abetted by the typical financial consultant (customer's man was the more accurate "title" in the first edition) at the brokerage house who also tends to reject the reality of today for the vague promise of tomorrow. "Let's give it another day" is the last sentence of many a phone conversation when neither customer (whose money is at stake) nor broker (whose ego is equally exposed) can bring himself to admit that the stock in question had better be sold right then and there.

After our earlier description of the selling decision as a "battle," it is not surprising to find a real battleground psychologically described in the same terms. Just transpose these words about Vietnam to the Wall Street arena: "The overwhelming desire for the success of policies to which a strong emotional attachment has been made also leads to an attempt to alter those facts over which one has control, making them consistent with the outcome that is desired. It is as though there is an expectation at a magical level that events over which one has no control will then also fall into the desired pattern." (From *Men, Stress, and Vietnam*, by Peter Bourne) In short, there's also a light at the end of the stock-market tunnel; we'll win in the future, so long as we don't have to recognize that something negative is happening right now. And even if we *do* recognize it, we remain convinced that it won't last. We develop a magical expectation for the future, rather than utilizing something over which we *do* have control: in the stock market, we control by our ability to sell.

How Do I Know When to Sell?

*I*s it even possible to know when to sell? Is there some way to separate hopes from real possibilities? It would be nice if there were an easy answer, a ready-made system to spell out. Sometimes you see something advertised that claims to have the perfect answer—but don't believe it; there isn't any. All those "how-to" books on buying stocks conveniently leave out the details of how to sell, unless it's something banal like "Oh, you sell when the stock has finally stopped doubling, and then you find another supergrowth stock to switch to." Chances are your broker skirts the question, too; neither he nor his firm's market literature advises you when to sell, though both will willingly hound you with buying enticements. That's because there are few moments that cry out for selling, and no simple way to lick the emotions that hinder cutting the cord. When the stock eases slightly below your purchase price, the situation is charged with doubt. Perhaps you *were* wrong, and should accept that small loss. But, then again, maybe it's just a temporary fluctuation: you bought a trifle too soon or a mite too high. And isn't the market due for a rally tomorrow? And how about the earnings report to be announced shortly? Or that exciting new product which was the reason you bought the stock in the first place? Such factors should be considered, but not to an unreasonable extent just because the investor won't admit he's made a mistake. Comforting one's self with "nice" thoughts is no substitute for confronting reality.

Take the common plight of the recent purchaser who declines the chance to settle for a small loss because it would be too quick an admission of failure. In the scale of things, losing a few hundred bucks isn't nearly the serious defeat that his churning emotions make it out to be. The purchaser, though, would rather hold, nurturing the hope that the stock will come back shortly. But it keeps going down, and before he knows it, the whole list is joining in the decline. As the price sags considerably lower, he shields himself with ignorance: he stops looking at the closing prices in the newspaper; he stops phoning his broker every day. Weeks later, as the crashing prices make the headlines and become the featured news on television, with anchors adding their own emotional tone and experts forecasting even more dire developments, hope finally goes down the drain. So, along with thousands of other panic-stricken investors, our investor dumps his shares into the abyss, and at last releases himself from his torture. He's taken a much bigger loss, but at least he's out!

This is the way major bottoms are often fashioned, leaving these bewildered investors in the lurch as prices turn around and shoot upward through a virtual vacuum—everyone who has wanted to sell has, by then, panicked out. With newspapers full of bleak headlines, who would be fool enough to buy stocks at this juncture? Yet someone obviously is, for the ticker tape shows prices bouncing sharply back upward. The buyer is certainly not our investor, who has desperately tried to hold and then finally given up in despair, for he has sworn off the market forever. Nor are the buyers the many other investors who were weeded out along the way down, or those who, with the tenacious courage of Beau Geste, defended their honor throughout and are still holding at substantial paper losses. On the contrary, these tattered individuals quickly toss their shares into the pot as soon as the rally manifests itself, believing it to be just another bear-market rebound designed to fail; if they get out without a loss, after the pain they've been through, they're delighted, and harbor no thoughts of buying even as they watch their stocks zoom on upward without them. So who has bought? there is a Wall Street truism of "stocks moving from weak to strong hands" which characterizes important bottoms: exchange specialists (who are required to buy anyway, according to the exchange rules, whenever there are no other buyers), and unemotional professional traders (who sense a change in trend brewing)—and those fortunate few who, having correctly sold long ago, are both emotionally and financially prepared to join those trading pros but with a longer-term (more value-oriented) view in mind.

A serious variation of this vicious cycle is recognizable through each bear market and back up through the next bull. During the rally, as the climate ostensibly improves, the public player (and even an all-too-human portfolio manager), vowing not to repeat his old mistake of selling too late, makes a new one: he sells too soon—as soon as he sees the slightest sign of struggling—because he doesn't believe the rally will continue. When it does persist, he makes amends for that 'selling-too-soon' mistake by making a different one: deciding that stocks will come back after a dip, he won't sell at all during the next phase. And thus he finds himself still holding at the top when that next dip proves to be the first decline in a brand-new bear cycle.

A Professional View

One explanation for why investors make certain mistakes at particular points in the trading cycle was supplied by a professional member-trader whom we'll call Charlie Fisk. "The public is most comfortable," Charlie said, "when they are sitting with losses." This is a judgment born of a dozen years as a customer's man dealing every day with amateur market players, followed by purchase of his own exchange seat. Now he trades for his own, and his firm's account, from a tiny office diagonally across the street from the exchange, with a day's collection of coffee containers on the desk near his only tool—the telephone that links him with the order clerk on the floor. It might be said, as the SEC once tried to insist, that Charlie is a typical member of the "they" club, "they" being that mythical body of money men the public suspects are always on the inside. "They" make a stock go up when "they" want to; "they" can always take it back down before the public gets a chance to get out...or so it seems. Before the SEC compelled the exchange to impose stricter trading rules, Charlie spent his day on the exchange floor and, while there, was a professional's professional, a man whom less nimble traders followed around to see what he was doing. So Charlie knows the market, the people who compose it, and how the game is played.

He has just conveyed to the floor a market order to buy 2,000 shares of Reading & Bates (which, when we first wrote this book, was a big-time stock). As he talks, he stares overhead at the ticker tape, which has the very same symbols and numbers flashing by that the public and its brokers also watch at the same time. Yet the end results are quite different, since Charlie Fisk makes a lot of money whether the market goes up or down. "Why is the public comfortable with losses?" he reflects, not bothering to relight the cigar jammed in the corner of his mouth; he is literally on the edge of his seat, watching. "Because if their stocks are down from where they bought them, they don't have to worry about selling them. Once he's got a loss, the typical investor is *sure* he isn't going to sell. He bears the lower price because in his mind it is temporary, even ridiculous; it'll eventually go away if he doesn't worry about it. So selling at a loss becomes absolutely out of the question. And since it is out of the question, and his mind is made up for him, the struggle of any potential decision vanishes and he's able to sit comfortably with the loss."

The phone rings as the floor broker reports the details of the RB purchase: 2,000 bought at 30 1/2. By then, of course, Charlie had already surmised which tick on the tape represented his order and had *begun to concentrate on timing his sale from the moment the stock was bought.* The smaller the degree of gain he's after—a point, even half a point—and the briefer the time span, the more significance each tick on the tape assumes. "Get me a fresh size," he snaps back into the mouthpiece. The specialist is obliged to give the size to anyone when asked—information about how many shares are bid for at the current best bid and how many shares are being offered at the lowest asked price, and this information has over the past decade become readily available via desktop machines in front of virtually every broker.

By then we ourselves can see RB repeatedly printing at 30 7/8 on the tape overhead. Charlie is concerned; he wants to see a trade at 31, the next round number, to keep the stock's upward momentum going, and it isn't appearing. "I worry about every tick," he mutters. "Don't like that one..." as 100 shares prints at 30 3/4. But it is followed by 400 more back at 30 7/8. "Isn't that okay?" we ask. The floor broker phones back with the exact size at the specialist's post; Charlie scribbles on his pad as he repeats: "Three by two, a half, seven eighths," meaning that the specialist has bids for 300 shares at 30 1/2 and is offering 200 shares at 30 7/8, even after we'd seen over 1,000 already traded at that price. Charlie scowls at the tape for a moment, then abruptly seizes the phone again: "Get me out." Then silent, brooding, he watches the tape until he spots 300 shares of RB printing at 30 1/2, followed by 1,700 more at 30 3/8.

"So I took a little loss." He shrugs. But why did he sell at that exact moment? "My business is trading for fast turns. All of a sudden the stock symbol stopped appearing on the tape and to me that said RB was having trouble eating up the stock offered at 30 7/8, let alone being able to get through 31. To me, a stock that can't go up must go down and I don't want to sit around holding it while it does. It could get rolling again this afternoon, but that's a different game."

The public, we remind him, is unable to go in and out on fractions of a point; they've got substantial commissions to pay on every such transaction. "Yes," he replies, "but the principle is the same: sell when the selling is a sound idea, when the stock no longer does what it is supposed to do. My expectations happen to have close tolerances. I take those 1/8 losses and half-point profits because that's my business. But to the public mind, selling is *never* sound. It always conveys the possibility of being wrong twice: first, admitting that they've made a buying error; second, admitting that they might be wrong in selling out. And if the stock has actually gone up, they're tormented: should they take the profit or hold for a bigger one? That creates anxiety, and anxiety breeds mistakes. But as long as they've got losses, and never have to decide, they can sit back comfortably and dream instead."

Public Misconceptions

Compare that discussion with a dialogue overheard one day while waiting for a tennis court in New York's Central Park. A couple seated on the next bench was reading the Sunday *Times* when suddenly the man looked up from the financial section. "Say, honey, remember the Jackson-Atlantic I bought at 14, and then it fell to 7?"

"Oh my God," she exclaimed, "you never told me that!"

"Well, I didn't want to worry you. No need to get upset; it's back up to 14 again, and made the 'most active' list this week."

"Great," his wife said, "now you can sell it and get our money back."

The man looked at her incredulously. "Sell it! Now that it's going up? I waited a whole year for this."

Whether the stock ought to have been sold or not sold at that point is a matter for discussion later in this book; certainly the facts that it then matched the original purchase price and that a year had elapsed should not have been relevant factors. Note that (1) having endured the loss willingly, he'd never even thought about selling until his wife raised the possibility; (2) he obviously expected her to be proud of him for having successfully stuck it out for a year; and (3) he now felt that he was being challenged to prove that he knew what to do about stocks.

He had willingly tolerated a 50 percent loss in his position on the grounds that "stocks always come back." Yet the manner in which they do, or the length of time it takes, to say nothing of the possibility that they never will come back *enough,* ought to be taken into account. The ranks of once-spectacular star performers that have never come back are legion. Total demise hit such popular darlings as National Video and Four Seasons. Memorex fell, in the course of three years in the early 1970s, from a high of 160 to delisting (and doubled twice while doing so, just to keep hopes alive), although it did survive as a company. And to these examples we can now add not only Wang but even, as a stock that'll be hard pressed to ever come back to the price levels many people paid: IBM itself. It took thirty years for the public's pet, American Telephone, to get back up from its depression low past its 1929 high. Nor does a company necessarily have to go bankrupt before being thought of as down for the count; if it was bought at 70, and now trades between 5 and 6, it requires a lot of blind faith to believe it should be held because "it'll come back" or to add, while whistling in the dark, "it's only a paper loss."

The Psychological Factor

*T*here is evidence that the typical stock-market player not only endures the irrationality of his behavior but actually *relishes* losing. The repetition of this phenomenon is so reliable that it has long since become one of Wall Street's most dependable indicators, codified in the Theory of Contrary Opinion and expressed in the accurate adage: "The market will do whatever it must to prove the greatest number of investors wrong." With its elements of reward and punishment, the stock market is an ideal arena for one's emotions; the *need* to be perfect, in what is an impossible arena for that quest; the striving to lose, stemming from an investor's subconscious, is a matter for psychoanalysts to define (guilt, sexuality, self-doubt, aggression, etc.). Our concern, as a different sort of analyst, is to recognize the phenomenon, and to use it for our own benefit.

For different reasons at different times in the market cycle, the average investor finds it difficult to accept a small loss or to lock in a profit before it evaporates. The formidable psychic struggle—to sell or not to sell—somehow invariably produces the wrong decision, selling prematurely when the advance has much further to go, and, having made that mistake often enough to decide it was a mistake, to leap to the other extreme with other holdings and refuse to sell at all after the top has arrived. Every once in a while the market tosses in some bait—like the pool or poker hustler who allows his victim to win a round or two—but for every person who sticks with a stock that continues to go up, there are dozens who lament that they never got around to selling "at 34 and now the stock is at 8," or the inverse lament, "had a double, so I sold it at 8, and now it's 34." Naturally, there are innumerable variations on the loser theme, one of the most frequent being the way a person, subconsciously seeking punishment, manages to sell his strongest holdings while sticking with his weaker ones because he "doesn't want to take a loss." Taking a fast profit (by selling a stock that's up) because of neurotic anxiety that the gain will "surely" be taken away is the path to seeing stocks that have been sold continue to rise while the ones kept remain weak. There is no rule that says a small loss can't become larger, or that a large loss can't end in bankruptcy rather than recovery. Yet as long as he doesn't sell, such market players reason that there is a chance for redemption, like sinners who are sure others may be punished but not them. "I learned early that you don't play day by day but year by year. If someone tells you they don't lose, they don't play. But a professional keeps losses at a minimum." Those words come from a professional gambler, yet they precisely apply to the game going on at the corner of Broad and Wall. Just as in poker, a key ingredient to stock-market profits is knowing when to fold—and not being distraught if that decision, too, backfires; knowing when to take a loss, and when to stay out for a while. But others, particularly the public player, dreaming only of a more rosy future, has yet to learn that what's happening right here and now is all that is applicable, all that counts.

The truth is that even the shrewdest professional on the floor of the exchange loses money at one time or another—sometimes when the dreaming of being perfect takes over, more often because the market itself is an imperfect game. To paraphrase the gambler: If you've never lost any money in the market, you've never played the game. But loss is not only ending up with less than you put in; loss is also missing a chance—a discernible, objective chance—to sell at a profit, for then you've given back money that could have been yours. Public players glibly proceed on the theory that they are playing with someone else's money, but since it would be theirs if they had sold at the sensible opportunity, that, too, is a rationalization.

It may not be surprising that the stock market, which has been a male province for so long, uses language that abounds with sexual imagery: getting married to a stock; glamour issues; love orders; as well as nicknames like Ma Bell and Bessie, ticker symbols like HUG and LUV. And there are, of course, a number of parallel patterns, too: the frequent mistake of selling too soon can be compared with premature ejaculation, of not being able to sell at all with impotence. Anything that goes up and down, with down being the losing side, certainly has sexual connotations, as does the gaining of money itself, the male manner of giving birth and proving power.

Too often, selling decisions are dictated by psychological factors rather than by what has been happening on the exchange floor. Consider the mathematics of the Jackson-Atlantic situation instead of the husband's own needs. Suppose this man sold at 12, when his position started to deteriorate, taking a loss of $200 (plus commissions). When the stock dropped to 7, he wouldn't have cared; in fact, he might have become proud as a peacock to have sold so well. Having already sold long ago, his mind would be clear and he could consider the possibility of buying this, or some other perhaps more appealing stock. Unlike a holder with a huge loss, whose mind is consumed with getting out when the price comes back, the investor who has already sold is both mentally and financially prepared to buy. That's an edge in itself. But let's suppose he had decided to buy back Jackson-Atlantic as soon as the stock began to show some life again. He might have considered that possibility when the stock was around 7, and acted upon it when it picked up some volume, buying, let's say, 150 shares at 8 with the $1,200 he got when he sold at 12. Thus he would own fifty shares *more* than he originally held. The Monday morning after his tennis match he could sell these at 14, the same price at which he stood to break even with his original purchase, and his net profit would amount to $700 ($900 on this trade less the $200 lost earlier). He would have grossed 50 percent on his original capital, with commission costs at least partially offset by the interest earned by keeping his $1,200 in the bank for a year. Besides which, and perhaps even more important than the cash gain, add the psychic profit of not having had to rationalize the stock's slipping further from 12 to 7. Yet there he was, wanting to be complimented for having nursed the stock back to the breakeven point.

This is not to be construed as advocacy of "dollar averaging"— but is, rather, to illustrate in simplistic fashion how selling frees. Whereas dollar averaging locks you into putting more money into a weak stock (the proof being its decline), what to do with one's money after a sale becomes a wide-ranging choice. Our ego-needy tennis player could have been twice gratified: the good sale, plus the chance to buy the stock (or any other stock) at a good price.

Tomorrow and Tomorrow...

*T*hrough the entire market cycle lurks the fear of finalizing the deed, of taking it from dream to reality by selling. This stems from the nature of the market itself—the great American indoor sport, a game which never ends. In a football game, the team that's losing throws a long "Hail Mary" pass on the outside chance that it might be successful; in hockey, in the last minute the losing team's goalie is pulled out in favor of another forward, in an effort to salvage a score before the final bell rings. In gambling, that's an attempt to win back all you've already lost with one fling of the dice. But the stock market goes on day after day after day, and never comes to a definitive end. In fact, the N.Y. Stock Exchange defines the market on the floor as a "continuous auction." There's always tomorrow, where the unfulfilled dream lies. By not selling, by tightly holding onto his stocks, the investor never has to face reality. Thus the nature of time itself—the actual past, the promise of the future—tempts the typical investor to refuse to deal with the objective situation confronting him.

The nature of the market as ever-ongoing can be used as a discipline rather than a day-dreaming arena. You don't *have to* sell to prove yourself. There will be plenty of times when the sensible decision is not to be pushed too hastily into such action, and plenty of on-going time to shoot for a high batting average rather than staking one's entire ego on each decision. But you have to pay attention and keep a clear head so that you are ready to sell when the warning signals arrive. You don't have to be on the edge of a chair like Charlie Fisk is every time he makes a commitment, watching every tick every day. Once a day, once a week, in fact, should be ample when you know what to look for and what to do. So let's find out how to determine the right time and the right price at which to sell.

Chapter Two

Right Is Wrong

*L*et's be straightforward about it: the widespread and deep-rooted neuroses that affect virtually all decisions in the stock market are the subject for a different kind of analysis. Stock-market analysis is *the task of separating real possibilities from mere hopes.* And the path to doing this successfully is by concentrating on what you *do* know because it is actually happening—current prices, volume, statistics, etc.—rather than on what might happen or should happen. *One forecasts from reality, not from expectations.* It is our expectations, our needs, which keep us from seeing things as they really are, and that includes recognizing that things are not going as we had dreamed they would.

Anyone who has a compulsion to be perfect, to be so free from error that every deed will prove him right, will be driven mad by the stock market. Sure, someone sometime has sold a stock at its very top, and someone, too, happened to buy it at its exact bottom, but it's not the same person doing both, nor is it likely that one person can score two such bull's eyes in a lifetime of trading. The stock market isn't that absolute. At the track the winner is known in a couple of minutes, the payoff is toted for ticket holders, and the race goes down in the record books forever. But the investment picture is always changing; each tick on the tape is like a grain of sand ebbing and flowing in an endless altering of the shoreline's appearance. As a result, there is always some way to go wrong in the course of just about every transaction. But it is only hindsight that makes the mistake clear; and we don't, of course, have the luxury of hindsight at the time the decision has to be made.

This means that one important thing to learn at the start is that no matter how hard we try to be right, we are in one way or another bound to be wrong. Assuming that you know what you're doing, that you're experienced, have a feel for what's happening, and have your emotions under reasonable control, the best you can do is be as perceptive and informed as possible for that particular juncture in time, and to act upon your perceptions decisively. Something else might pop up a single tick later, but (1) you can't snatch the act back, and (2) you shouldn't fret about what might have been. With proper discipline and intelligent observation of the information that's available, *you ought to be able to make more money than you lose, and in the stock market that's the only measure of being right.*

Take the case of an off-floor trader named, let's say, Lesser, who has the reputation of knowing what he is doing. He and his brother comprise Lesser Bros., Inc. One, the exchange member, works on the New York Stock Exchange floor, while the other sits "upstairs" at an ordinary desk in the middle of an ordinary downtown board room, surrounded on all sides by ordinary retail brokers constantly calling up their customers. But Lesser has no customers; all he does, day in and day out, is trade the firm's capital; it's a job, moving merchandise in and out quickly and profitably, and he has done it well enough over the years to be considered a rich man.

Ignoring the patter of the salesmen around him, he heeds only what the tape is saying and how those transactions relate to the charts of each stock spread out in front of him. In April 1972 Lesser was holding the hot stock of that era, Levitz Furniture. Having paid 50, he was uneasy when he saw that each rally following a normal dip was failing at a successively lower level—first at 54 1/4, then 50 3/4, and again at 50 1/4. That's it, he thought, and on the next rally (which lifted off from 45), he sold out his position at 48 for a small loss. What's more, it became increasingly evident that 45 was an important price level; if broken, LEV could plummet a long way before finding its next level of sup-

port. So, at the same time that he liquidated his long position, he
went short a like number of shares.

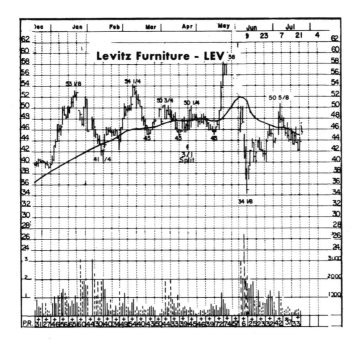

But, as you can see on the chart, LEV refused to break 45 in
three straight swats at that level. Then a major brokerage firm recommended purchase and that "expert" confidence in a company
whose stock was already up from 10 to 50 in a little over a year
induced several big buyers to begin chasing the price up wildly.
Seeing the strength materialize, Lesser quickly reversed his reversal, covering the shorts at 51 for his second loss and going long
once again. LEV boomed ahead, creating for him a profit large
enough to offset both the previous losses. Coming to work one
morning, Lesser decided the run-up had been too much too fast
and it was time for him to nail down his gain. But when he got to
the office, the "broad tape" carried word that the SEC was investi-
gating Levitz and was, consequently, suspending trade in the

stock. Once that news was disseminated, and trading resumed, LEV was not to reopen until a torrent of sell orders could be matched with buyers back under 50.

That gave Lesser his third straight trading loss, and yet, in reviewing his decisions, he couldn't spot a thing he did wrong. He was, in fact, right about having sold the first time, and right about having gone short (the stock ultimately went to 1 1/2), and right when he covered and went long, since LEV shot up more than 10 points afterward. Yet each time, the market—and a bit of fate— proved him wrong. With hindsight we can see what he might have done differently—namely, kept the short position on the grounds that furniture in concrete warehouses isn't exactly a glamour industry. But hindsight is not available as a tool. Lesser did what seemed objectively sensible, based on a style of trading which had produced a high batting average over the years; although he was wrong, Lesser remains confident that his overall market approach is correct.

In this moralistic-technological culture of ours, we've been brought up to believe that there is a right and a wrong about everything, and that if Judeo-Christian values don't tell us which is which, then modern science can conveniently punch out the answer. *But there is no such absolute in the stock market.* There, measured against a perfect score, one is destined always to be wrong somehow. That fact of Wall Street life must be pasted across your mirror, because that's what coming to grips with the act of selling is all about.

An alert institutional money manager would have sensed, during the great bear market of 1973-74, that the fancy glamour stocks selling at super-high price/earnings ratios were potential disasters, and then, even if he hadn't acted upon his own simplistic measures, he would have seen them actually collapsing all around. If he sold his block of, say, Hewlett-Packard when it broke 80, he would have slept well as it plunged into the low 50s. Look at how right that selling was—until, during the first upwave of the new bull market, HWP not only recovered that lost ground but went up to a new all-time high over 100. Virtually alone among the glamour stocks, Hewlett staged a remarkable performance:

last to break down, best on the ensuing upside (showing *relative* strength both ways is a not untypical sequence). In hindsight, he might have wished he'd held; in reality, he was right to protect his capital by selling, and would have been doubly right if he'd bought back as the market climaxed. The test of a good sale always includes what use the money was put to thereafter.

The history of Memorex illustrates "right" and "wrong" in reverse. If you finally got around to selling MRX at 30, or even 20, long after it was sliding from its record peak around 160, you sure looked slow-witted, but not so wrong when the stock plunged to under 3 and then off the board entirely. Subsequent action made even that laggardly sale at least relatively right.

In each of these examples it is easy to see what the perfect path would have been, just as Lesser could see, afterward, where absolute rightness lay in Levitz. But he knows he did what needed to be done *at the moment.* "I did it based on all the evidence available at the time," Lesser says, "and I'd do it the same way again. The only way to win at this game is to be consistent."

Since, indeed, the stock market is nothing but a game, with players on both sides of each transaction, with a score in money-points, and with winners and losers along the way, it is often revealing to compare it to more familiar games. Take baseball: the manager who orders a sacrifice bunt knows it won't work every time. The batter might pop up, a fielder could pull off a brilliant play, or the runner might die on second anyhow and he'd wish he had that batter back again to swing away. But he knows that the law of averages, developed over similar past situations, is on his side, and he can, based on his own experience and insight, refine the odds by considering other factors, such as the bunting ability of the batter, the speed of the base runner, the skill of the next batter, how late in the game it might be, and so on.

Strangely, the same fan who appreciates that the manager is playing percentage baseball is unable to translate that approach to the game he is playing—the stock market. Instead of looking back over his own record of success and failure to see which technique worked and which didn't, or what frame of mind affected each decision or failure to decide, he tends, in the market, to repeat his errors time and again. "Next time," he insists, after striking out again with the winning run on third, "it will be different."

Next time he ought to keep his eye on the ball that's being pitched and not stand there visualizing the adulation that will come from his game-winning hit. Sheer hope that it'll be different next time, instead of learning from experience, is changing what could be a reasoned decision into a gamble. To be sure, we've heard brokers, traders, investors, rationalize their gambles; the stock market offers infinite opportunity for making excuses. A good reason is the sugar coating that makes emotion easier to swallow: if you don't want to sell, can't bring yourself to sell, why, then, it's simple enough to find a reasonable excuse for that non-act. Here's one: the classic "I'm locked in" heard so often from the investor who insists he can't sell now because the stock has already fallen. Of course, he could pick up the phone and sell in an instant, but he's created that concept of being "locked in" as the reason behind his emotional inability to accept an already very real loss. Others use the same phrase: "I'm locked in because of the taxes I'd have to pay if I sell." That investor's emotion has convinced him to give back his profits rather than pay a portion to the government.

Not all emotions are misplaced in the market. After all, we're not entirely crazy, and many times our feelings may parallel stock action. Sometimes, one's instincts may be perceptive—and the emotional problem may be in an inability to act rather than an inability to confront the reality of the stock's action. But we'll bet those insights usually come when you have no personal stake in the matter. "Levitz looks like it's topping out up there," you can wisely tell your neighbor, but if you already owned LEV, could you be so blithe about it? Rather than being an evaluation of any supposed (and impossible to ascertain) value, the price of a stock at any given time is essentially a bet on what the price will be sometime in the future, so both the buyer and the seller have an emotional stake in being proven right. That's when all those "reasons" can be conjured up from the Wall Street culture.

If you want to make profits on balance, year in and year out, you can't afford to be taken in by such self-serving phantoms. You have to learn to recognize them for the excuses that they are. Nor can you trust that somehow you'll survive simply because you deserve to; if the market were that compassionate, would so many upstanding citizens, and deserving widows and orphans, have lost so much money to it?

Because everyone has his own style of becoming a victim, it is difficult to establish definitive guidelines which will rein in emotions. Confronting your own stock portfolio will require some hard study and, probably, some painful facing up to facts. Try withdrawing from the market for a while, and thus unburdened, sit down and analyze your decisions over a period of time. A convenient way to do this is to use your income tax Schedule D reports for the past several years, since these represent an unarguable situation. Then honestly detail all the factors you can think of which affected your selling judgment—both when you didn't sell and when you finally did—with particular attention to non-market factors (a marital spat, a job change, etc.), as well as to market influences (too quickly snatching that two-point profit). We'll bet that a pattern emerges which you'll find both startling and, we hope, edifying.

One person who did precisely this sort of self-analysis was a floor trader on the New York Stock Exchange. He was compelled to make a choice between being a trader full time or merely being a floor broker representing orders for others. In the course of reviewing his records to see which activity was the more profitable, he perceived that his trading on the long side was only mediocre but that he made a mint whenever the bear took hold. He decided to forgo working for commission dollars, and he also made it a policy to tread very carefully when the market was bubbling bullishly. But when he caught a whiff of an impending top, and could start selling short aggressively, he knew just what to do and milked declines for all he could.

With experience, and with some grasp of what has consistently affected your judgment in the past, you should be able to determine at which times and under what conditions you function best...and when you should be extra-careful, or even stay away entirely. One important thing every professional knows, or ought to know since it is his business to know, is that he doesn't have to play the game every single minute of every day. The advent of desktop machines and their ability to present right in your face what is actually happening every single minute of every day—and some with bells and whistles to call your attention to some petty and momentary thing that has just happened—has had its effect, though: the less experienced, the less disciplined, have become increasingly short-term oriented and excitable, more, in fact, akin to what we believed in the past that the public could be criticized for, of playing a game, of having a predilection for continually being in the market in one way or another. "Isn't there one stock worth buying?" was a common question during the massive 1973-74 bear market, and still is. *There is no rule that says you always have to have action;* yet that is perhaps the most disastrous of all the common errors we've noticed. Rather than continually confronting the market on its own often inscrutable terms, stop and ask yourself what you know, whether what you know is enough to act upon, and how *you* are relating to it. Maybe it is a period when the market's personality conflicts with yours, or something in your extra-market life is hampering your ability to view stock action objectively, or, simply, perhaps it's a time when the market's course isn't clear to anyone. Then it is best to step aside. You owe it to yourself to find out exactly how ready and able you are to play, because it's yourself you end up playing against.

Mental Mistakes

What has all this to do with knowing when to sell? Well, if there is no perfect time to sell, no absolutely right end-of-the-rainbow moment, *the important task is to avoid the wrong time.* None of us can ever get rid of our extra-market dispositions entirely, but we can identify them, recognize them when they attempt to interfere, devise individual rules of play in advance to keep them at bay, use them when they can be of service (such as knowing when to become aggressive), and, if we lose our concentration and make a mistake, understand how to get back into gear with what's happening instead of perpetually berating ourselves.

The classic Wall Street fable that illustrates this is about the man who, back in the 1920s, was so invariably wrong that his friends secretly arranged with his broker to be called whenever he placed an order, so they could do the opposite. In September 1929, he sold, so they all rushed in to buy. Battered thereafter, they asked him how he had managed to come up with a sensible order. "Oh," he answered blithely, "I realized that every time I did something, I should have done the opposite, so this time, when I picked up the phone to place a buy order, I forced myself to sell."

Without attempting to be all-encompassing—the variations are infinite—here are a few examples of potentially harmful mental attitudes to keep in mind and perhaps to uncover within yourself:

One of the more significant is the tendency to view the market as if it weren't played with real money. There's no contract to sign when making a transaction, Wall Street being one of the last bastions of the belief that a man's word is his bond, so it is easy to spend tens of thousands of dollars, sometimes simply as part of what seems like a casual conversation with one's broker. Besides you can "charge" it, inasmuch as you are not required to settle the deal for five business days. And even then no cash changes hands; writing out a check to pay for a purchase is less wrenching than pulling dollar bills out of a wallet. If you are using margin, the paper-money effect is even more pronounced; borrowing automatically from a brokerage house doesn't seem at all like going to a bank and taking out a loan (although it is much like it) and so the reality of any loss becomes postponed and blurred. Wrong decisions thus become readily tolerated.

Another mental diversion is using the stock market as if it had totemic powers. The children's game of "step on a crack, break your mother's back" is not much different from selling a stock (or refusing to) to teach your wife a lesson. Then there's the "last of the ninth" fantasy, in which the game is won with a home run just when a loss seems inevitable. Men have seen a basket swish through the hoop at the buzzer enough times to project the belief that being behind in the stock market can be reversed in the same way. "Why sell when there's still a chance" is the rationalization then expressed. (Without this history of gamesmanship, women seem to come to Wall Street with a more open mind, learning to play the market by its own rules, and thus often doing better than men.) Once you've become more aware of your need to use the market for your own nefarious ends, you'll be in much better mental shape to see what is actually happening.

The Market vs. Individual Stocks

*E*ven as you come to feel comfortable with the ebb and flow of the averages, you're bound to be frustrated that no matter how easy it is to foretell their direction, your individual stocks are still giving you headaches. The averages are merely the backdrop of the game; the real contests are waged over stocks themselves. Even in its broadest consensus, the market is never completely unanimous. Certain stocks will invariably be out of phase, either still going up (as many glamours were until late in both the 1969-70 and 1973-74 bear markets) or topping out ahead of the Dow-Jones Industrial Average (as "hot" stocks like Levitz and Bausch & Lomb did in 1972). By the time the blue-chip average hit its bottom in late May 1970, DuPont was already starting to rise emphatically in defiance. And from May 1971 through November of that year, the market underwent a severe intermediate-term correction, although you wouldn't have known it from the action of the mobile-home stocks, which kept going up and up and up. Obviously, you cannot be alone in your opinion—not when millions of shares trade—and hope to survive for long. Nor do you have the millions of dollars needed to hold a stock up by yourself. The question always comes down to the unrepealable law of supply and demand: *Who is more prevalent, buyers or sellers?*

There are two aspects of this law: current and potential. As for the *current* battle, that is what you see on the ticker tape and read about in the newspaper stock tables, both the price changes and the degree of volume needed to produce those changes. You've got to learn to recognize the times when the tide of battle has shifted, with sellers first stemming a rally and then beginning to press their advantage and sending a stock tumbling back down. *Potential* supply and demand is more familiarly described as support and resistance. These are price levels which were developed during the past action. If, for example, a lot of people bought Polaroid between 38 and 44 on its way down from 150, thinking it was by then a bargain, and then stuck with it painfully down to 15, you could look at that 38-44 area as a potential resistance area, a price level where many of those sufferers would be likely to sell their shares as soon as they could get even. And, of course, this potential source of sellers becomes an actual one as the current stock price closes in on the prior area of activity. Therefore, if you bought Polaroid at 15, you would be alert for problems as the stock neared 38 again.

Once long ago we were invited to attend, as an observer (little realizing that one day we would actually participate in), a typical brokerage house morning sales meeting, this one composed of a number of institutional salesmen (in those days, all men) gathered to hear what their firm's fancy research department had to say. They can have quite an effect on the market, since institutions (mutual funds, insurance companies, pension funds, bank trust departments, and the like) are the largest influence on supply and demand. The salesmen, on that particular morning, were anxiously hoping for a "story" they could sell, something exciting from the researchers that they could get on the phone with and use to generate a buy order from one of their institutional customers. As it happened, the analyst had a less than mediocre story about a textile company to deliver, but since he'd been scrutinizing the company for months and was being paid an unusually large salary to produce ideas, he had to deliver a report on something. The result was a recommendation to buy a stock he had previously recommended some 5 or 6 points higher, insisting—this is a classic remark—that "if I liked it at 33, of course I'm going to like it at 27."

This line of reasoning (as compared to admitting a mistake) can cost investors fortunes. Indeed, the clients might have appreciated a (rare) bit of "sell" advice, rather than a buy recommendation based solely on the rationalization that the stock's price drop had discounted the industry's, and the company's, hard times. Despite the cliche that "the market never discounts the same thing twice," the reality is that it often does. Tobaccos, for example, got pummeled with fresh waves of selling every time the cancer story made the headlines, discounting the same thing, by our count, seven times (at the time of first writing; by now, the story has reached the courts, and on each new headline, more selling appears). The salesmen around the table, as you can imagine, swallowed this particular story hard, but salesmen, after all, need commission income more than they need to ask questions with difficult answers, and so we watched this group rise from the meeting, march to their desks, and start dialing assiduously.

This is one way demand can be created—and you can see the effect, often, of such salesmanship in the way a particular stock will open for trading that day. For even though the textile story was, shall we say politely, thin, salesmanship brought in some buy orders and the stock started to go up. At first the advance was relatively uncomplicated; almost all those holders who had wanted to get out as the price dropped had done so already, and so a decent sized institutional order would be able to gobble up all the stock offered for sale from 27 to 28 and still be looking for more to fill the order. As it turned out, the salesmen managed to give the stock enough of a push to get the price up over 30 in a few days, a bullish jiggle which seemed to justify the earning of commissions. (After all, if the call was made when the stock was 27, and it went to 30—that makes the call "right," doesn't it?) But just a glance at the past history of this particular stock, as recorded on a chart, showed a large area of potential supply in the 32-36 area, where the stock had traded for many weeks before breaking down again. As a result, it was not hard to predict that by the time the stock got back up near 32 most of the salesmen-generated buying would already have taken place and a lot more sellers would show up. At that point, therefore, supply became stronger and the tide of battle shifted; indeed, as sellers spotted the weakness of the buying, they pounded into the breach in their haste to get out, driving the price back down sharply the next day.

Typically, the way institutions buy their stock is to try to accumulate it bit by bit. Oh, sometimes they run amuck with their emotions, like any other humans, but unless there happens to be a large block for sale in a stock they're interested in, the order on the exchange floor is usually filled over a period of time, as they gather in the desired number of shares while trying to keep the price from leaping until they're done. But when they do their selling, they are not so patient; having accumulated those thousands of shares, institutions usually want out as soon as the decision to sell is made. This desire to flee involves a rapid search for someone on the buy side who'll be interested in the shares—other trading desks are called, computerized systems are put up on the screen. Lacking an easy out, the block to be sold will be sent to the exchange floor, where the floor broker handling the order will take the specialist aside and see if anything can be worked out to get such a big block sold quickly near the current price.

Let's picture the floor broker standing at the trading post with his 100,000 share order to sell written on a deceptively tiny scrap of paper. He may not want to overly influence what is happening, so if another broker were to come along with a mere 100 shares to buy, he'd let the order go right past him for someone else to sell to. But an order for 1,000 shares or more to buy would be a different story; he'd step forward, sell, scratch out his running total on the scrap of paper, and scribble in the new number of shares he has left to sell. Thus, even though the price of the stock might be staying up there unchanged, or even advancing slightly, a close observer could note that there was a lot of selling volume in the stock. Indeed, the balance between buyer-initiated trades and seller-initiated trades could be calculated by adding up the number of shares traded at an "up" tick (a price higher than the last sale price) or a "zero plus" tick (a price higher than the last different sale price), which would be trades initiated by buyers, and compare the total to the number of shares sold (those which traded on "minus" ticks, or "zero minus" ticks). A sequence of 100 shares at 2...100 shares at 52 1/8...another 300 shares at 52 1/8...200 shares at 52 1/4...followed by three prints of 100 shares each, also at 52 1/4, would take the stock up one 1/4 of a point on

1,000 shares. If the next tick on the tape were 1,000 shares at 52 1/8, the broker would have done his job well, selling 1,000 shares without disturbing the price of the stock for future sales. In fact, he'd be pleased to accommodate any buyer of size by selling even more at 52 1/4, and even then his selling would be masked because the price would be "up." This action on the exchange floor gets printed on the ticker tape, and then gets summarized in the newspaper, and finally is translated graphically (for use by the technically minded) to a chart of the price fluctuations.

The Law of Supply and Demand

Take a look at the Eastman Kodak charts for mid-1972 here and on the following page.

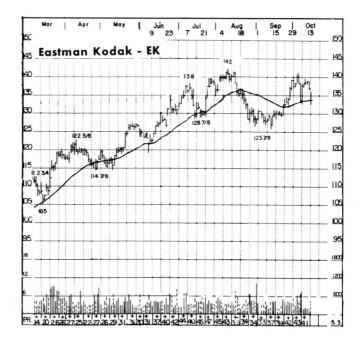

Suppose our broker is trying to unload 100,000 shares of EK but, with the market rising and Kodak having just made a new all-time high, he doesn't feel the need to hurry. Initially, near the end of July (on the daily chart), he sells 5,000 shares just to get his feet wet, and then steps aside to let the stock drift up to the 140 level, where he is a more active seller of bigger pieces while letting small orders keep EK up. Indeed, it even straggles up to a new high at 142; he's been a seller around 140, and nearly two weeks later, he's disposed of 90,000 shares. That's about it, he thinks. Even if he just dumps the last 10,000 shares abruptly, he'll have done his job well, since the falling price would make the rest of his selling look brilliant to the institution. The chart shows his activity as the stock slips to 135.

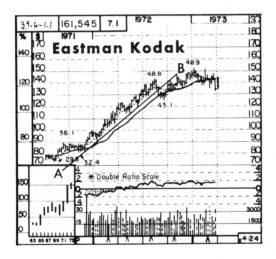

Buyers come in under 130 and become persistent in the 126-130 range, eventually proving strong enough to drive EK back up to 140, where there is now enough supply to halt the advance again; the battle is between the willing buyers around 130 and the sellers 10 points higher. Who will win? Who will prove the stronger? At least theoretically, sellers would seem to have the advantage since potential sellers can arise from every single share of stock outstanding, while potential buyers must come with money from the outside. The sell side has yet another advantage: motivation, for while fresh buyers may be scarcer after such a rise, the rise itself has increased the number of potential profit-takers (both long-term and those who bought a few days earlier near 130).

The truth is, however, you don't really know who will win at this point. But you *do* know certain details: (1) that for the first time in nearly a year, EK is failing to move on to a new high after a normal pullback; (2) that, instead, the stock is moving sideways for the first time in that entire span; (3) that any uptrend line drawn (for example, A-B on the weekly chart) has now been broken by this action; (4) that the same is true for the long-term Moving Average line, identified on the weekly chart as the heavy black line (Moving Averages will be discussed in detail in a later chapter); (5) that even if buyers were to emerge triumphant from this tug-of-war (by taking EK up to another new high), it wouldn't alter the evidence of a loss of momentum taking place—thus the "best" one can say is that it is late; and (6) that you can recognize that sellers will have won if the 126-130 support areas, where buyers had been strong enough before, gives way.

Thus although you don't know "right" or "wrong," you can see that there is some observable and objective evidence in the market. The basic law of supply and demand is the best objective counterweight to all those emotional reasons that otherwise create losses. No rule said Eastman Kodak at this time was worth 140, no more, no less; that it became a bargain at 130 or deserved to sell at 160 eventually. But there are certain details that can be ascertained.

Even so, the market doesn't make it easy. A new high, for example, may be a sign of renewed strength, or it may, with hindsight, turn out to be the "head" of a head-and-shoulders top. A judgment has to be made somewhere along the line. You may want to ask, at this point, if you should be looking for all those chart patterns you've heard about—head-and-shoulders, diamonds, triangles, rising wedges, *etc.* Because the mannerisms of buyers vs. sellers often repeat themselves, certain chart patterns also reappear consistently. If you want to delve into this aspect of the market, we strongly recommend *Technical Analysis of Stock Trends* by Robert D. Edwards and John Magee. But remember: all chart patterns are no more than individual peculiarities in the way a stock signals the underlying changes in supply and demand. You could keep it all in your head, as many professional traders do. A chart is history, helpful as a reference to where potential support and resistance can be expected, and even more so in portraying the action objectively so you can resist taking the emotionally appealing bait. "Look! the stock is going up again," you may cheer, and buy at 131...and therefore think nothing of selling instead, so pleased with yourself you would have felt when the company reported a 21 percent jump in earnings, surely a good reason to continue to be bullish. But it just so happened that *that* report came the week the stock failed to make a new high, and instead sold off 5 percent. *That* decline was excused as "nothing but profit-taking on the good news," except that on a longer-term basis EK continued on down to double digits.

Many investors (and analysts) become confused because they try to link corporate developments with market action. One says: "Eastman Kodak has been a great stock to own because the company has been doing so well." But the stock's performance has nothing to do with that reason, except insofar as the company's fundamentals create a group of people willing and anxious to buy stock. A stock goes up in price because of the *buyers,* to because of the balance sheet; if we see their buying on the tape we don't need to know their motivation, just their numbers. Furthermore, the willingness to act upon whatever reason the buyers may have is boosted because, if you will, there *is* a bull market in progress. When the bull starts to fade and then is toppled, so too does Kodak join the decline; even though earnings may continue to grow, even though the balance sheet may be just as robust, that reason is no longer valid. The law of supply and demand has asserted itself. Maybe everyone who wanted to own the stock has already bought, and a few of those, having paid 70 or 80, would now like to sell on the "good" news they anticipated; others may simply feel that 140 has become too rich. For whatever reason, *sellers* have shown up in Eastman Kodak. The question "Why does a chicken cross the road?" is no joke on the Street; when someone asks, "Why is that stock going down?" the *objective* answer is, "More sellers than buyers."

Therefore, if the law of supply and demand—the one thing you can keep track of objectively, the one tool that is devoid of emotion—tells you you're wrong, it's wise to accept it. You may think Kodak is going still higher for all those "becauses," but if that support level gives way in the marketplace and the price falls to 125, don't fight it. "Can I bear to take yet another loss?" "Suppose I sell and the stock goes back up?" "How can I sell such a nice company?" Can't you just hear those echoes? But the rule is as applicable to the stock market as it is to real life: *Do not rationalize failure.*

If you root for stocks in the market game, there is nothing wrong with being a fair-weather fan. The decisive act of selling may turn out, with hindsight, to be a mistake, but the indecisive act of *not* selling can turn out to be a disaster.

Chapter Three

Market Cycles and Selling

*E*ver since the first corporate share was purchased, it has been a credo of American culture that the road to wealth is the patient accumulation of stocks in growing corporations. As the country expanded, steel, oil, mining, and railroad ventures paid off handsomely. For years, railroad shares were considered the premier investment for those who'd made their pile and wanted to keep it safe and sound. More than one will of the pre-depression era specified in unbreakable terms that the heirs were to entrust the family fortune only to railroad shares. As it turned out, railroads were safer than buggy-whip or streetcar companies, but by the time the country's massive industrial growth began to produce a comparable boom in the stock market, railroads weren't the thing to be in. Industry—products—became the fashionable investment; railroads, especially as disaster struck in the thirties, lost their respectability and became speculative. One generation's gilt became the guilty dross of the next.

Despite such shifts in fashion, it may seem, in that era of extraordinary growth, that *any* investor who bought into the market was bound to have profited on the trip upward. Not so; someone who bought the Dow Jones industrial average (of the thirty leading industrial giants) prior to the 1929 crash and held on to them through thick, thin, and thunder would have had a net loss twenty years later of over 52 percent and would not have gotten even until 1954, a quarter of a century later. Going from 161.90 in 1949, when rising prices began to bail out the pre-crash investor, the Dow moved to 679.36 in 1959, for a decade's gain of 320 percent. That was a great decade, but it was *not* as so many took it to be, testament to the ultimate virtue of squirreling stocks away. The next ten years (1959 to 1969) also contained a prolonged and benign bull market, yet when it was over the DJI had advanced a grand total of 120 points, an average of only 12 points per year! And 12 points is a move the DJI often makes in a single day.

If, bewitched by how marvelous everything seemed to be in the early sixties, an investor bought the Dow industrial average at the outset of 1966 (at 995), he would have taken an immediate loss, but would have gotten almost even by the end of 1968. Then a third of his capital would have been rapidly snatched away. By the end of 1972, he'd have struggled back to being even again (actually getting ahead for a couple of weeks in early January 1973), but he'd have been taken on a roller-coaster ride scarier than any at Coney Island, down 20 percent and then back up, nine months later, at the original (995) level. But the worst was yet to come for those who assumed they had bought good stocks and who confidently put them away. Less than a year later, by the fall of 1974, the Dow toppled back down below all its achievements of the entire decade of the sixties and was even impinging (at 580) on 1958 levels! To complete the examination of this decade: by January 1976 the Dow managed to return to the level of January 1966, but inflation was beginning to strip away about one third of the real value of the investments, for an actual loss of 33 percent in buying power (a loss of buying power further magnified during the next few years, as well).

The same sad story is true of individual stocks, even the bluest of blue chips. Consider having locked 100 shares of U.S.Steel in a safe-deposit box in the early forties (original cost about $1,000). By 1959 the virtue of believing in this country's economic growth would seem to be confirmed, with those shares being valued at $10,900. Little more than ten years later, though, locking those shares up wouldn't have seemed too wise, for they'd fallen back to a value of $2,500—still a gain, but a far cry from the peak value.

Even though the strongbox approach may in the end yield gains, especially on paper, *maximum* profits are seldom taken.

And we would like to know, right at the outset, how anyone in the world can identify which stock can be tucked away for a generation, sure that it'll be *the* winner among all those other equities that are bought and sold along the way. Certainly U.S. Steel is a substantial company, not likely to disappear and thus decimate one's entire investment, but its stock has ups and downs like every other. And for every "buy it and put it away" investment in a company like U.S. Steel, there are a hundred others bought because they seem to have had vast potential at the time of purchase—perhaps as the current blue chip (the "IBM syndrome") or the exciting name that is being touted as the blue chip of the future. Remember that old favorite Cinerama, the concern reputedly destined, in 1961, to revolutionize the motion-picture industry? Up the stock shot to 22 1/2; down it went to 2. Another widely ballyhooed stock of its time was Kalvar, the photocopier fledgling which was to outstrip Xerox. It went to over 300 on that promise, and down to under 3 on the reality. Then there was National Video, bought on the thesis that it would carry color television to new heights; its own height was near 125, but those shares are now just so much fancy wallpaper. Even as this is being rewritten, we can expect Andrea Electronics to qualify for such a comment, as Centocor already has, along with other marvelous upshoots and collapses—enough to fill a room with wallpaper.

To be sure, over the years the market has gone up, and just as surely there have been profits to be made and kept. In earlier times, stock-market wealth typically came from being on the inside of shenanigans. It was not nearly as important to ride the cycles as to ride the coattails of the great manipulators of the nineteenth century. This was true even through the Roaring Twenties, when pool operators and their buddies were the adventurers to follow. "The SEC has since put a damper on such conduct," so we wrote in the seventies, "and the theory of investing is a nobler activity." Those words, of course, are an embarrassment as we re-write after the eighties; how can we have been so naive? Nobler, it is not; discernible, it is. It is always essential to pay attention to *both* the day-to-day trading *and* the cyclical rhythms of the market *and* the emotional content of those trends. It is the combining of those disparate factors that is our ultimate task when confronting decisions.

Whereas the 1929-1949 period would have resulted in an overall loss of 58 percent to those who believed in the "lock 'em up and leave 'em alone" approach to investing, had you bought at the bottom and sold at the top of each of the three major bull markets that occurred within that twenty-year span and stayed out of the market completely the rest of the time, your *gain,* not including dividends, would have been 1,700 percent! (And, having sold, you really should include the mental profit of not having had to suffer during the down periods, plus some added interest earned with your capital while out of the stock market.) Similarly, though buying in 1949 at a supercyclical bottom and holding until that cycle peaked in 1966 would have produced a quintupling of funds, the investor who swung with the shorter but still major tides, selling out in 1956, 1962, and 1966, when the market reached important tops, and buying back at subsequent bottoms, would have done nearly *four times* as well! Nor does any of this include taking advantage of the bear via short selling for further capital protection and enhancement (to be discussed in a subsequent chapter.)

Similar comparisons can be applied to individual stocks, though with far more varied results. Each bull market has had its own hot stock; clearly, anyone who bought this winner in its time and sold as it made its top would have been best off. But that's perfection; let's study one example of a strongbox stock—International Business Machines—to see what would have happened had it been traded in and out at major tops and bottoms, rather than tucked away throughout the cycles.

We're not talking about the kind of in-and-out trading a member on the exchange floor does, nor of the activity of "hedge" funds, but of something more long-term. In 1949, brokers were recommending Alcoa and Du Pont as the growth blue chips; IBM was considered speculative. A decade later, however, IBM had become the leading light, and you could have bought in at around 80 (adjusted for subsequent splits). If you sold ten years later, at its top of 370 in 1968, that would have been a profit of 360 per cent. But if you had traded in and out a mere three times during this period, here's what would have happened: bought around 80 in 1959 and sold at the 1961 top around 160; back in at the 1962 bottom around 90 and out again at the 1966 top near 180; in again at the 1966 low at 150 and out again at the 1968 top close to 370. That's 100 extra points—125 percent more on the original investment—and a hefty reward merely for paying attention.

That exercise of buying IBM at the bottom of bear markets and selling out again at the top of bull markets—as you will read later, we do indeed believe it is possible to identify such major turns—lasted until the 1987 peak. *The moral in 1993* is a much more serious one than just illustrating how to make a few more bucks. It is also important to realize that stocks "die"—just as Alcoa and Du Pont, although still considered "blue chip" names, have never returned to their 1949 roles as market leaders, it finally became IBM's turn. Had you sold out at IBM's forever-peak in 1987, you'd have bought back in after the crash only to find that you had a laggard on your hands. By 1989—having traced its course from speculative, to emerging growth, to *the* growth stock, to becoming an institution—the stock began trading badly, although it was still "IBM." Its market underperformance was "saying" rather clearly and emphatically that something was wrong with the company. It became time to reap a different "reward merely for paying attention"—our words in the preceding paragraph—by recognizing that the game was over: time to sell and to *not* buy back in on the seductive rebounds and devoted brokerage recommendations. The *Wall Street Journal* in 1991—*at IBM's 140 rebound high*—headlined "The King Is Back" on the exact day it was time to switch regal loyalties. The moral: you really can't lock any stock away forever. Market action, not fundamental comments, tell you when a stock has changed its characteristics so that you can, indeed, sell in time.

IBM, as you now know, had lost its ability to keep up with the changing technology-times. You must similarly consider, we went on to write in the first edition, that the country's economic fertility is rapidly becoming exhausted after 200 years of growth. No longer do acorns drop from the tree of free enterprise and immediately sprout in rich native soil. The sudden surge in conglomeration in the late sixties, by which additional paper money was created out of existing corporations that were already fully capitalized, showed as much as anything else how little prospect is left for fresh growth. It can be done, of course. Clever financiers and novel ideas can still pull millions out of a hat. Examples at that time were Diners Club, McDonald's, and Electronic Data Systems, all of which succeeded by selling convenience, exploiting the needs of an economy of plenty. But what had once been considered the vital, and basic, growth of the country—steel, mining, oil, railroads—has been relegated to cyclical roles. Technology has become identifiable as growth because it alone has the capacity to keep changing; new concepts are constantly coming along in telecommunications, computerization, and the like...while the "hot stock" conglomerates (as well as the leveraged buyout games of the eighties) are being downsized, and broken up, often into their original pieces again. In the nineties, investors have become seduced by the same arguments—*in reverse*—that were used to make conglomeration a "great" concept in the sixties.

Clearly, the investor who squirrels away his stock certificates because it worked in the past is betting on the future in a highly dangerous way. He must believe that each company he selects is going to participate fully in whatever growth lies ahead, and that such future growth is inevitable and will continue unchecked and that nothing new will come along to supplant even the best of ideas. The United States itself has already become, in a manner of speaking, a mature company; what used to be growth pains and then middle-aged aches, now shows bureaucratic signs of arthritis. Were it a common stock, one wonders who would buy "America" (ticker symbol: USA; earnings: negative; management: questionable; long-term debt: enormous; potential for bankruptcy: increasing) on the grounds that it still merited a growth stock's price/earnings ratio.

Not to sell, therefore, is perhaps the riskiest investment approach of all. Nevertheless, it is surprising how many naive investors still venture their capital on the assumption that there's indiscriminate growth ahead. As growth itself becomes a struggle—and for every company that flourishes, scores of others have the market equivalent of Andy Warhol's "fifteen minutes of fame"—it will be all the more difficult to pick the few companies that will survive with their earlier promise intact. It is far better and easier to learn to sell at the sensible time, a time predicated not so much on earnings growth as on the market's and the stock's "natural" fluctuations.

The Theory of Market Cycles

*T*hat word "natural" is placed in quotation marks because the ebb and flow of securities prices is obviously a man-made phenomenon, even though it gives the impression of responding to a higher order. So prevalent is this impression, in fact, that a number of observers have spent years earnestly trying to calculate the periodicity of market fluctuations, like so many astronomers puzzling over the universe. One vast cyclical concept was developed by a Russian economist named Nikolai Kondratev who, early in this century, isolated a sequence of wars, types of governments, and economic activity that, as it turned out, had demonstrable pertinence to the stock market. But Kondratev's approximate fifty-year cycle anticipated another deep depression sometime around 1980-1981—a watershed period for a market leadership change, the beginning of an open-ended budget deficit and the beginning of the end of Communism, events far different from what his theory would have expected. Changes—and sometimes major change—is what keeps the stock market (and our interest in it) alive.

Another cycle student, R.N. Elliott, applied his studies solely to the stock market and came up with something that has become known as the Elliott wave-cycle theory. A follower, and explicator, Robert Prechter, made a big splash in the eighties by successfully applying wave theory to that rising bull market. But then, as is the market's style with such achievements, when the theory finally became popular it went astray, almost as if to punish the host of amateurs who believed without knowing. Like any analytic approach to the ongoing market, a depth of not only understanding but practical experience enables the practitioner to respond to change. In our opinion, the theory, although useful, is too tenuous to be used in stand-alone fashion; only *afterward* can it be applied with any degree of certainty. But the market *does* move in waves, so in its simple form it can provide a relatively clear notion of where the market has been and thus where it might be, and that's rare enough information in itself, even if its moment-to-moment timing is too erratic for us.

The basis of the theory can be traced back to the thirteenth century mathematician Leonardo Fibonacci, who determined that the ancient Egyptian architects of the Gerat Pyramid at Giza had followed a specific arithmetic progression in the pyramid's design. The series starts with the numbers 1 and 2 and continues with the sum of the previous two numbers: 1, 2, 3, 5, 8, 13, 21, 34, 55, etc. One characteristic of this series is that the numbers bear a ratio, one to the next, of 1.62 and, reciprocally, of .62. These are, remarkably, relationships also found in nature. Limbs branching out from a tree are said to increase by Fibonacci numbers, as do the diameters of the spirals in sea shells, the number of rings on an elephant's tusk, etc. The Western musical octave also is comprised of Fibonacci numbers: 13 keys on a piano, with 5 black and 8 white.

In 1939 Mr. Elliott published articles in which he applied the Fibonacci series to stock-market movements, showing that what appeared in nature and at Giza could also be found in the market, although sometimes a bit of shoving and squeezing (and re-interpretation) are needed to make the cyclical terms fit. Elliott defined market movements by stating that there is always one large overall cycle in effect, consisting of a bull and bear market within that cycle, and, further, that the bear market will have two downswings and one upswing, while the bull market will have three upswings and two intervening downswings. In turn, those waves would, if examined closely, be found to break down into lesser waves of Fibonacci numbers: 3, 5, 8, as they got progressively smaller, 13 yet smaller, etc. Elliott and his followers have come up with extraordinarily arcane variations on this theme, market phenomena "identified" as flats, inverted flats, and reverse inverted flats, to name a few. We are innocent, and simple, perhaps, because such extensions and applications we find confusing and complicating. For our purposes, however, the fundamental theory of three or five waves comprising important cyclical swings is empirically consistent and hence worth paying attention to.

This is especially so since some remarkable forecasts have been made by Elliott disciples. In 1961, Hamilton Bolton, publisher of *The Bank Credit Analyst,* analyzed the then-prevailing market as follows: "The advance from 1949 should be complete when 583 points (161.8 percent of the 361 points of the 1949-1956 rise) have been added to the 1957 low of 416, or a total of 999 DJIA." This target, of course, was hit squarely on the nose five years later, in 1966, coincident with what appeared to be the required number of waves for the entire upcycle which had begun in 1949! (We say "appeared" because there was, in late 1968, a return to that approximate level in the Dow, although wild speculation at that time carried unweighted averages to much higher peaks.)

Considering that the end of the fifth wave (third upwave) of a bull market within a larger five-wave bull cycle marks the end of that entire cycle, it was time, according to the theory, for a new super-bear cycle. Sure enough, along came the 1966 smash (call that the first bear market), followed by a bull market of speculative dimensions (wave two, up), and then a second and much more severe bear market (wave three, down). *At the time,* therefore, Elliott's theory would have provided perspective to warn many investors that the worst wasn't over simply because there had been a bear market in 1966; it wasn't going to be just another interruption in a constantly rising market, as so many then thought to their subsequent regret. What's more, application of the theory indicated that the 1969-70 bear market was sure to go lower than the 1966 bottom, as indeed it did. And along the way, had you scrutinized such swings, you'd have found that Elliott's requirements had been met in simple fashion. During the 1969-1970 slide, for example, there were the requisite three waves down and two intervening waves up, with each, in turn, displaying the lesser waves in approximate Fibonacci harmony. The problem then—and the problem typical of trying to *interpret* an ongoing market—is that it wasn't clear whether to measure by the 1966 or the 1968 top. The former seemed more valid at that time, and if so, an orthodox conclusion would have been that the low in 1970 completed that super-bear cycle. But in hindsight the 1966 bear market didn't seem very significant—1968's gunslinger speculation made for a much more dramatic top—and then, too, the action at the bottom in 1970 didn't seem to be that of an end of a major bear cycle. We could confuse you all the more by continuing this discussion—but when the bear market of 1973-74 crashed below the prior (1970) low, it was evident that *this* was but a continuation, at its virulent worst, of the entire super-bear structure. Theoreticians still argue about 1966 or 1968, but in practical terms it was enough to know that the end of the super-bear cycle was likely to come with the end of that particular 1973-74 bear market. That suggested, in turn, that the ensuing bottom—formed in October/December '74—was going to launch an *entire* new super-bull-cycle. Waiting for extra waves so as to fit a preconceived count requirement is dangerous, just as becoming prematurely anxious before enough waves have been seen is unnecessary.

On the evidence, it is good to know just about where Elliott's wave theory says the market is, within a super-cycle, and even within a major wave, but clearly it is not a system to bet the rent money on. After Prechter's publicized successes in the eighties, a whole school of followers decided they could do it better, without realizing the limitations of using this theory alone. It is, after all, an abstraction of market behavior, so that the more one gets into trying to "count" the smaller wave movements, the more the market, in its perversity, makes sure the math is wrong in one way or another. What it does illustrate is that the stock market does not go straight up or straight down. One wave is never enough: stocks move in a *pattern* of waves, and these flows *eventually* and *inevitably* reverse, and then *eventually* and *inevitably* reverse again. That is a vital perspective to maintain, especially when one's emotions argue otherwise.

Long-Term Waves

Just as a surfer picks certain waves to ride in preference to others, an investor, knowing that stock-market waves come in all shapes and sizes, should analyze which ones are likely to give him the best ride for his money. There are four basic types, each with its own advantages and disadvantages. *Super-waves* last for many years (e.g., the super-bull-cycle that ran from 1949 to 1968), encompassing lesser, though major to us, bull and bear waves. These major bull or major bear markets are *long-term waves*, often accurately called the *primary trend* (e.g., the bull market that ran from 1962 to its top at the outset of 1966, or, in turn, the bear market of 1966 or the Kuwaiti bear market of the latter half of 1990). *Intermediate-term waves* usually last several months, like the intermediate-term uptrend within the major bull market which lasted from December 1970 until the end of April 1971, followed by an intermediate-sized correction, or downtrend, from that point until Thanksgiving 1971. (A more recent, similar, sequence was the intermediate-term rise that began when the Fed eased in December of 1991, which lasted until June '92, and was followed by an intermediate-term decline into October 5th of that year.) Finally, there are *short-term* swings within intermediate-term waves. For example, that 1971 correction consisted of a drop of over 100 Dow points from May to early August, when an interruption, fed by Nixon's game plan, caused a short-term swing upward for several weeks, followed by a decline of 130 points from that intervening rally—all, we remind you, as part of an intermediate-term downtrend within a major bull market, which existed within a super-bear cycle.

Each such wave, big or little, offers its own buying and selling opportunities. Our task is to determine which, according to its own characteristics, is most productive to follow. First, however, we must dismiss the strongbox approach, for that hides even from super-cycles, and anyone who doesn't want to sell his stocks before a super-bear cycle sets in is too self-destructive to save.

Similarly, riding super-waves is (as we briefly demonstrated in discussing Elliott's theory) an enormously difficult predictive task. It is particularly dangerous because of the emotions attached to the late phases of such super-waves: glowing, in a bull phase; hateful, when the market has been bearish. An example of the former is the way investors, having gotten used to the notion of interruptions along an eternal path upward, believed that the worst had passed in the summer of 1970. Indeed, many bank trust departments and huge university endowment funds were accused of not being equity-minded enough at that time, and so the theory was developed—by amateurs, we might add—of owning only "one-decision" stocks, stocks so good, so lovely (like a bride at 20), that they could be bought (in a form of marriage) and held through anything. The result was that they got clobbered in 1973-1974. And then, of course, they were so distraught that they were unable to bring themselves to buy anything at that super-bottom. Super-cycles cannot be accurately defined, and so are useless as timing tools; there are much more useful waves.

The primary trend, at least, is discernible to a considerable degree; certain indicators, to be discussed in subsequent chapters, speak at the tops and bottoms of such waves, and the length of time involved in a primary trend—a couple of years or so: 1962-66; 1967-68; 1970-72—is not so long that you are likely to lose track of the overall context (bullish or bearish) in which you are dealing. It may sound overly simplistic to say, but that doesn't alter how sensible it is to try to buy near the bottom of a major bear market and to sell near the top of the ensuing bull market.

But it is hard to stay sensible when in the midst of a primary trend. It's been a long, profitable ride upward, you wish you hadn't been so cautious before, and then, toward the end, comes the most excitement. Now's your chance, you salivate. Speculative stocks start zooming, new issues crackle, good economic news abounds, your neighbor's got a hot tip for you, and optimism becomes pervasive in the media and on the Street. It's tough not to be swept up in that sort of climate, particularly when, as in 1972, the speculative fever is in blue-chip stocks. Even if one is sophisticated enough to realize there'll be a piper to pay sooner or later, the temptation is strong to keep playing, so long as hot tips, booming prices, and locker room tales of quick fortunes pour in. In such an atmosphere it takes a slide itself to provide evidence that the end has arrived, and even then, the first slide is taken as just another opportunity to buy. When prices continue on down a lot of stocks prove to have been bought at their highs, a lot of losses pile up, and a lot of those bull-market profits have gone down the drain.

Not only is an ebullient state of mind hard to control at such tops, but the technical evidence of the demise of a primary trend is, by its nature, often lagging, coming *after* the top has been completed and the decline has started. After all, the first downward whack looks like just another temporary correction, no different from the pullbacks that had previously interrupted the bull market. Not until the next rally *fails* is it clear that the primary uptrend is over. One example of how this delay affects long-term technical analysis can be seen in the fact that the venerable Dow Theory requires *two* signals to "prove" that a primary uptrend has ended: one or the other of the Dow averages—Industrial or Transportation—must fail to make a new high while the other does— but then both must breach prior support, confirming each other that a new, now down, trend is in effect...thus further delaying the signal. The investor who prefers to ride out intermediate corrections and hopes to swing only with the primary trend must wait for such signals to appear, and then, caught in the midst of a sharp decline, feels he needs to wait for the next rally before selling, and then, typically, the next rally isn't quite enough to suit, so he waits for more, but the feebleness of that rally is in itself a further confirmation, but by then he's becoming trapped in a genuine, and destructive, bear market.

Furthermore, trying to identify the top of a bull market in the averages, such as the Dow Industrials, is hard enough, but many times the averages will not be consistent with what your own individual holdings are doing. For instance, Bausch & Lomb, a huge winner in the early seventies, started falling apart many weeks before the Dow hit its own definable peak in January 1973. With the averages still advancing, it would have been tempting for a holder of BOL to persuade himself to stay with it as it tumbled, arguing that the continuing bull market would bring it back up to the high he'd missed. Perhaps such a holder would have recalled how the beginnings of the 1969-1970 bear market were totally ignored by a dozen or so of the Street's flossiest glamours, which waltzed upward virtually by themselves throughout 1969, oblivious that the music had long since stopped and, in fact, the ballroom was on fire. If you'd held on to Bausch & Lomb through 1972 because you were watching the behavior of the Dow for the sign to start selling, and because similar high-fliers had kept going well past the Dow's peak on the previous bull-market top, you'd have tossed an awful lot of your own money back into the pot. *There are always similarities, top to top, but not consistencies.*

Thus, another impediment to tracking the primary trend is that *no general market move encompasses every stock simultaneously.* The discrepancy between your stock and the average (and the need to make a decision about yours while eyeballing the average) is one of the most constantly frustrating elements of the market, particularly if you are holding a portfolio of several different issues, each one out of phase with the others *and* the averages. Adding to the difficulty is that it isn't this way at bottoms, where stocks tend to start going up in relative unison; at tops they expire one by one. Most bottoms are made when the market tumbles as a whole, as it did in the avalanche that ended in December 1974 or the October '87 crash. During such phases, signs of a bottom tell you to start buying just about anything from Abbott Labs to Zurn. That's why the dart-throwing system actually seems to work: at major bottoms it is hard to miss a big winner unless you miss the page entirely.

What goes on at bottoms is not even remotely applicable to having to judge individual stocks as each in turn forms a major top and then starts down. Over the years we've observed that about one third of all stocks register their bull-market tops ahead of the averages, another third at approximately the same time, and the remaining third after (sometimes long after) the averages have already turned down. So your chances of being right in regard to your own portfolio, even if you correctly identify a major top in the Dow to the exact day, are apt to be no better than one in three.

It is vital to be able to convince yourself to sell a stock regardless of how the averages look. Continuing to hold while it is already on its way down could cancel out any advantage gained by correctly holding other stocks that are still in gear with the averages, especially since stocks have a way of going down much faster than they go up. By the same token, you don't want to liquidate so completely that you dump the very stock capable of moving ahead in defiance of the overall market. A classic example of such action was American Research & Development (since merged into Textron), which was actually a tremendously profitable *buy* as the extensive 1969-70 bear market got underway. The DJI started rolling over and going down, while ARD was breaking out on the upside for a rapid doubling in price! A lot of people who sold that stock in late 1968 and early 1969 were dead right about the market and dead wrong about the stock.

The opposite situation is illustrated by another popular issue of the late sixties, University Computing, which hit its all-time high in 1967 well before an overall bull market had completed its cycle; as the bull went roaring ahead, UCX went the other way in its own private, long-term, bearish cycle. There were, however, swings of *intermediate-term* duration in which UCX actually doubled (and more) on the upside; while it worked its way inexorably down from a peak 185 to under 5, it experienced rallies from 55 to 110 and a gain from 14 to 38. While others hope and pray that such rallies will keep going until they get even, the reality is that these rebounds must be recognized as selling opportunities for anyone holding such a weak stock, regardless of the action of the averages at those times.

Obviously, the anomalies of the marketplace are enough to drive anyone to an early grave in potter's field. One views the long-term action of the averages and of individual stocks, but there's no apparent way to link the two consistently. Besides, the emotional pressures created along the way by intermediate-term waves sorely disrupt the equanimity of the investor who is trying to follow the major trend.

To illustrate the bewilderment that can arise when you deal strictly in primary trends, let's go back to the turbulent spring of 1971. You've just had a rousing rally that has emphatically confirmed a new bull market so, in accord with the market's primary trend, you elect to hold onto your stocks that spring. You reason that, while a correction is due, that's about all it should be. Why get involved with taxes and steep commission costs by going in and out? And then there is the very real difficulty of trying to catch the next bottom. Indeed, your judgment seems to be right when the market slides from the Dow 950 level to nearly 840; that, you think, is enough. Then along comes Nixon with the first of his economic game plans, which gives the market quite a boost. But another downleg soon sets in. At first, you can accept this as evidence of a more severe correction than you expected—one in keeping with an Elliott pattern of two downwaves and one intervening upwave. But suddenly, with prices tumbling, a reason for the decline becomes apparent: by November there is a severe international monetary crisis, generating headlines and driving stocks even lower. The 840 level has cracked as if it were no support at all; there is talk of worldwide disaster. Would you retain last April's confidence, holding on to your stocks in the belief that "it's just an intermediate-term correction; the primary trend will reassert itself soon"? Actually, that's all it turned out to be, but our point is that it is extremely difficult to maintain perspective in the midst of collapsing prices and a churning stomach. Too many investors lose track of their original decision and panic in exactly such situations. *The risk of an emotional defeat after an objective decision is a serious problem for those who follow primary-trend moves.*

With the benefit of hindsight, we can add another problem: the market, and its tastes, is always changing. That simple pre-correction peak in April 1971 proved to be the actual peak for many individual stocks, as measured by the cumulative advance/decline

line. (That indicator, to be discussed in detail later, is a simple measure of the underlying trend for individual stocks.) An unusually large number of stocks made their highs that spring, and were already in downtrends as the Dow made its top eighteen months later. The moral: there is always a second decision to be made about individual stock holdings.

The goal, clearly, is to be positioned so that the least risk is assumed for the most potential reward. But this is a delicate balance at best. Trying to catch tops at their very peak might yield maximum reward, but the risk is increased considerably. On the other hand, surrendering the possibility of a large reward for the calm of risklessness is better accomplished in a savings account. To make good money in equities, one is obliged to take risks, but these risks should be based on as much information as possible. When the situation becomes diffuse, as it does when you are trying to devote yourself to a trend that might well last a couple of years or more, it becomes difficult to be decisive and more likely that emotional squalls will batter your judgment. Sometimes you'll jump and dump; relying on your broker's, or your own, computerized message machines can intensify this moment-to-moment thoughtless responsiveness—"do it now!" or feel as if you've missed it. At other times, you'll procrastinate. Waiting one day, and then another, for enough evidence is like continually swearing that your next cigarette will be your last. Acting on a moment's momentary input, after you've sworn you're a "long-term" investor, can be foolish; indecision, though, is habit-forming, and can be injurious to your wealth.

In sum, there are a number of complications when you invest in primary uptrends. First, a substantial portion of profits probably will have to be given up before it's proved that the uptrend is over and that many stocks should long since have been sold. Second, once the decline has set in, the belated arrival of long-term reversal signals generates a desire to put off getting out until the next rally, and a feeling of being locked into the very stocks you wanted to profit from near the end of the primary uptrend. In turn, this increases the chance that when the rally does come, you'll be convinced that the uptrend has been renewed and thus will compound the mistake of doing nothing. Third, there's the perplexing problem of trying to time your particular holdings to the action of the overall market, because there is no such animal as the average stock. Fourth, you wave the opportunity to greatly enhance total profits by selling before intermediate-term corrections set in and buying back later at lower prices. Finally, trying to peg decision-making to a judgment of primary trends can leave you exceptionally vulnerable to having the wrong emotions at the wrong times: gloom, despair, and hopelessness traditionally mark the time bottoms are formed; blinding optimism and Lourdes-like faith in the future, at tops. Since *no* stock goes from A to Z without first stopping at H, retracing to D, bouncing on to N, coming back to F, or even A, the simple appeal of the primary trend is, in fact, highly problematic. This Mexican jumping bean way of making decisions can be as risky—speculative, if you will—as betting that you'll never have to sell at all.

Short-Term Swings

Given the problems of following primary trends, it might seem feasible to take the opposite tack and to get out at the first hint of weakness and back in as soon as strength returns. In this short-term way, the future can be shrunk to a few days, or, at most, a couple of weeks, so even if you're wrong, you're never *that* wrong. Many amateur players believe they're protecting themselves against big problems by dealing strictly in short-term swings. "No one ever got hurt taking a profit" is their theme song. They may have taken a bath in a Levitz or University Computing before, so they swear it'll never happen to them again, because they're going to take those profits as soon as they're made and then get out. But once you buy a stock in the afternoon at 20 and sell it the next morning at 23, you're apt to get hooked on a very dangerous game, best left to professionals...and best suited for lining your broker's pockets with a steady stream of commissions.

Just as long-term investors pooh-pooh market swings as not affecting *them*, short-term traders exaggerate the significance of every little twitch, convinced that looking at the market through a microscope will disclose its secrets. *This need has been intensified by what seems, to such traders, to be the almost magical solution—that is, computers.* Nowadays, you can actually put those twitches up on the screen like a dentist scrutinizing an X-ray: this "molar" is healthy, but look, over here, three downticks in a row in your "left lower bicuspid." These tick by tick, or moment-to-moment charts have all the appearance of reality, and can, indeed, be "read" the same way as a daily or weekly chart...so the trader believes in them far beyond their usefulness. They cause over-trading, and all losses lead from *that*. They create a belief that one knows what one is doing, when it is really *the noise* of the trading floor and trading rooms around the country that one is staring at. (This criticism/warning is of course not only valid for charts of options, futures, and stocks themselves but also for indicators, especially those oscillator types that ring "signal" bells all day long and then again overnight.)

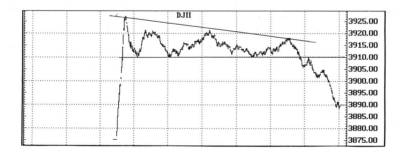

In this intense environment each downtick triggers apprehension; each uptick may be the last chance to sell out; every minute the stock is not on view on the tape heightens anxiety. What will happen next? And next? The answer is not something meaty to chew on but, rather, a peanut or potato chip that one can't stop eating. The more fluctuations one sees, the more one feeds on them. "Better grab that profit while I can," the amateur mutters, unable to let a potentially big winner develop through bouts of selling. In this Lilliputian world, every 1/8 of a point is a milestone. The uneasiness is incessant and may even be exactly what such a speculator desires. Some folks have an ego gratification need to be right, even if it is only for 3/8. Others have an ego need to be constantly stressed out, even if it is only down that 3/8. Many, in fact, have both such needs; it seems to give life itself significance.

The short-term trader feels obliged to keep close and constant watch—during his lunch hour, at business meetings, even while he's incommunicado in the dentist's chair, or, as dentist, leaving you with your mouth locked open while he answers a call from his broker. Some people wear watches that give prices because stock-market injury (or opportunity) seems to take place repeatedly at just those moments when one's back is turned. We can always get a laugh from portfolio managers by saying, "the market's going to take off next week because we're going on vacation." Indeed, prices often move decisively on partial holidays when bank trust departments and insurance companies are closed, and on those odd days, such as the Friday after Thanksgiving, when few people are around to pay attention.

Moment-to-moment anxiety is compounded by compulsiveness, for such a trader is driven to have a bet down even when the market is dull, hard to figure, or even perilous. Most professional traders, however, like most professional gamblers, recognize that there are stretches when the game isn't worth the risk. They may not know what the market is going to do next—and they'll admit it. They are quite willing to step aside for better odds. They may even acknowledge that they are in a slump, or that the market is throwing them its own form of curve balls. Many times a professional trader will leave the exchange floor early, just to keep away from temptation after he has decided he doesn't want to do anything more that day, preferring to wait for more substantial, more understandable clues, before choosing the next direction and/or a lower-risk time to play.

A revealing parallel comes from a professional gambler whose work consists of studying the entries each day at race tracks around the country. He is employed by a number of big bookies as a handicapper (an "investment" analyst of sorts) and supplements this income with his own astuteness in betting. There are days when he personally doesn't make a wager, even though he keeps feeding advice on every race to his clients. In the vast majority of races, he explains, there simply is no clear-cut choice. Although one horse might handicap out as a shade more promising than the rest, that isn't good enough for him. Nor does he bet if two horses look much better than the rest of the field, or when the odds on a horse he favors aren't high enough. He bets *only* when all the aspects come together favorably; as a professional, he tries to reduce chance as much as possible and realizes that there will always be another race. Yet the public throngs to the track and feels compelled to bet on every race, with the daily double, exacta, trifecta, and all else thrown in for good measure.

So, too, in the stock market, where the gamble is the same, although the atmosphere is more polite. Short-term traders think they should always have a bet going on some ticker symbol or other, a need that is encouraged by brokers who stand to capitalize on the easy commissions generated by such gamblers. Even in a bear market, short-term traders will hope they've found the one stock that will beat the odds. In difficult-to-discern or trendless markets, they'll buy puts *and* calls, they'll put on spreads, sure that the answer is in just doing, doing. For the public, the hope is too often just hope.

A professional trader on the exchange, whether on the floor or sitting "upstairs," can take short-term losses as part of his daily business because, as a member, he pays no commissions. (Taking into account transfer taxes, clearance costs, and other similarly small items, the cost usually comes to little more than an 1/8 of a point, meaning that if he buys 100 shares at 20, decides he's wrong and sells at 19 7/8, his loss is approximately $50.) But to amateurs, such a small loss is compounded by the additional cost of the round-trip commission; even using a discount broker, that can amount to $100 or more. The result is that a person with a slight loss tends to hold for a fluctuation back up—until he perceives stronger proof that the situation is bad, which leads him to lose 2 or 3 more points while waiting for that proof. Thus, even when played close to the vest, the typical short-term loss can easily turn out to be a hefty $500 or $600 per 100 shares, plus commission costs. But that's only part of the bad situation. To recover that 4-point loss, the trader has to chalk up an 8-point gain, because profitable transactions, too, get clipped for two-way commissions. He has to hit two winners as big as his small loss *just to stay even.* Even worse, we hasten to add, is the psychological problem of taking such a deep loss. Remember, his ego is at stake, too. Many such errant trades turn the trader into an *involuntary investor* while waiting to be proven "right."

From time to time we meet someone who boasts about how well he trades—this winner, that winner, but never a word about losses. (Only his accountant, and his Schedule D, know the truth.) The conversation has the tone of a gambler to it, just back from the thrills of Vegas. But the hard truth is that short-term trading is a profession in itself, requiring total concentration, discipline, and even then such a trader cannot do what an exchange member can do. Not only are a member's transactions commission-free, but he has the added advantage of being in direct touch with the floor, either in person or on the phone to a friendly floor broker who handles his orders and is familiar with his style, so there is a two-way flow of information. It is not that he gains any time advantage (your orders can get executed just about as promptly), but his questions get answered, and salient bits of trading information flow back to him. He is geared, and poised to act decisively, which is less taxing when there is little extra penalty for being wrong. And, of course, it's his job, and that gives him the psychological advantage.

Because the professional appears to fare better, some public traders who have the need, and greed, but not the time, turn their accounts over to registered representatives who have built up a reputation for such trading (particularly, nowadays, in options). In that way, they get the thrills and emotional involvement without the burden of personal decision-making. Sooner or later, though, even the most red-hot broker handling such an account is bound to find himself in a jam. He'll buy a stock for his customer's account that looks ready to make a quick move, but the stock doesn't produce immediately. There's nothing wrong yet and it still appears ready, so he decides to give it a further chance. To pay for it, though, he has to sell something else from his client's fully invested portfolio. Not wanting to show losses in the account if he can help it (*his* vanity and *his* guilt feelings are also at stake), he opts to sell a stock which shows a profit, regardless of whether that position is ripe to be sold or not. What's more, such brokers often use the arcane aspects of the options game to try to make amends—they'll sell calls against the position they're stuck in, for example, or, worse yet, sell puts on the theory that they're willing to buy more shares now that the stock has fallen to a "better" price. It takes only a few such switches and maneuverings before the customer finds himself no longer a free-swinging trader but an involuntary holder of weak positions, bereft of those stronger stocks which had been (and probably still are) going up. Often, a surrogate's emotional involvement in buying ("Got to make that loss back before the account gets taken away") and in selling ("Can't take another loss or he'll murder me") is as destructive as your own. Instead of the inner anguish of being able to blame yourself, you now have a handy scapegoat: *he* did it to me. But the losses are still your money.

We might add a variation to this theme: people who are only part-time gamblers, akin to those who blow their bankroll only when they visit Las Vegas but are otherwise solid and cautious citizens. These traders get caught up late in the game, when excitement and a lot of action and tales of a neighbor's profits, lure them in; they take a flyer here and there, lose, and withdraw, swearing never to play the market again...until the gambling itch comes back during the next cycle. There's probably no way we can convince a compulsive short-term gambler to find a better strategy short of recommending Gamblers Anonymous. Our warn-

ing is directed at the less neurotic. Playing short-term swings is, for
a non-member of the exchange, a sure way to losses. There will
be seductive profits during some phases, and small losses, which,
taken singly, won't seem like much; but over a period of time such
in-and-out activity will leave your capital in tatters and your nerves
a wreck.

Intermediate-Term Waves

*B*etween the two extremes of short-term in-and-out trading and
the blurred long-term investment view lie intermediate-term
waves. Though sometimes obscured by the peculiarities of the averages or the quirks of the marketplace, they are always there, and
are always discernible, as moves in the market which last from
several weeks to several months before exhaustion sets in and a
countermove ensues. An intermediate-term wave contains within
it several short-term swings and can be in gear with, or contrary
to, the primary trend. And, we would add, it has three consistent
characteristics: (a) as it culminates, it scares—down waves do
something (violate a closely watched level, break an uptrend line)
that scares potential buyers away; up waves scare short positions
out just as the move is becoming exhausted; (b) it lasts longer than
expected; and (c) and it can be identified in relation to market indicators.

Herewith is a chart of the Dow Jones industrial average from
December 1968 to mid-1974 with each of the intermediate-term
waves identified.

A number of intermediate-term waves are readily apparent.
We've labeled, as A, the final intermediate-wave onslaught of the
1969-1970 bear market. You can see, within this, a total of five
short-term waves, three down and two up, with the final slide the
longest as that bear market came to an end (so that its intermediate-term characteristics coincided with the end of a long-term
move). Once the base for the new bull market was complete, the
first intermediate-term upwave (labeled B) was inaugurated; it is a

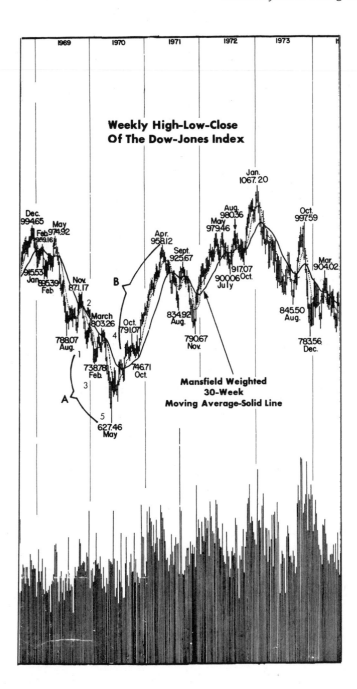

Weekly High-Low-Close
Of The Dow-Jones Index

Jan.
1067.20

Aug.
980.36
May
979.46

Oct.
997.59

Dec.
994.65
May
974.92
Feb 969.16

Apr.
958.12
Sept.
925.67

Mar.
904.02

915.53
Jan
896.39
Feb

Nov.
871.17

B

917.07
900.06 Oct.
July

845.50
Aug.

788.07
Aug.

2

March
803.26

Oct.
791.07

834.92
Aug.

4

790.67
Nov.

783.56
Dec.

1

738.78
Feb

746.71
Oct.

Mansfield Weighted
30-Week
Moving Average-Solid Line

3

A

5

627.46
May

1969   1970   1971   1972   1973

particularly fine example of an intermediate-term rally sustained for several months without real concern (except for the anxieties of holders) before suffering a reversal. Indeed, all three uplegs of this bull market are similar (with the moves in 1970-71 and again in 1971-72, each from the end of November to the end of April, virtually identical), crisply defined, recognizable for what they are, and, as we'll discuss later, clearly foreseeable at their outsets via technical indicators. So, too, were the corrections against the primary trend which intervened: note how this totaled five intermediate-term waves—three up and two down—within the long-term bull market, just as the intermediate-term waves themselves had three or five shorter-term waves, in keeping with Elliott's wave cycle theory.

Indeed, this entire charted period represents a super-bear market cycle, depicting as it does two primary waves down, with the above-described intervening primary wave up being nothing more than a contra-trend bull move within that bear cycle. Unlike long-term and short-term moves, intermediate-term waves are relatively precise in form; they last long enough and are sufficiently identifiable to be outstandingly adaptable moves for selling purposes. You can also see—and we are adding this identification (X) to the chart—what has become the classic example of a contra-trend rally within an ongoing bear market: the rise from August into October of 1973; it looks like a clear failure in hindsight but at the time consensus sentiment became wildly bullish, insisting that the bear market had ended and all was right with the world again...even as they were sitting in gas lines blocks away from the filling station. Perceiving this move for what it actually was—nothing more than an intermediate-term contratrend rebound—made it easier to accept, to believe, to act upon, the simple indicator sell signals (negative divergences abounded) which appeared that October.

Let's go back to the chart's bottom in '70 for further analysis. Dow lows were made in late May, early July, and finally in August, thus forming a base, and the new bull market was launched on a decisive upside breakout across the 790 level in December '70. Given the base-building that had taken place, and the decisiveness of this breakout, one can be confident that the rise isn't going to collapse abruptly. Instead, the first minor reversal can be presumed to be nothing more than a short-term reaction, during which profits are taken by nervous traders, augmented by selling from those who were so scared by the prior bear market that they want to take this opportunity to flee. In 1971, this phase occurred in February, lasted five days, and retraced a mere 1.3 percent, the market equivalent of blinking one's eyes while speeding through a small town. In 1972, the comparable initial correction lasted less than two weeks and declined about 3 percent. (We have observed over the years that volatile swings against the trend—sharp, scary, short—are characteristic of the *early* stages of intermediate moves.) The quantitative difference between the '71 and '72 swings reflected the fact that the second came much later in the overall bull cycle and hence the market was not as powerful or broad. Such tidbits of deduced information are, to the practiced eye, subtle but highly significant clues about the market's future. Having witnessed a brief short-term correction, you can expect the second, as it comes, to be somewhat more extensive, but still merely contrary to the intermediate-term uptrend in force, *not yet* the beginning of a serious reversal.

In 1971, the second correction came in March; if you squint at the chart you might see it, but then the steep *intermediate*-sized uptrend resumed into its April peak. Consistently, intermediate-term uptrends in a primary uptrend flow through those five short-term waves (three up, two down). Investors following this course must become alert after the second minor correction to the potential end of this particular cycle and be prepared to sell into the third and final portion of the rally. (However, intermediate-term moves *against* the primary trend—up in bear markets, down during bull—usually encompass only three shorter-term waves. You can see this clearly and dramatically in the intermediate-term correction which followed that April 1971 peak: a sharp decline that wasn't enough, an intervening rebound that sucked money back in, and then the second leg down into that November to complete the correction.) It is during the third upleg of an intermediate-term upwave that smart money starts to cash in on their profits while

naive newcomers, finally convinced that the rally is going to endure forever, start buying.

In simple terms, therefore, selling into the strength of this last
short-term wave up of an intermediate-term rise is an efficient way
to take profits at good prices. But sometimes such identification is
not clear, sometimes the bullish emotions of the moment are blinding. *The advantage of intermediate-term moves is that the
stock market's various technical indicators work best at those
extremes.* As an intermediate-term top (or bottom, for that matter) is approached key indicators change their readings, and begin
to signal a market change of direction. The moves that follow are,
as the chart illustrates, substantial enough to make it worthwhile
having acted. (When a reporter wants to know how far down we
think the correction is going to be, our answer has become,
"Down enough to make you glad you've sold.") A correction such
as the one from April to November 1971 also has a second effect:
fewer stocks will subsequently rebound well during the remainder
of the bull market. By selling at the top of intermediate swings,
you get a chance to restructure your portfolio for the next advance. The value of this is conspicuously demonstrated by that
April high because it proved to be the *breadth* peak (as identified
by the advance/decline line), and thus was the peak for many individual stocks even though the averages chugged upward once
again to their higher highs in January 1973.

You can also see that although intermediate-term waves are
sometimes no more than that, at other times they *coincide with*
the end of major cycles. Extreme emotional and fundamental factors underlie major-trend reversals; the end of a cycle *requires*
Wall Street to be so hysterically keyed up for a *continuation* of
the trend that the stage is set for a refusal to recognize the turn,
when it comes, as valid. Anyone looking for evidence of a shift in
the long-term trend will, therefore, insist on a lot of proof and
there is, typically, never enough, when bullish fever is running so
high. But if, instead, realizing that the genuinely *definable* move is
an intermediate-term leg, you focus on whatever clues can specifically point to such swings, rather than the diffuse and laggardly indications of the demise of the primary cycle, you'll catch the

major-trend's turn much closer to the time of reversal. Indeed, you may not yet believe that the major trend itself has reversed—you may be as enamored as everyone else that all is marvelous "long-term" even though you know that your intermediate-term messages call for a correction. But that's all right, so long as you act. On your side, helping to protect you from emotions, is the unalterable fact that *every long-term bottom and top must also coincide with the end of an intermediate-term move.* By playing such intermediate term waves, the big swings will take care of themselves.

The indicators that warn of intermediate-term trend reversals are almost purely technical in nature, stemming, for the most part, from the actual behavior of the market itself—the main exceptions being influences of monetary statistics—reflecting, directly or by inference, the prevailing psychology of supply and demand. (We'll discuss these in detail in subsequent chapters.) Since these technical indicators are objective, in that they are formulated from the actual announced statistics (such as the number of advances and declines), they help expose any emotional biases favoring a never-ending continuation of the trend. And, naturally, when such signals coincide with the rumblings suggesting a possible change in the major trend, they add timing to that aspect as well. Therefore, a policy of trading in and out in concert with intermediate-term trends will help prevent you from being fooled by a major trend reversal; you'll be out of the market well before the long-term picture comes into focus, which most investors were *not* as the market rolled over in early 1973. Furthermore, if you play intermediate-term trends, you'll get some help in trying to time the action of individual stocks as well as the averages, a critical factor apt to be absent in relating to the market's primary trend and utterly deceptive in shorter swings. You'll be on your toes and, watching the waves and being alert for impending changes, you're much more apt to recognize trouble that begins to form in a stock you own.

In the years we've espoused trading intermediate-term rhythms, there has only been one consistent objection: that the intermediate-term has a bad, almost deliberate, habit of lasting a mite *less than* the required holding period to achieve long-term capital-gains tax status. For a long while—chiefly because the bull market from 1982 onward was so prolonged—this did not seem to matter as much as before, but in 1993 it is assuming importance once again. And the problem is real; you might well find yourself with a serious sell signal within hailing distance of the IRS's requirement. Note, on the Dow chart, how both the 1971 and 1972 uptrends expired just short of the long-term capital-gains goal. Unfortunately, the market, with its typical disdain for our personal needs, doesn't give a hoot about your taxes. Of course, nowadays derivative products provide alternative strategies, but generally speaking, we're on the market's side. The important thing is not to let something extraneous, such as the calendar, affect your decisions; only after you have analyzed the market, and your individual holdings, should you factor in tax considerations.

As we get into the chapters regarding individual indicators, you'll see how consistently they've been able to give signals near the peak of an intermediate-term uptrend. Since these clues can be matched with the discernible waves of typical cycles, paying attention to these trends is the soundest way to add timing to your tactics. As you watch those signals materialize at a time when the waves have been completed, you'll know it's time to sell. Do that once and see the market tail off into an intermediate downtrend—that'll make you a devotee of such swings from then on.

Chapter Four

Protecting against Losses

*B*ottoms are made when just about everyone who has decided to sell has done so. On the way down, prices try to lift their heads, but more sellers appear, taking advantage of rallies to unload. With virtually every single share of stock outstanding constantly available for sale, by discouraged long-term holders as well as by short-term traders, it's tough for prices to go up much when the bearish psychology holds sway. But eventually such sellers are exhausted and the bottom is reached, often followed by a sudden rush upward through a vacuum, such as the initial whoosh of about 30 Dow points the day after the May 1970 bottom, or the action after the December 1974 low, marking the end of the catastrophic 1973-74 collapse. In January 1975, the DJI gained 87.45 points, setting a record at that time for the largest point gain in any single month. That record lasted only a year; in January 1976 the Dow shot up over 130 points, reflecting the fact that during late 1975 all those who were scared that the stock market was going to collapse again sold out. The market was so explosive in August 1982 that it became the major front page headline for several days in a row. Once the selling was absorbed, buyers far outweighed sellers, and the scramble for stocks was on.

In earlier days, sold-out conditions such as these often created what was known as a "selling climax." The ticker tape would run extraordinarily late as every last share was wrung out of panicked holders. This type of bottom invariably presented less risky buying opportunities and used to be the easiest to identify, especially if you'd long since sold and were calmly watching for signs that all the remaining suckers were getting scared to death. In 1962 the ticker ran several hours behind floor transactions, and it wasn't until hours after five in the afternoon that anyone knew what price he'd bought or sold at. Since then, the exchanges have taken steps to install higher-speed tickers, as well as measures designed to reduce the number of characters needed to be printed on a late tape. As a result, the ticker no longer cries panic.

Nonetheless, intermediate-term bottoms are characterized by a concerted, and at the time seemingly endless, bout of selling. Astonishing declines—as measured in Dow points—have occurred in the space of a few hours: the crash itself; the UAL-bred mini-crash in October 1989; morning declines that followed the Russian coup, and on October 5, 1992. The lack of a truly-late tape is what has changed, but not the degree to which massive selling becomes culminating. In May 1970, the clue was that, with the Dow off another 10 points to what turned out to be its low, upside and downside volume were equal when downside should have far exceeded upside on that day. At the time of the '87 crash, the clue arrived on the morning of the second day—Tuesday, October 20th—when, after an up opening, renewed selling turned to panic, so much so that specialists on the exchange floor began to halt trading in many leading stocks. Everyone who wanted to sell was trying to get out the door at the same time. By lunch time, the specialists were matching the weight of those sell orders with buy orders—at whatever lower price such matches could be made— and thus cleaning up all the sellers. (See Chapter Seven for a further discussion.) Such a bottom was as terrifying to buy into while simultaneously being about as easy to identify as we will ever see. It had the characteristic of stocks acting in unison on the dump 'em side, so that all an astute investor needed, besides nerve, was ample buying power (from intelligent prior sales). We are often asked, at important market tops, for places to hide. The preferred answer always is "cash;" one profits during a bear market best by the prices one buys back at.

But what makes selling far more difficult than buying is that tops don't provide comparable conveniences. Owners have only a limited option of what to do with their particular stock—sell or hold. With billions of shares of common stock outstanding, all eligible to be sold, and compared to which average daily trading volume is miniscule, it takes a lot of time to form a top. The Wall Street word is "distribution:" holdings need to be sold shrewdly and carefully to late and naive buyers, keeping the price up as well as possible while getting out. It can take days, weeks, sometimes months, of shares tossed into the pot before it boils over. As the size of positions has increased multifold over the past decade, even block trading desks must take their time working off large sell orders. One by one, stocks stop going up. Some shareholders may begin to worry—"why is my stock not going up when the averages have been making new highs?"—yet they hold on due to greed, stubbornness, inertia, denial, or simply hope; reasons are found to explain why an individual issue is lagging, bounces come along to keep hopes alive. The first round of weakness is stemmed by those who believe the lower prices, compared to the previous peak, constitute bargains. A new upward trend ensues, though noticeably less broad, fed by newcomers whose dream of profits has been stirred by the previous vast rally and who now look for stocks to go still higher.

Although incipient cracks can be detected in the rise, savvy professionals stay with the trend, switching from tired holdings to newly emerging favorites. They recognize that certain categories of stocks may be out of it, but other groups are still going up. Often such pros are so sensitive to underlying shifts in sentiment that they discern prospective trouble weeks, perhaps even months, before it actually becomes worth worrying about. Look what that does! failures begin to appear on the charts of those stocks they're worried about; the stocks they switch into assume leadership. Although alert to an impending reversal, they keep at the bull, bypassing those stocks which have become particularly vulnerable. Their buying power becomes concentrated in fewer issues, which, in turn, display more spectacular gains, thus buoying the general optimism. If IBM, say, is up 12, who cares that Woolworth has eased 1 1/4?

Such is the process by which intermediate-term tops gradually develop, with weakness hardly noticed at first, the excuse being that the stock has simply paused for a well-deserved rest and will catch up to the rally later on. But fewer and fewer contribute to the rising action as the advance in the averages continues. Rarely has this divergence between individual stock action and the leading averages been so apparent as in 1972. Overall upward movement carried the Standard & Poors 500-stock average up nearly 5 percent. Yet only fifteen stocks accounted for that gain, while the remaining 485 stocks actually averaged a .5 percent *loss* during that period! An investor who was convinced on the basis of the averages that a bull market truly lived was wrong. The divergence widened in a final frenetic rally at year-end, with all the speculative money pouring into those few conspicuous stocks which dominated the DJI and the S & P averages. Meanwhile, the stage was being set for the worst plunge since 1929.

One can readily see how the public tends to lose money during such periods. Every night on the news the announcer enthusiastically reports the day's gain in the averages ("The Dow was up again today"), but no one bothers to add that the gain was a dangerous distortion of what was really happening on the exchange floor. At the same time, the financial press digs deep into its bag of cliches, referring to each interruption in the uptrend as a "technical adjustment while the market digests its recent gains," or "a necessary consolidation prior to a resumption of the advance," or, in the ultimate of shrugging, "a bit of profit-taking." And brokers insist that "with the outlook so cloud-free, now is the time to invest in common stocks." In 1993, the phrase became, "the best of all possible worlds for equities" even while Merck and Philip Morris had been cut in half, and IBM was even worse. Naturally, the amateur remains confident that it is still safe to participate; those who were frightened by losses in a prior bear market are finally convinced that it is safe to own stocks once again.

Someone, though, is selling. Someone has to be distributing shares to meet this public demand. Someone has to be in the way with sell orders to prevent this stock or that stock from making a new high. The professional, grasping the deterioration that's been going on underneath the mask of the averages and those few eye-catching gainers is perfectly willing to let go of his own positions.

Indeed, he needs naive buyers to absorb all he may want to sell; invariably there's a sizable increase in the number of secondary offerings in which holders of large blocks are willing to sacrifice a peak price (and to pay an extra commission) just to get the whole lot sold in a hurry.

And while this is going on, who is worrying about you? The only person looking out for your well-being is you, make no mistake about it. (Indeed, your broker is probably trying to get you to buy what the big guy is trying to unload.) Kicking yourself later for having missed a selling opportunity may be a self-satisfying punishment/pleasure, but psychic currency isn't spendable. Yet converting paper profits into cash or selling out at a loss when a deeper loss is threatened is not a difficult feat.

"They" vs. You

*I*t is dog-eat-dog on the Street (and it is!), who are the big dogs? And rather than running away with our tails between our legs, can we join their pack? Indeed, we can, for *one of the keys to selling success is to be able to view all developments through the eyes of professional traders,* the market's most invariably successful operators, the fabled "they" who always appear to be "doing it" to the little man.

Just as the folklore of finance has it that the "gnomes of Zurich" manipulate the foreign exchange and the gold markets, a popular belief of public investors says that "they" rig the stock market in such a manner that the public always loses. No sooner have we bought a stock that "they" take the price down and make us panic out at a big loss. If we put in an order to sell at a certain price, "they" won't let it get there; and if we do sell, "they" spring some fresh news that skyrockets the stock on up without us. Those nagging suspicions are not totally unfounded. "They" did fleece the public during the late 1800's and early 1900's, as well as via insider pools in the Roaring Twenties. The 1929 crash and various assorted and associated scandals led to the creation in the early days of the Roosevelt Administration of the Securities and Exchange Commission, which virtually put an end to blatant market rigging. Even so, despite efforts to change things, there's still "inside info." Of course, there are inevitable leaks that constitute the genuine article (the nephew of the company chairman tells his girl friend about a merger offer); in many other cases, it may more accurately be described as "advance" information—that is, knowledge about an analyst's recommendation, or a company's surprise earnings results, begins to spread around the Street...and gets to John Q. only when an actual announcement is made. The intense concentration of activity in the hands of institutions has become a problem in market domination. But, by and large—*and all the more so, as instant dissemination has become the rule*—the specialists on the exchange floor, traders, various analysts and others in a position to "know," no longer have a real monopoly of power or information. "What's going on in XYZ?" is still a frequent question, but it is based on action all can see, and almost always has an answer that can be dug out, or perceptively surmised. Professionals consistently make profits, not through deviousness, but through skill, constancy, and discipline—traits any of us would do well to emulate.

As the major bull market of the '80s wended its way into the '90s, such achievements increasingly became the province of money managers of varied styles—hedge funds, momentum players, value managers, etc.—but at the time of our first edition, much of the "they" was comprised of member traders who kept cashing in profits with such astounding consistency that, in the early 1960s, the SEC branded them parasites on the grounds that simply being able to make a capitalistic profit wasn't a useful function. The SEC alleged that they contributed little to the orderly functioning of the market but, rather, stood around skimming the cream off whenever and wherever they could. It was possible to clamp down because these men weren't closely connected to the exchange's power elite (many were former clerks who'd made their way upward; others were the nouveau riches who had bought seats after the war); there was even an element of anti-

Semitism involved, against a number of floor traders called the "Catskill crew." As a result, when the SEC's new and restrictive floor-trading rules were adopted, many floor traders were driven off the exchange floor upstairs, where, at their desks, they were able to trade aggressively, outside the strictures of the new rules.

But there are always bright young lawyers coming to work at the SEC, and in the late sixties the issue was reopened. The commission analyzed the trading activity of these off-floor traders, and the study showed that a number of them were, in fact, buying the same stock at about the same time and often selling out at about the same time as well. There were tidy profits involved: 5,000 shares bought at 15, say, and sold a few minutes later at 15 1/2, for a $2,500 gain, less only some minor bookkeeping and transfer tax costs, for a nice day's pay. The SEC noted that most of these trades took place after noon and concluded that the evidence clearly showed that "they" were getting together at lunch and plotting which stock or stocks they were going to run up that afternoon.

The SEC staff refused to believe that the explanation lay not in a conspiracy, but simply in the way the market worked. However, a further investigation was carried out, and the conspiracy theory was laid to rest. This is the gist of what was unearthed: instead of catching one particularly successful off-floor trader as he returned from lunch with his cohorts, the researcher found him sitting at his desk day after day with the wrappings of a corned-beef sandwich and an empty coffee container at his elbow. "I can't afford to leave the tape while it's running," he said. "Maybe SEC lawyers can take a lunch hour, but not me." Each of these alleged conspirators was asked if he ever spoke to any of the others about what was hot. "Haven't said a word to him," one sneered, "since we were on the floor together." Another insulted trader responded, "I don't want to know what the others think. If I knew, it would affect my judgment." Still another said, "If God himself told me what to do, I wouldn't do it until I saw that I should on the tape." None of these professionals went out to lunch with any other trader; they never even talked to each other about what they were buying or selling; and they never fixed any market sequence whatsoever.

Then how *did* they manage to buy the same stock at about the same time, and sell at a profit in similar fashion? Because, as it turned out, each acted from what he saw on the ticker tape. Everything that's done on the floor—buying or selling, 100 or 10,000 shares—is revealed on the ticker tape, yet in any given trading day there are only a handful of situations which can be translated, from tape printout to reflex action, in a quick profit. (That is all just as true in the '90s as it was then, but tape-reading is not quite that simple any more. The number of actual tapes to "watch" in various offices is diminished, and in some cases has totally disappeared; desktop information machines enable one to program a select batch of ticker symbols to serve as a Reader's Digest selection of what to watch; the constant blinking on such machines serves to distract one's eyes to any old-fashioned tape reading; volume, an important aspect of such reading, is far less visible, both on the machine's blinkings, which only tell of price changes, and on the tape itself, which usually deletes smaller transactions; and because so much of the machine's info is pre-selected, one can readily lose—and not even notice the loss—the wide-ranging freedom to "learn" that old-fashioned tape-reading provided. We have, as you can tell, the classic prejudices of growing old and believing that things were better in the "old days.")

Even so, the principles of such "readings" remain the same. A trader would notice a certain stock, as one put it, "pecking away"—17 3/4, 7/8, 7/8, 7/8. This pecking, or "nibbling," to use another favorite word of traders, would suggest the possibility that if the price hit 18 it had a good chance of running further faster, provided, of course, that recent prior action (which he had also been attentive to) had primed the pump for such a move. One trader would snatch up his phone and ask the broker on the floor at the other end of the line to hustle over to the post where that stock was being traded and get a size (the number of shares bid for and offered at that time) on the stock; if 100,000 shares were offered at 18, it would be unlikely that demand would be great enough to eat up all those shares and take the price higher, and if it were only 100 shares, it would be impossible to purchase in sufficient quantity for the effort to be worthwhile. (Of course, really sensitive tape reading, like Luke Appling being able to foul off eleven straight strikes until he got the one he wanted to hit, can sometimes "feel" that the nibbling is but preparation for an institutional buy order about to take that 100,000 shares all at once.) Another trader, spotting the same nibbling, might watch with his hand on the phone, to see if the stock could actually trade at 18 on some confirming volume. Yet another trader would simply shoot down an order to buy 5,000 at 18, in an effort to make the impressive (or initial) print himself, and hope the splash on the ticker would, in turn, attract more interest. If the stock ran to 19 amid spreading board-room excitement, those traders would be selling just a few minutes later to all the buy orders generated by excited brokers calling excitable clients. The process can be so quick and profitable that it is no wonder that the SEC and the public feel taken in by the "they" who gain. Yet there is nothing in any of this to prevent you from noticing the same patterns on the tape, watching the same charts, analyzing the same company's fundamentals, and darting in with the same alacrity. The chief difference, day in and day out, is that "they" act—and the public hesitates...and that is true not only for such day trading but when buying, or selling, with any time framework in mind.

How Professionals Minimize Losses

Blaming "them" is a psychologically and socially acceptable way to avoid blaming oneself. Yet professionals can, and do, make mistakes. When they buy a stock and it doesn't go up (even if it doesn't go down), that's wrong enough for them, simply because it did not perform as expected. The pro reasons that the stock went against his judgment, so he sells it. And he doesn't expect to be perfect, any more than a professional baseball player expects to bat 1.000. Knowing that losses are inevitable, he seeks to minimize them at all times. To be sure, his ability to take a small loss is enhanced by the benefit of not having to reckon with commission costs, but even so, if he were relatively incompetent he wouldn't last long in the business; the loss might be less, or slower to pile up, but the return on invested capital would be dismal enough eventually to send him into another field.

Rule One of the professional trader is: *When a stock doesn't do what you expect it to do, sell it.* No hesitating, no questions or doubts raised, no conjectures of the way it should have turned out, or might still turn out, no dreams of how it will do what it was supposed to do "tomorrow." The pro never says, "I'll watch it one more day." He doesn't phone an analyst who's been following the company and ask, "What's happening? Is there any news?" All too often, the delay in searching for the "why?" is costly. The desire to be perfect is one of the prime bugaboos of the stock market, but it's a compulsion that belongs on the psychiatrist's couch, not on the exchange floor. And that means no berating yourself for having bought it, should it then go down, and no remorse for having sold should the stock turn around after you've gotten out and finally do what was expected. We once watched a trader jettison an entire position because it had retreated half a point. "Not acting well," he muttered at the time. But then, an hour later, there it was, roaring not only through his sale price but also through his original purchase price, and going higher still. The trader didn't stop to berate himself; he immediately bought the stock again at the higher price. Since Wall Street is a game without end, he saw the situation for what it was: a brand-new chance.

Typically, though, the amateur confronted with the same sort of performance takes the stock's behavior as a personal affront. Instead of dealing directly with the new information the tape is providing, he will stare disconsolately at the tape (or scowl at the newspaper tables the next morning), inveighing against the "they" who stole his stock from him—and then got rich while he could only watch helplessly. Obviously, this is not how it is done. An unemotional, consistent program for minimizing losses is the *sine qua non* of learning to sell efficiently. (The same, as we'll discuss in more detail later in this chapter, is equally true of selling to capture your profit before a sagging stock takes it away from you.) Unless one accepts the inevitability of some loss, one is destined to wander in the world of would be, waiting, stock in hand, for tomorrow. Whereas one of the amateur's most immediate concerns is not to look foolish, the professional's foremost interest is not to be trapped with widening losses. He sells to be safe, to be able to keep on playing. To him selling is like taking out insurance on his capital. To be sure, you cannot always be as prompt as a professional who can leap the moment he sees one tick. Nor should you. You have more important things to do than watch a bunch of numbers all day. You cannot react to that single tick without having seen all that came before, just as you cannot settle for a half-point profit. But adjustments *can* be made, and once you make them, you're on the way to developing your own means of reacting to the market through a trader's eyes.

Sometimes finding out that a stock hasn't done what you expected it to do requires going back to the notion you had when you bought the stock in the first place. Suppose your expectation of profit was news-oriented: the earnings were going to be much higher, or a new product was due, or a rumored merger or tender offer was going to make the stock worth more. Once the news you bought for becomes public knowledge, the test is at hand. If the stock fails by not doing what you expected it to do on the news (that is, doesn't go up), then you've been suitably, albeit subtly, warned: either no one else cares enough about the news to buy, or too many knew and had bought already, or there are enough sellers anxious to use the news to unload. There are also times when a stock is doing so well your inner voice confidently predicts: Tomorrow morning it is going to break right out on the upside. But when the opening comes, the stock denies its promise and sags instead. Assuming your expectation made market sense, the stock's failure to follow through is a sign something may be wrong.

Market action itself can tell you that your stock isn't behaving as well as it should. For example, when the stock fails to make a new high, when renewed rallies show shrinking volume, when the market averages are spurting ahead but your stock simply isn't participating, or when, after holding well at a certain level during a correction, it finally sells at lower prices. These are all circumstances relating to failed expectations. Essentially, the stock has been unable to do what was reasonably expected of it, and that is one of the first, and often the best, clues that it is time to consider selling.

Using "Stop-Loss" Orders to Minimize Losses

We are concerned here with taking our lumps—selling at a loss when the reality of the situation (failure of some sort) calls for that action. We'll try to keep the loss as small as possible, giving the stock just enough rope to hang itself, but no more. One way to cope with the amateur's handicaps of time and distance from the market (and the nagging suspicion that your broker is not paying enough attention to your account) is to commit yourself unswervingly to a predetermined selling point. Then, when the stock doesn't go up as you expected it to but goes down instead, you react to that failure by automatically selling out. Such a system can deal directly with disconcerting and destructive emotional responses (i.e., refusing to see the failure, or hoping it will go away if you ignore it) by eliminating any chance they have to get in the way.

One such arbitrary formula involves the use of a sell "stop" order, or, as it is more popularly called, a "stop-loss" order (even though it can serve to protect a profit, too). This type of order is placed beneath the current market price and is automatically set off (the term on the exchange floor is "elected") if the stock falls to that price. Thus the stock is sold without any further decision-making; you set the price at which you want to cut your loss *at a time when you can be objective about the situation*, rather than when you are under the pressure of the stock failing. A properly placed stop-loss order can help you match the self-imposed discipline of the professional trader without having to remain riveted to the tape all day every day. It will help you sell a stock that doesn't do what you expected it to do, with no questions asked and no procrastination permitted.

A simple format is sometimes adopted for this emotion-free system, merely by putting stop-loss orders in at 10 percent below your original purchase price, on the grounds that a 10 percent loss is the most you would be willing to incur with any given purchase. If you paid 50, you would enter a stop at 45; if you paid 15, the stop-loss order would be entered at 13 1/2, and so forth. By entering the order immediately after purchasing the stock, you would *never*, despite your inner struggles to hang on grimly, take a bigger loss than that 10 percent.

Moreover, if your stock rises as expected, the same automatic formula can be continued: each time the price advances a certain amount, you cancel the old stop order and enter a new one, maintaining the 10 percent differential between the current price and the price set on the stop order; if the stock then falls 10 percent, that is indication enough that it is having difficulties and you would elect to get out. With this elementary formula, a sufficient rise after purchase will guarantee you out at a profit; if the stock doesn't go down 10 percent before it goes up 12 1/2 percent, you're in the game. Meanwhile, you've been protected from a loss that could get worse while you're too paralyzed to sell.

Of course, the above is too simple for practical use. The stock market is man's most beatable game, and putting the odds to work requires common sense, not just a formula. For example, common sense in poker (man's second most beatable game) tells you that the chance of pulling a flush with the last card in five-card stud is nearly one in five; you already have four, so there are nine others from the same suit left of the forty-eight remaining cards. Nine chances in forty-eight comes to 18.75 percent. But of course the odds don't hold if other cards in the same suit are already on the table—or if none are. By the same token, relying on an automatic formula to place sell-stop orders won't produce predictable results, either, if contrary evidence is on the table in front of you.

What good is relying on a system based on stop-loss protection, for instance, if it serves to make you feel safe about buying stocks at the wrong time? "I'll take that chance," the gambler-investor tells himself, "since the most I can lose is 10 percent." But if the stock has been running wild, *that* may be his reason for placing the bet—emotionally walking into the situation just when the fling down is due. Sometimes, the bet is made by guessing at a bottom in a downtrending market—and that's like placing an order for a loss on purpose. Often those who want to seek out bargains when they shoot for the bottom in stocks that have already fallen wind up getting stopped out (or scared out) very near the real bottom. Many of their choices, particularly in a final panicky dumping, have that 10 percent more to go on the downside. This can be a very painful and unnecessary loss right at the bottom of a bear market.

Often, too, at the end of a massive bear-market decline, many stocks will appear to be starting to hold—the guessing-at-the-bottom phase—only to undergo serious last-gasp slides before immediately turning around and starting a strong advance. Sometimes this sequence forms the left shoulder and head of a head and shoulders bottom chart pattern; at other times, the downside break occurs from a triangle pattern. Chart purists have continually been baffled by this phenomenon, and call it a "false downside breakout," since what technically should have been a renewed decline inexplicably reverses into a big new bull move. The action of Merrill Lynch in the last half of 1975 is a flawless example; we were charting the stock at the time and the action was so dramatic

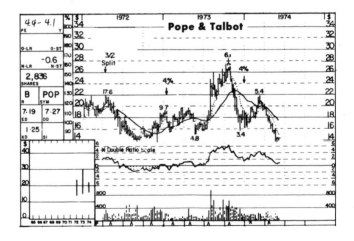

that we've never forgotten it. Since then, we have spotted so many triangular patterns with this effect—*the first direction is "false" and the stock then reverses to move in its "real" direction*—that we've dubbed it the "Bermuda triangle" effect.

But you can see how the initial downside breakout, coming late in a bear move, blindsides investors who dump, and then fail to see how bullish the subsequent action consistently is; there's nothing like being distracted by being proven wrong to cause you to miss the next chance to be right. And in such situations, you wouldn't want to have been stopped out just before the rise because of an arbitrarily placed 10 percent stop-loss point. Consider the accompanying chart of Pope & Talbot during 1973, a rather typical example. Here's a stock that looked fairly good; from November 1972 through April 1973 POP had refused to join in the general market plunge, which therefore made it an attractive buy candidate. But if you had bought in April at around 19 and used a formula stop point 10 percent below—at, say, 17—you'd have been stopped out on the abrupt drop to 15 5/8 in late May, just before the big upsurge to 28 began. How or why "they" did this to POP at that time is irrelevant; all we know is that any arbitrary users of formula stop orders would have been knocked out of what later turned out to be one of the market's best long-side trades of that dire year.

Careful observation of everything that is on the table as well as in the air, plus a sense of timing, are just as critical in the market as in poker. This being the case, it makes better sense to use *calculated* stop-loss points whenever possible, rather than purely arbitrary ones. An earlier Pope & Talbot chart would show that the entire area around 15 had provided support for the stock going as far back as the 1969-1970 bear market. It would have made more market sense to have placed a stop-loss order just below that major support area, on the theory that if the stock broke *that* level, after holding so many times successfully, it would be a sign of fresh and highly significant weakness. Contrast that with an arbitrary stop at 17 based not on the stock's behavior but on the relatively accidental price the purchaser happened to have paid.

In some instances, the calculated stop-loss point could be as little as 4 or 5 percent under the purchase price; in others, as much as 20 percent. *The former may seem like a temptingly "good" (little to lose) bet, but our experience has been that such close stops are quite likely to be set off before the stock goes up.* More obviously, a high percentage (more than the arbitrary 10 percent) suggests that the stock is over-extended, and thus should serve as a warning to wait for a temporary dip in the stock before buying, so that the protective stop legitimately could be placed closer. *The effective use of protective stop-loss orders requires a sensible purchase in the first place.* A stop-loss point that has to be placed too far below the current price often suggests the stock is too high to buy. The buyer who chases a stock that has been running wild has already lost control of his emotions and has no rational guideposts to help determine whether or when it should be sold. Such a hapless individual can be whipsawed right into the poorhouse, as is shown by the chart of Alberto-Culver. After holding through the summer at 5, while the rest of the market was crashing, ACV made its first false downside break at the end of

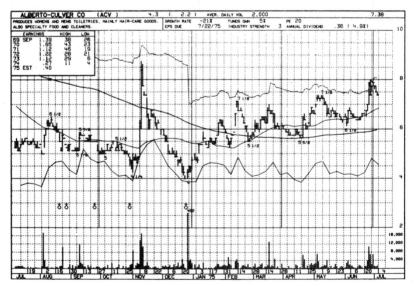

October, seving to frighten away premature purchasers. It then instantly doubled, from 4 1/4 to 8 7/8 in two trading days, so that anyone who chased it as it got hot and paid over 8, let's say, and protected that purchase with a stop-loss order at around 5, would have suffered a huge loss on the subsequent plunge to a new low at 4. But the stock then turned right around and straightened out again.

Indeed, there is no proper place to put a stop order in ACV until after that second "give-up" move down to 4. While a bottom is being formed, erratic and extremist moves such as those two swings down—one might even describe them as "shake-outs"— are not unlikely and ultimately turn out to be all part of a base. When no sensible stop point is available, you need to track the stock more closely until the opportunity develops. For this, reference to a daily bar chart does the job best, as it will pinpoint specific price levels. Sometimes a weekly chart will do, but often the scale of such a chart is too compact, making it difficult, even with squinting, to determine the exact price level permitted.) As a rule of thumb, a sell-stop order should be placed just below the lowest price of the stock's prior support. Generally, such a "lower low" can be considered *the price at which the market is telling something has gone wrong.*

While a base is being formed, any stock is capable of enduring a last gasp shake-out. Hence, if you buy while a bottom is forming, a stop order would be premature. However, when the stock breaks out, completing the base, you should then look for the price at which the market would tell you the rise was false. Using ACV as an example, the gradual improvement was encouraging, especially as a series of higher lows began to develop; when previous highs began to be exceeded—say, on the move to 7 3/8—a stop could initially be placed at 5 3/8, and upon the further rise to 8, it could be raised to 5 7/8. The stock then needs to advance again, beyond the prior spike high at 8 7/8, before the stop level can be lifted, and even then one must wait for a valid level to appear. (Those familiar with these Daily Graph charts will note the 200-day moving average line arcing under the price level as ACV turned positive; this line can also serve as a meaningful message as to where to place stops. A combination of the most recent low that has held, *and* the longer-term moving average line, works well.) As proof that a particular level has attracted important buying, a meaningful support area should be confirmed by at least three days of a subsequent rally. If the next decline were then to drop below the level at which buying had previously been found, it would be an objective indication that the stock was in trouble— enough of a failure, perhaps, to call for selling the stock out. We want to add one *caveat* to this discussion: some stocks have their spike-down shakeout *after* the uptrend has begun, rather than while still in the basing phase as ACV did; after a valid upside breakout—and thus early in a new bull move—one ought to give a

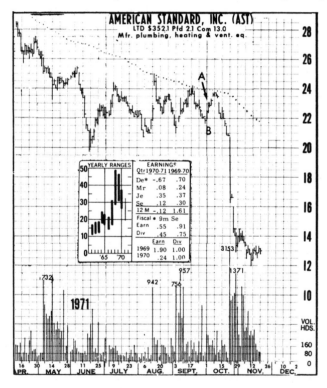

stock more leeway; violent but short-lived whacks are typical of such situations.

When it comes to objectively protecting capital, the stop-loss order is an invaluable tool. Interestingly, a tabulation of thousands of stop orders we've seen shows that almost all are simplistically placed either at the whole number or, somewhat less often, at the half-point fraction. Therefore, a congestion of potential sellers is likely at those intervals, possibly leading to poor executions. The least used, and thus to be preferred, fractions when entering stop-loss orders are 3/8 and 7/8. Further validity for the use of these odd fractions is that the public also concentrates its limited-price buy orders at the round number and at the half-point level, so your stop order should be entered underneath, not wanting it to be set off while there are still potential buyers around but only after they've lost the battle to sellers. Lastly, we feel so strongly about wanting to be under a round number, especially a "zero" round number (20, 30, 40, etc.), we would even stretch a bit to go under that level, to 29 7/8, for example, rather than a closer 30 3/8.

Another illustration of the placement of stop-loss orders comes in the chart of American Standard in 1971. The stock had already tumbled from 40 to 20; there it began to look as if it were building a new base of support, bolstered by an intriguing sequence of rising bottoms: 19 3/4, 20 3/4, 21, and 21 5/8, indicating increasingly assertive buyers. It seemed like a reasonable speculation that the 50 percent decline was over and that a new upward trend lay ahead. Let's suppose you bought at point A on the chart, at around 23, as the stock began rising again after holding that fourth time at 21 5/8. The sense of this was bolstered by the ability to enter a protective stop-loss order quite close to the purchase price. Our choice would have been just under that most recent low; we would have entered an order: "Sell at 21 3/8 stop" (point B). True, one could have aimed all the way down to the 19 3/4 bottom of the previous June, entering the stop at 19 3/8 and awaiting a violation of the entire area as a definitive sell signal. But it is usually the *first* sign of trouble in such a situation that is the tip-off to developing weakness, and in this case, one can draw in an uptrend line connecting those rising lows, a chart pattern suggesting that an initial break would spoil everything. And, we add, even if one had opted for the 19 3/8 stop level at the outset, the failure of the rally to exceed the previous high—halting at 23 3/4, short of the prior 24 1/4—would have been a warning to raise the stop at once to 21 3/8 as closer protection of your capital. At that point, the uptrend line would have been broken to the downside, contradicting that hitherto bullish sequence of rising bottoms. Once the trend has been changed, a move in the new direction is usually sharp. To be sure, there are always those exceptions, where the stock manages to be saved before falling apart. But we are not here to take such risks, and indeed, we've noticed that

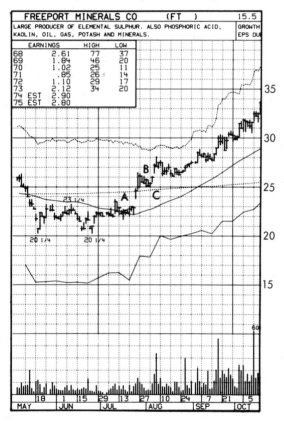

even the seemingly saved stock often gives way at a later date. For our money, we want out as soon as trouble is *first* registered, because that's the way a professional would act.

Let's take another illustration: Freeport Minerals, during the bear market of 1973. The market was getting progressively better that summer (it turned out to be a large-scale intermediate-term contra-trend rally) and a prospective buyer of FT could have jumped in at about 23 in July. Noting the twin lows, a sensible stop-loss order could then have been placed at 19 7/8, which would have been nice and neat, not only because it was under two levels that had successfully stemmed sellers before, but because it was also just under an important round number (20). Notice, by the way, that someone who paid 23 for FT midway between those twin lows and applied an automatic 10 percent stop would have been taken out unnecessarily on the second dip to 20 1/4.

Some people are wary of placing stop orders on a specialist's book, suspecting that those market-makers on the exchange floor deliberately drop prices just to be able to scoop stopped-out shares into their own accounts before a steep rise is to begin. This view of specialists as arch-conspirators is another version of the "they" syndrome, suited to the needs of amateur traders anxious to be able to blame someone else for their own losses. On the evidence, the fear is specious. The specialist could theoretically take advantage of stop-loss orders in Freeport by dropping the stock another 3/8 of a point to 19 7/8 and buying all the stock thus elected for sale. But how could he engineer this? In the first place, he'd already have to own some stock in order to have some to sell to drive the price down; if he did force it under 20 by his selling, he'd be giving himself a paper loss in his remaining position, as well as passing up the chance to sell those same shares at 22, where the stock was then trading. Secondly, there would have to be some buyers down at the lower level other than himself, because he could not sell to himself; it's a violation of both exchange rules and federal law to be on both sides of the market.

Suppose he didn't own any shares at the time, could he manipulate the price down? In the old days, there was such a thing as "gunning the stops," by letting other sellers have their way until all the orders were cleaned out. But now the specialist is expected to—and the exchange conducts computerized surveillance to see that he does—interpose himself to prevent a disorderly market. Granted, a specialist prefers to get ride of a pile-up of stop orders on his book because they could accelerate a sell-off, but it takes *outside* sell orders coming into the market to make that action a reality. If such sellers succeed in driving the price down until it hits the level you specified, thus electing your stop, it would be because the exact circumstances you were protecting yourself against had come to pass. In effect, it would be proof that the stop was needed.

None of this should be taken to mean that the use of stop-loss orders is perfect. Rather, we believe, their application as a consistent tactic is a particularly professional way to play the game. Upon occasion, you'll get stopped out and the stock will then turn around and shoot upward without you. There's nothing you can do to avoid such situations; just chalk them up to "the way the market is" and don't sit around moaning. Remember: a reversal indicates that sellers have been cleaned up; it may be appropriate to buy the stock back as soon as you realize the market has tricked you. If you apply stops intelligently, following a style similar to the one outlined, their primary virtue will be that they can save you from losses that could become devastating. For our money, that insurance is well worth an occasional whipsaw. Take another look at the Freeport chart: the alert trader, admiring the breakout at A, and the way the stock held during the next few days, could reasonably buy near B, with a stop order placed at C (24 7/8) under the pullback low and also under the stock's long-term moving average. A break below 25 would announce that the rally had been spoiled, and you'd be out of a questionable position with a minimum of damage.

On the face of it, it may seem as if the same ends can be accomplished in your head without invoking specific stop orders (e.g., "I promise myself that if XYZ goes down another point I'll sell it and the hell with it. Nothing will change my mind then.") but you've heard that litany often enough to recognize it as an emotional dodge. All too often, the user of a mental stop point is able to tap a stream of justifications for continuing to hold on: the stock is due to bounce back; it's selling for only three times earnings; the yield is so high it's silly to sell; good news is due out next week; and so on.

For the more experienced and disciplined, one compromise method is worth mentioning: the mental stop order utilized by John Magee, the dean of technicians. This approach is based on the closing price only, so that brief intraday whipsaws can be avoided. If the stock *closes* below a pre-selected point (and here again this point has to make *market* sense), then a market order to sell the stock is entered prior to the next day's opening. In this way emotion is curbed because the order is entered while the market is closed, when you can still be objective, and there's the added advantage of selling at the opening (to be discussed later). For those confident of their ability to act decisively instead of wasting time rationalizing, this variant may be suitable.

The principal advantages of a non-arbitrary formula are (1) it reduces the emotional turbulence of the decision, and (2) it effectively protects you against taking an unnecessarily huge loss. First of all, it is worth repeating that purchases should be made only when you know, in advance, that there is a sensible place to enter a protective stop-loss order. If the stock hasn't yet proven that it wants to go up, or if it has already leaped, any prospective point for a stop order would be a whopping distance away and you would have a wise constraint on buying at that time. Later, when the stock is ripe, if you can place a protective stop order within, say, 10 to 15 percent of the purchase price, you're in business. Having made your purchase, you are now protected against absorbing an unnecessarily gross loss if the stock doesn't perform as you expected.

What's more, now that you have already entered a sell order, there is no likelihood that if and when a loss must be faced you'll be unable to utter the order to sell. Nor will your broker be in a position to complicate matters. Many is the investor who resolutely has made up his mind, only to hear his broker respond, when he says sell, with a questioning sigh or a peculiarly intoned "Oh?" "Why not?" the client replies. "Don't you think I should sell?" And then, of course, the door to disaster has been opened wide.

If you place a stop-loss order whenever a sensible point becomes available, the order will be there on the exchange floor and, if need be, it will be executed. Indeed, if such a properly placed order is entered, the stop point should *never* be lowered. If you can see that an expected overall market correction is likely to take you out, you've got a good signal that it would be wiser not to wait but *to sell instead at the current and higher price.* For example, if FT is at 30 when the various key indicators (as described later) warn you the bear market is about to resume, perhaps you'd wish you could change the stop order back to 19 7/8, foreseeing that FT could get walloped back down to its prior base. But is that not telling you—since you objectively can visualize the stop at 24 7/8 being "set off"—to sell at 30? And once it's sold, accept it as a fact of life, with no regrets even if the stock eventually proves you right by zooming back up. Like a successful professional, you've acted on the evidence that something has changed. Whatever the reason (which might not become public knowledge until *after* the stop has been elected), you'll have been protected.

Using "Stop-Loss" Orders to Lock In Gains

Once you've learned to cut losses short, you'll be ready to carry the use of stop orders into the profit side of the ledger. Let's say you've perceived the bottom of the bear market in mid-1970 and have selected Champion Home Builders for purchase (bought at about 5—point A—adjusted for subsequent splits). CHB then rises to the upper teens for a sizable gain. If you'd used the arbitrary 10 percent formula for protecting that gain, you would have garnered the bulk when stopped out at around 14 in March 1971 (B). Indeed, having nearly tripled your investment, you might have felt the system had worked—except that there were over 100 more points to go! To follow CHB up another notch, a 10 percent formula trailing stop order entered after the next rally to 31 would

have been executed at 27—and you can see how costly that would
have turned out to be.

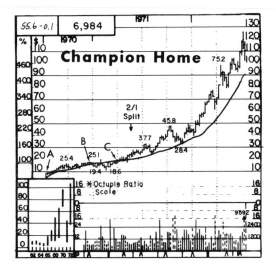

There is not always an opportunity to buy at such historic bottoms, so let's consider a more typical purchase—in this case, as
the stock staged a major breakout across 19 (C). Note the black
line on the chart which represents the Mansfield Chart Service's
thirty-week Moving Average line, a graphic technique which
smooths out the course of the primary trend by calculating its average price over the past thirty weeks. Here it can be seen that on
four separate occasions the price of the stock tickled that Moving
Average line, but then bounced back up away from it, showing
that the M.A. was serving to define the rate of support. Obviously,
any stop-loss order placed just below this well-tested thirty-week
M.A. line would have served as an excellent guide, keeping you in
the stock until, as can be seen subsequently, the line was finally
penetrated. In addition to support areas, the M.A. line can verify
the stock's expected price action, and thus can be used as an intelligent guide to placing stop orders. (An added aside on published
moving average lines: Mansfield's, as noted above, is a thirty-week
weighted line; the charts published by *Daily Graphs* use a conven-

tionally calculated 200-day moving average line. We prefer the former, for its earlier messages, but have found that individual stocks which do not track well in relation to the moving average line in Mansfield often have their useful relationship to the 200-day line instead. We have found no such reliability in any shorter-term Moving Averages—whether 5- or 50-day.)

You might note that CHB's corrections along that upward route had a specific sequence too: there was the dip from 31 to 27, a steeper one from near 50 back into the 30s, another from 50 to 40, the sharp break from near 80 to almost 60, from 100 to 80, and, at the very top of the chart, from over 120 to nearly par. Not one reaction went lower than the preceding one, or, to put it another way, *each reaction low was higher than the previous one.* Had a holder who wanted to stay with the stock as long as there were no danger signals simply adhered to a policy of raising the trailing stop order to just under each reaction low (and under the M.A. as well), he would have had enormous profits locked in, and he would never have been stopped out all the way to the stock's high at 130. That's perfection!

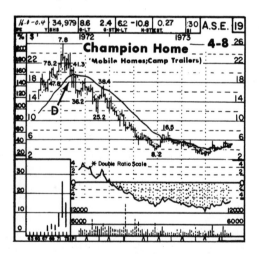

The second chart has been adjusted for a 5 for 1 split in the fall of 1971 (thus the high at 26 equals the high of 130 on our first chart). The M.A. remained unbroken during that correction to 20 (100 on the old chart) for several weeks until, at last, a sharp drop breached the pattern at point D. The investor, pegging his trailing protective stop order behind the action, would have applied a combination of being just under the M.A. and just under the prior reaction low—probably placing his stop order at 18 3/8—and sold finally, automatically, for a grand profit.

Few stocks behave so impeccably for so long, but then, not all stocks go so far up toward that pot of gold at the end of the rainbow. No matter how far, or for how long, the stock's rise, the investor who uses this technique to make sure he harvests at least a portion of his blossoming profit is likely, over the years, to fare a lot better than the unprogrammed holder who says to himself, "That's enough. The stock is too high, I'd better sell." We want to sell, but not so emotionally and arbitrarily. Reliance on objective clues to determine when the stock has begun to lose its virtue is what we want. Stop orders aren't foolproof, but with CHB all the way back down to 3 (the equivalent of 15 on the first chart!) as the next bear market took its toll, it's clear that using a stop is a lot better than passively riding the roller coaster up and then back down again.

Recognizing Realities

*P*laying the market would be wondrously simple if all stocks behaved as neatly on the way up and down as Champion Homes did in 1971. Yet it should be noted that even CHB could have been sold out and bought back many times along the way by an aggressive trader, so long as he was alert enough to get back in. For instance, Champion's penetration of the twin highs at the 50 level provided a key re-entry point for those ready to buy back in once the corrective action had run its course. Those who sold earlier often want to buy back in brilliantly—near the correction low, so that a rebound becomes aggravating. But the player should always remain alert in case a whole new field of play opens up. The trouble is that it is more common, having sold, to hope the stock then goes to zero; the further down it goes, the more triumphant the feeling. Emotional rooting can blind you to what is actually happening; make a point to observe your stocks as objectively as you can.

Sometimes a stock's uptrend will be so dynamic, as was Champion's, that it's hard to do the wrong thing as long as you stay with the trend. But at other times there are complications. The accompanying chart of the daily action of United Airlines, Inc. provides a more typical challenging example of life on the Street.

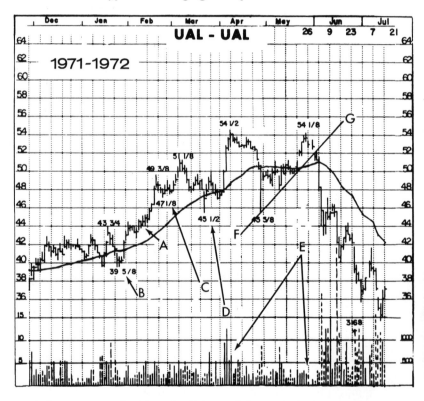

Suppose you had bought UAL in February 1972 at 44 (A), and immediately thereafter, following the suggested guidelines noted

above, you had placed a protective stop-loss order at 39 3/8, just
below the twin lows made in January (B). UAL does what you expect it to, shooting upward, but at first there is no apparent place
to raise the stop level to. Perhaps you might have considered the
47 1/8 low (C) but at that time it would have appeared insignifi-
cant, having been established only fleetingly. In March, though, a
sharp pullback was stemmed authoritatively at 45 1/2 (D), so the
stop logically could have been raised to just below that support, at
45 3/8 or 44 7/8. Many investors become itchy when the stop
order must be entered so far below the current price—that's their
profit, they greedily "reason"—and so they resort to a closer but
dangerously arbitrary price. That's a bit like telling the market how
it should behave. Such presumptuous acts have no technical significance and hence will be far less rewarding over the long run than
waiting patiently for market-derived stop levels. You can see how
anyone who had pressed upward impatiently by using the insignifi-
cant dip at point C would have been stopped out on the drop to
point D, since it was not until that drop that a suitable price for a
stop order appeared.

Does the placing of even a suitably deduced stop allow you to
sit back and relax? It had better not! Sell-stop orders are a useful
part of an overall approach to success but they are not magical,
nor are they the be-all and end-all. Anyone who relies on them
solely will be missing other clues of weakness. In UAL's case, in
fact, that sudden plunge to 45 1/2 proved to be the first warning
that some serious sellers were on the other side of the fence. Even
though it quickly straightened itself out, the stock logically
shouldn't have gone down so far; even more worrisome, the same
thing happened again in April following a satisfying spurt to a new
high. If UAL was still healthy, buyers should have appeared on the
scene at a higher price level, but they didn't. Now, although your
stop order is still unexecuted, the near miss should serve to alert
you to a precarious position instead of allowing you to heave a
sigh of relief and go back to sleep, as so many amateurs would.
The third clue then confirms your suspicions: the failure to make a
new high on the next rally—54 1/8 vs. the previous 54 1/2. And
there is yet a fourth clue: the greatly diminished volume during

that second rally (compare the action shown by the arrows at E). At this juncture, the aggressive trader would have acted wisely if he had simply cancelled that distant stop order and sold the stock outright.

An alternative would be to scour the chart for any other clue as to where a stop-loss order could be sensibly placed closer to the current price. The moving average line in UAL's instance is evidently too erratic a guideline, but by drawing a line across the April and May lows, a chartist would have discerned an uptrend line (F-G) which was defining the *recent* rate of gain. A tight stop-loss order could be placed at 51 7/8, but we would have respected that little area of supportive sideways action at 50 and given ourselves a little more leeway by placing the stop at 49 3/8. If you cover the rest of the chart with your thumb, you can see that a break below that level makes the chart look much more negative than it had been looking. That's a tip-off to get out safely. It's much more important to *be* out than to quibble about a point or 2, especially in view of the fact that the stock went down to 16 not long after. Throughout the years, we've learned that heeding the early subtle clues has been far more frequently significant than sticking such troubles out for a later reward.

Using the Dow

One more exercise in the use and placement of sell-stop orders may be helpful in emphasizing the need for perspective. Let's look at the daily bar chart of the Dow industrial average for 1970, a year which included a major and complicated bottom, analyzing the DJI as if it were an individual stock.

Following a serious decline in 1969, many investors were avidly looking for the bottom. The 740 level in the DJI had considerable historic validity and seemed reasonable, which is why the decline was initially stemmed there at the end of January. Let's suppose the sideways movement throughout most of February, which suggested that the market was through declining, enticed a trader to

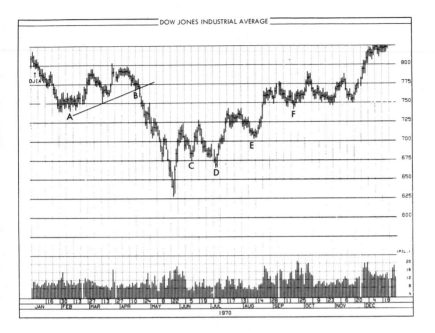

buy. He would have placed a protective stop-loss order just under the prior lows at point A. A modest rally ensues; indeed, the correction in March seems normal and prices advance even further. But there's increasing evidence of faltering by early April; the momentum has gone out of the rally and the trader needs protection much closer. By using the trend line created from the sequence of rising lows, a stop can be placed just under that line which would get a trader out at point B for a modest profit and, more importantly, before a loss-invoking smash arrives.

Indeed, as May rolls around, the situation has become so steeped in gloom that every analyst, it seems, expects ruin just around the corner. Bleak financial news abounds and more is developing, exactly the kind of disheartening atmosphere typical of important bottoms. But that's a hard truism to honor when the headlines are so frightening. (No one says you are forced to buy at such a difficult juncture; our primary concern here is to make sure you've sold your holdings long before that moment arrives.) In time, a wild reversal to the upside arrives, but armed with bad economic news, the bears insist it is just a "bear-market rally" such as occurred in 1930. The Penn Central debacle unfolds on the front page along with rumors that other major companies such as Chrysler are on the verge of collapse as well. The middle section of the chart—of the DJI from the end of May to July 4—shows how the initial rally ran out of gas, corrected, tried again, failed, and broke the prior low in the next wave of selling, indicating to the bears that the decline was on the verge of being renewed.

Notice the relatively high volume at the end of May, signifying panic dumping. Months of moderate volume on the way down lulled stubborn holders into believing that there was no real selling pressure and hence no need to sell. But when the magnitude of the decline finally became scary, volume accelerated. A huge increase in the pace of trading is usually a component of a bottom area; the subsequent fling back upward is made easy because the heavy dumping has left a temporary vacuum of sellers overhead. But when that rebound is exhausted, a second component of such a bottom arrives: a successful test of the prior low on considerably less volume. This happened in early July, when the Dow held above its May low, even though the Penn Central mess lingered. As the market rallied, it performed its function of discounting the bad news and anticipating the future. To grasp that this is what the market is doing is called *having perspective;* without it, it is hard to understand what is going on under the surface; one is left to repeat mistakes over and over again.

One mistake commonly made at such junctures is fearfully putting stops too close under the market because of nervousness that the bear market will resume. Having perspective—in this instance, seeing the classic messages of a bottom arriving (note how different the action was from that of point A)—should guide you into giving stocks as much leeway as possible. One does not want to be shaken out as a base is forming. Thus, by this time, a stop under C would be the wrong tack to take; not until the bottom had been successfully tested and the prices moved away from the July low was D established as a point of reference for placing a stop order. Notice, on the final segment of the chart, that the 740 level, familiar from the prior February, becomes important again, this time as resistance (it's natural to expect supply to come out at that level from those who are now able to get out "even"). Then, when the next decline holds at E, above the prior low, you can move protective stops up under that level with some confidence that they are in no danger (unless something goes radically wrong, which is why you need the stop in the first place) of being set off when the DJI moves sideways in September, October, and on into November. Again, notice now important that 740 level is, for it is once more holding the way it did in February. It may seem mystical, but it is empirically evident that these trading areas are meaningful to market forces. The market is, after all, a phenomenon of mass psychology, and that mass has clearly agreed on the significance of such levels. What's more, not only does 740 affect prices, but so, too, does the upper level around 790 assume increasing importance; it beat back the winter rally and now has successfully resisted this latest upside effort. A tug of war is still going on. But you may objectively back up your perception that this is a new bull market by buying and holding stocks, and not taking the unnecessary risk of buying too far away from useful stop levels. By the time October rolled around, we would have thought that the ability of the market to hold at point F meant stops could be raised to that new and higher level. All those still rabid bears simply lacked perspective at the time. It's obvious that if the 740 level were then to break, they would have been proved right; but it never happened. In the meantime, the objective trader would have already positioned himself on the long side, with practical protection via stops just in case. Identifying that key level of 740 for his own stop-loss purposes would have made it even clearer to the investor that the successful support from above that level in October and again in November was increasingly bullish and that he was on the right track.

Knowing where you are in a market cycle is vital to any intelligent market approach. Sure, you have to weigh what the bears are worried about, but so long as you have the proper perspective on what has to happen to prove their case—and what has to happen to prove the alternative—you can proceed wisely. This is so not only at bottoms, but holds true later in the cycle as well, after an extended bull market, when optimism and blind confidence surge to the fore. As the Dow soared above 1,000 in January 1973, all you could read or hear about was how marvelous business was, how rapidly earnings were climbing, and how far up the Dow was going to go. One analyst confidently predicted that the DJI would leap to 1,500 by April. The first January issue of staid *Barron's* ran a now famous headline, "NOT A BEAR AMONG THEM," as it interviewed a panel of experts on what 1973 was to bring. It was to bring, of course, the worst market decline in the post-World War II era—and the key to foreseeing it was perspective…which is a fancy word for keeping your head.

What Doesn't Go Up Must Come Down

Given ample opportunity to rise during a bull market, the failure of a particular issue to move upward in gear with the averages can be warning enough in itself that something is wrong. Laggards are losers. Speculative flings in search of "something that hasn't moved yet" can sometimes sweep up a laggard issue or two, but by and large, the hope is that what did not happen yesterday and today will happen tomorrow—only because the market seems so marvelous—and as the bull surges on without that stock, the reality becomes progressively more urgent: *a stock does not have to go down first to show that it is becoming weak. Merely not going up is, under most bullish circumstances, a sign of trouble brewing.* Once again, it's time to flog your built-in desire to keep on hoping with that old pro's question: Is the stock doing what it was expected to do? And if some churlish voice inside responds, "No, you stubborn ninny," it had better be heeded. You can give a laggard ample chance when perspective tells you it is early in a primary uptrend, but anyone waiting for his stock to catch the last train to success has been seduced by the optimism around him. If anything, *this* is the time to bring stops up close. Indeed, it may even be sensible to sell out on the very next rally. As one professional trader remarked about instances when experience tells you the stop is inevitably going to be set off anyhow, "Why not sell *now* at a higher price?"

Stops are valuable protection, but they should not be substitutes for making a decision. Sociologists might call over dependence on stop orders a self-fulfilling prophecy. The order is first entered in the belief that the purchase is so marvelous it'll never be elected, but subsequently it takes on a life of its own that it will eventually be executed. Given that inevitability, the emphasis (subconsciously, at least) is on the waiting, not on what the current market situation suggests should be done. In this guise a stop order can be a method of postponing the inevitable. So when you have a stock that's been acting poorly, the first question you should ask is, Would it be better to sell the stock outright? Furthermore, the situation is also altered when the overall market begins to act tired. Once you start to get negative readings in the various indicators, it is the act of selling outright which provides the protection, while holding on becomes the "just in case."

Yet there are times when that churlish inner voice is apt to argue: "Are you kidding? Sell here, when the market is still terrific?" No matter how much that dreamer tries to persuade you to keep on holding, don't listen. You've simply got to learn to set aside personal entanglements with a stock. One test is: Would you buy it when it is dawdling so drearily? No, you undoubtedly wouldn't, you admit. Would you sell if you had a huge profit in it already, now that it looks as if a top is forming? Yes, you nod. Well then, sell it. The truth is, *the price you paid for a stock is absolutely irrelevant to where and when it should be sold.* The level you bought it at has to do with a personal past act only, and brooding about the price (or gloating) cannot be allowed to impinge on analyzing its current behavior. No one else—neither broker, specialist on the exchange floor, accountant, nor the person who's about to buy the shares from you—cares what price you happened to have paid.

And, of course, if the price you paid for a stock has no practical significance, then neither does the price you sell at, except for your taxes. Grasping this point is the key to dealing with your own emotional involvement, for price is the peg that emotional hats get hung on. We must learn to view the market as cold numbers rather than as emotional dollars, just the way the Dow averages are read as abstract points. Mistakes will still be made, but maybe there will be times when you'll be lucky, too. Luck will get you the top 1/8 of a point once in a lifetime; a rational approach will keep you ahead of the game year after year.

No one says it's easy. But you can learn and practice how to avoid making emotionally-bred mistakes by using stop orders to control the fear of taking a loss. Observe *before* you buy where the sensible price to place a stop order is so you can make sure you aren't buying after the stock has already run up too far. (But never buy a stock just because the stop can be placed so close the loss would be minimal.) Having bought only when the stop can be placed a reasonable distance away (10 to 15 percent is desirable, using as reference not only the previous point at which the stock found support but important trend lines and the long-term Moving Average as well), and giving yourself the added advantage of the odd fraction when you enter the order, you'll have established objectively determined protection against the possibility of a big loss.

It is not enough to make sure you aren't going to get destroyed by a collapsing stock; the stop order is a strategic device that can tell you when the stock has failed to do what it was expected to do. It's supposed to go up, isn't it? Well, the stop says that if it doesn't go up, but is going down instead, you *must* be a seller. Of course, you should also be alert to raising the stop price whenever a new and sensible level materializes, and remember that it is not a crutch to be leaned on so you don't have to make a decision. You must always consider the possibility of selling out directly, at a higher price, when the stock isn't acting as expected, rather than waiting helplessly for the stock's stop to be set off.

If you can't be a professional trader all day every day, using stop orders in this manner is the practical alternative. It will keep your losses modest and make sure you get sold out of any stock as soon as it starts to turn into a losing position. You can see where this policy can lead: to a portfolio in which the losers are kissed goodbye, so that you are constantly weeding out the worst and holding only stocks that are working well for you. You will have stocks you've purchased so recently that they haven't had a chance to prove themselves yet, perhaps a stock or two that are wobbly (but you know that you'll be out promptly if the situation gets any worse), plus a whole batch of stocks showing gains. In sum, you won't have to lose sleep over losses any more; they'll be taken in stride. Your problem, pleasurable as it is, will be learning how and when to cash in all those paper gains.

Chapter Five

When to Sell (I)

No kind of selling advice can save you from losses if you persistently buy at the top. But if you follow the prescriptions in the previous chapter you should gather a portfolio studded with gains. That being the case, the next aspect of selling is how to tell when *the market* gets into trouble. Remember, the adroit use of stop orders is giving you objectively determined downside protection in individual stocks. With that as practical and mental support, let's develop the means to identify market tops so we can do our selling while the stocks are still up there.

The investment community is easily fooled by its slavish dependence on the Dow Jones Industrial Average as the signifier of what the market is doing. No matter how many other averages are more representative of the behavior of stocks as a whole (or of the stocks you own), it is the Dow which one's broker always cites when queried, the Dow which the news announcer reports each night. The Dow is even headlined in a newspaper that prints the chart of another average: *The New York Times* publishes a picture of the S & P 500 while its columns invariably refer to the Dow industrials as what "the market" has done.

Because the Dow is so widely watched and worshipped, it has its place among analytic tools. As an average, it reports on what a specific supposedly blue-chip segment of the market is doing; in addition, it serves as a standard against which other statistics can be compared in order to determine market timing signals. First, let's examine the DJIA itself. It is comprised of only thirty stocks, all of them large, well-known companies; some components have changed since the first edition of this book; a few of those remaining are troubled companies. Totally absent, for instance, are the new-era technology stocks—Xerox was never included, nor are today's leaders such as Intel and Microsoft. McDonalds and Minnesota Mining have joined; Union Carbide and Westinghouse remain. Some lopsidedness exists via three international oils, and there is a modest tilt toward more cyclically-based companies such as Alcoa, Bethlehem Steel, Du Pont, and the like. Chrysler was deleted as it neared zilch, but had it remained, its recovery would have caused the Dow to have gone even higher than it has. More of a distortion than what the components represent is the way stock splits and changing companies have affected the way the average itself is calculated. The "divisor"—adding up the thirty components and "dividing" so as to get the *average*—constantly gets adjusted with every significant change to the extent that it is now not a divisor at all, but a *multiplier*. Thus every small change has a material effect on the average, to the extent that—as we write this—if all thirty stocks were to go up 5/8 of a point each, the average itself would be up 42 points! Four stocks each up 2 points can make up for nine other stocks closing unchanged. Thus the math masks narrowness.

But for all its flaws, the Dow is representative of a certain core of the market, much the same way as Middle America is representative of "the people." The stocks included in the Dow are powerful companies and popular stocks; their market value used to add up to approximately 20 percent of total NYSE market value, but that has diminished as, proportionately, more and more other stocks have become listed so that it now ranges between 8 percent and 12 percent. However, individually they trade in considerable volume and thus have the liquidity—the ability to get in and out of the stock quickly—many portfolio managers desire. If they can't move, or do move, it tells you *something* about that core of big cap name brand stocks. So one should not dismiss the Dow, but understand that it is a real average no matter how easily criticized—often narrow, sometimes deceptive, but one that is so widely followed that faith in it can be turned to our advantage as a form of litmus test.

If the Dow and the other market details we'll come to shortly are performing in gear, we know that there's nothing inaccurate about the market trend the Dow is depicting. But when something goes askew and one or more of our other indicators is no longer in phase with the Dow, we term that a divergence. Time after time, throughout market history, such divergences have represented key signals that the trend is about to change. Another way to phrase this is "non-confirmation" or failure: when such indicators as the high/low differential, or the advance/decline line fail to confirm the direction of the Dow, it is a failure of the of the bull or bear (at bottoms) case. What happens is that while the Dow makes the market look as if the trend remains intact, other forces are shifting under the surface. If you can learn to see the divergences while others are blinded by the Dow's apparent health, you'll be able to take advantage of the forthcoming change in trend, instead of having it take advantage of you.

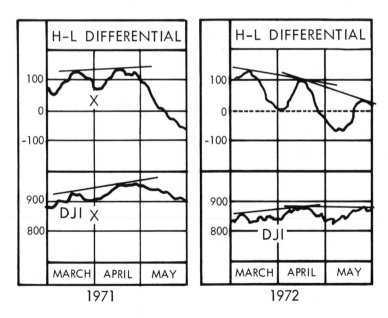

Take a look at this revealing illustration of divergence. It's the high/low differential compared to the Dow during two three-month periods of 1971 and 1972. In order to make the comparison with the Dow over an extended period, and to smooth out any abnormal action on any one day, a ten-day Moving Average is applied to the statistics. To do it yourself, simply add the number of new highs for the latest ten trading days; add, similarly, the number of new lows, and subtract the lows from the highs. The difference, divided by ten, provides the current reading. The next day, drop the first day's figures and add in the eleventh day. If you want to plot it on a graph, it will be on either side of zero, depending on whether new highs or new lows are winning the market battle. The key signal to watch for is divergence from the Dow, showing that stocks are not behaving in confirmation of the blue-chip average. This can be read statistically, with a graph, simply by noting the days when the Dow makes new highs; early in a market rise the high/low differential will be in gear, rising too; later, the Dow will make a new high, but you'll notice that the differential has fallen short of its previous peak. You're on your way to spotting a divergence.

In the first chart (March through May 1971) the initial divergence appeared at points X, where the H/L differential sagged considerably more than the Dow did; and then, as illustrated by the slope of the trend lines we've drawn in, you can see that the Dow rose much more sharply. Lastly, the differential fell away much more severely than the Dow—the average dipped to point X; the differential plunged far below that previous level. From this chart it was apparent that the overall market was doing much more poorly than the Dow's behavior suggested. This divergence was followed by a trend reversal; the DJI underwent an intermediate-term decline to 790 that autumn.

The second chart, showing the same three months of the following year (after a rally which had begun from that 790 level), reveals how the DJI was still going up into April while the H/L differential was already drooping badly. Three market rallies, one each month, kept the Dow going up, but there were fewer and fewer new highs, producing a divergence of considerable significance. The Dow fell into a stupor for the next six months, while hindsight shows that the high for most stocks (as measured by an all-inclusive unweighted average) was actually occurring in that March-April period of 1972.

The rule with the high/low differential (as well as with the other indicators that follow) is that *such divergences are never to be ignored*. As you can see, in both years the alert investor could have caught two successive intermediate-term tops right on the nose by following this one indicator, taking but a few seconds of calculation each day.

How does the high/low differential work? Its signal doesn't appear mysteriously from nowhere at the appropriate time; rather, it has its roots in typical stock-market behavior. During the first months of a bull move, stocks rise, and so does the high/low differential. More and more stocks join in and chalk up new highs while far fewer make new lows as the rally progresses. All is harmony. But no bull market is infinitely expansive. Eventually, purchasing power wanes and profits are sitting there like ripe plums *while* many are *already* fully invested. Now comes the first minor dip. Latecomers, seeing that prices have backed down from their highs into a more buyable range, step forward; their buying sends stocks up again. The averages go to new heights, but because their bargain-hunting is more concentrated, there is usually a slackening in the number of new highs; perhaps only a few fewer, as in 1971; perhaps more conspicuously, as in 1972. Folks are still bullish and toss their money into the pot; the Dow goes to another new high, but some holders are taking profits on this recovery by using the stock's recent high as a guide to where to get out; their supply is in the way of the stock making a new high. More stocks look too high to attract new buying; still others are sold by those who want to switch to enticing new items on the menu. By this stage of the market rally, the ranks of exciting stocks to buy have thinned, and buying is channeled into far fewer issues. This phenomenon makes the market look very exciting, with big gains in those individual stocks and new highs in the DJI, but it also leaves a whole batch of stocks sitting it out like wallflowers; suitors are after only the best looking. What is developing is a classic case of divergence. This kind of "failure" will occur *during* bull markets, forecasting an *intermediate* length correction. Ultimately, though, the non-confirmation will also coincide with a market top, and thus is predicting the first leg down in what will prove to be a new bear market.

This sort of pattern unfolded in December '72-January '73, when the end of the Vietnam war was thought to be highly bullish for an already rising market. When the DJI crossed 1,000 for the first time in history, the consensus was that 1,500 was not far away. Were you buying then instead of selling? Merely watching the high/low differential would have spared any optimist from the disaster that was to follow. When fewer and fewer stocks make new highs, the odds that your particular stock will make a new high have now mathematically diminished. Thus, divergence from the DJI is telling you that the chances for a further profit have shifted against you, despite the apparently lively market atmosphere. That's the sort of message we want from the indicators, because it is objective, contained in the statistics themselves, rather than being emotion-laden. Something has gone wrong, and it is time to sell.

If you want to refine the high/low differential a bit, it's helpful to scan the list of new highs and lows in order to omit, as irrelevant, new listings, when-issued securities (which naturally can make new highs and/or new lows promptly—sometimes both on the same day), and preferred stocks. We now have the *Investors Business Daily* to supply those "common stock only" lists for us. We've kept these statistics in relation to the over-all numbers and they generally give the same sort of signals at approximately the same time, but you may feel they are worth keeping as an additional tool.

Indeed, that newspaper makes studying the lists themselves easier by grouping the new highs (and new lows) by industry group. It would be a sign of collective weakness, for example, if several steel companies were to pop up together on the list of new lows. Note whether the lists—on either side of the ledger—feature blue chips, or glamours, or cats and dogs, or cyclicals. You'll get a picture as to where the market's substance or softness lies. Particularly look for stocks that *first* appear (the yellow blinking light) and those that have been re-appearing (the red light). For important names, you may want to go back to the listings to see if the new high was made by 1/8, and if the stock closed down for the day. This subtle form of failure is a warning that the rally may have become exhausted, compared to spotting that stock on the new high list for the very first time, shooting up a couple of points on heavy volume for a genuine upside breakout. Pay particular attention to stocks on the wrong list. If the market is in a strong uptrend, any common stock among the handful of new lows is sounding a solitary alarm which it would pay to heed.

In Defense of Technical Analysis

*T*he high/low differential is an example of a technical indicator, as opposed to fundamental analysis. Don't be put off by the word "technical:" it is not nearly as magical as the uninitiated seem to think. It's premise is that the market, as a game, yields to the study of risk on a game-theory basis; that is, from the market's action itself. Indeed, it has always seemed to us that fundamentalists, with their scrutiny of corporate balance sheets, cash flows, and economic conditions, have much the harder row to hoe, with far less chance of being right. One of the single most important distinctions to understand about the market is that you are never buying or selling a company; you are bidding and offering in an auction of its shares. Prices are not determined by boards of directors, by an illustrious company name, or by an exotic product line, but solely by whatever amount someone is willing to pay or accept for that stock at any given moment. Now, of course, the real person behind those orders may have based a decision to buy on the grounds that the earnings associated with that particular ticker symbol are desirable, to his or her way of thinking. If so, the market action itself will tell us that someone wants to buy those shares. It's far more important for us to know *what* such buying interest is aiming for, and *how* powerful it is, than to know precisely *why* the order is forthcoming. And then, of course, the subsequent action will show us how *easy to buy*—someone is ready, perhaps eager, to sell to that order—or hard to buy (the order has to be raised in price until a level at which a seller is found). A stock that is "hard to sell" is sending a message that you ought to sell it. The market is the sum of everything that everyone knows, believes, or feels, about every company—and acts upon. So the buying and selling forces are all there, summarized by the market's own internal data.

That is not to say fundamentals don't have their place; they do, but it's a precursor-place. Fundamentals are useful, for example, when, after already having a sense of the market's (and an industry's) future technically, you want to decide which of two companies to buy. Fundamental knowledge was of the essence at the '87 crash lows, when some stocks—*if* you knew the companies—were being "given away" at that moment. Basically, fundamentals are the concerns of businesses themselves, and economists. They relate to stock trends in the sense that so many moneyed decisions are based upon them, but they have virtually no forecasting validity for the stock price. If the next earnings report is going to be terrific, it should be *already* reflected in the stock's chart: in volume, in an edging upward, in a "feels like it's getting better" tone to the action, or even, "it's already up in expectation of that news." Fundamentalists revel in positive corporate results, and cannot conceive of selling during a rosy time. Yet the peak of good news is often the time to be selling, as in the winter of 1972-73, when corporations were reporting record earnings results. More recently, the auto companies came in with record-breaking results in the first quarter of 1994, and promptly got clobbered.

If a fundamentalist approach worked on its own, the price/earnings ratio, cherished by those analysts who must justify their desk space and carpet on the floor, would be a consistently accurate basis for buying and selling. But a glance backward shows how undependable it is: what used to be value at ten times earnings in 1973 became a huge loss in 1974 as the same stock slipped to sell at five or four or even two times earnings. At other times a stock which seems overvalued at thirty times earnings shoots up to 100 times earnings before fading—or before living up to the reason why its ratio was so high in the first place. Because so much of the market depends on mood, fundamental analysis can be the deception at important turning points. "Sell on good news, buy on bad news" is, like other cliches, a truism not to be casually dismissed.

It is, therefore, the fundamentalists who are playing the dangerous, and often subjective, game. Their slick 100-page institutional research report includes an analysis of the plant in Peoria but omits what is actually happening on the exchange floor where the stock is being voted upon. Balance-sheet analysis can be taught, can even be the basis for a particular buy or sell order, but in the end it is nothing but a game of subjectively trying to decide what price is reasonable for that particular stock. Is eight times earnings cheap? How about ten times rising earnings? Is twenty times too much? Or is twenty times earnings a bargain since the stock sold at forty times earnings during the last bull market? or because other stocks in the same industry group are selling at higher multiples? And how much should we pay for information that is being leaked? or is it "in the market already?" It's all a guess as to what value the market itself will place on the stock next week and next month. Technicians, on the other hand, want to know such objective data as to whether there are more sellers than buyers, and how strong each competing side is, and who—professional or odd-lotter—is on which side. Then we know how to play the game with the least risk.

The technical approach is based on whatever the market environment itself discloses: more sellers than buyers, optimistic odd-lotters, fewer stocks making new highs. Behind the various indicators is the consensus of those who presumably know about value, the intricacies of Federal Reserve monetary policy, the prospects of a new product, etc. Collectively they have the strength to exercise an influence on stock prices. In order to profit from their knowledge, they have to act in the marketplace by buying or selling; whatever conclusions their opinions bring to the stock market become technical evidence. Similarly, other indicators measure the emotional responses of amateurs, who have a track record of being wrong when it counts. Thus, in a manner of speaking, the technical analyst has the benefit of Wall Street's best thinkers at his beck and call, and can also determine which advice and activities to stay away from. You think you've got the greatest "information" in the world, and the stock isn't going up—then you'd better believe that the market knows more than you do!

A Contrary Indicator

*L*acking interest in such seemingly glamourless work, the big money managers botch up selling, time and time again. Long ago, we visited the offices of an esteemed mutual fund management group, a relatively successful one as such organizations go. The offices were perched in one of the city's loftiest aeries, with a stunning view of New York harbor. Dwelling within were a brood of impeccably dressed, well-spoken young men (and the obligatory woman), deciding what and when to buy, and what and when to sell. There was no desk in the chief's room; it would have been too imposing, or, he would say, old-fashioned. Without a desk, office meetings tended to be more relaxed, he believed, and, therefore, his subordinates wouldn't be intimidated, would tell him what they really thought about this stock or that. Such attention to detail obviously helps a bit, since over the years this fund has performed a trifle better than most of its counterparts, although, incredibly, not as well as the public could do on its own.

During the market's steep intermediate-term correction of 1971—from Dow 950 all the way down to 790—this team of money managers sold enough stock to put their fund 15 percent in cash. That doesn't sound like much in the face of sharply falling prices and accompanying losses, but it was twice as good as the mutual fund industry's average. To be that much more alert involves some skill, but very little of it stemmed from selling techniques. Like virtually all big institutional investors, this fund's style is heavily oriented toward optimism. Selling is an annoying, even alien, concept, used to take a profit and hence tolerable, or to admit that the stock picked was a disaster and hence anathema.

Selling is a stressful act in contrast to the romance of stock selection, with its exciting stories, jealousy of other winners, and spy-like intrigue. Very few institutional salesmen ever try to talk to mutual fund managers about selling a block of stock, even though the commissions should be roughly the same, and there is a chance to earn a second commission with a new buying recommendation. Indeed, so deeply ingrained is the predilection toward buying that the manager of this fund told us that, if he were assured that the market was about to go down, the only effect it would have on his decision would be to cause him to buy "a little slower."

This fund's modest ability to outperform its rivals can be attributed in large part to the formal setting of upside objectives: the price they feel each selection should achieve if it works out perfectly. On those occasions when all goes well, they manage to cash in at a robust profit. Other institutions don't indulge even in this rudimentary discipline. As a result, they can often ride stocks up, but then they ride them all the way back down again. Funds tend to stay relatively fully invested regardless of the market climate; indeed, by the 1990s this had often been codified by their clients to a requirement. The main reason for their selling is usually to conceal their blunders. That is, they'll liquidate a disaster (the shares of Levitz they bought at 47, when it has fallen back to 9) to keep it out of print at quarterly reporting time, so that the huge loss is buried, sometimes without any notice that they'd been in and out at all! For the most part, they rely on their belief in the inexorable upward thrust of the economy to enhance their assets.

But this upward thrust has not been inexorable; the averages have had their bear markets, and market sectors have had their leadership moments followed by being out of favor for years. The game is a matter of timing and choice and style. Up until about 1984, most funds were unable to get ahead of the game; a couple of better years were then offset by the crash of '87. Considerable struggling resumed until after the Kuwaiti war when, thanks to sharply lower interest rates, a couple of years of outperformance were achieved. (Indexing a portfolio to the averages became popular because it seemed like a simple way to ride a market that was supposedly going up forever.) Their difficulties typically come at crucial periods, precisely when one wants, and is paying for, the help of a professional money manager. This can be attributed to the same trouble that besets the ordinary investor: being human beneath his modish suit, the big-money manager is also caught up in emotions and prejudices. He buys heavily near the top of a rally because that's when everything is stimulating and seemingly safe; at bottoms, when it seems the decline will never end, and his job is in jeopardy, he finally panics and dumps blindly into the market.

From the predictability of foibles such as this comes valuable stock-market timing devices. Although not as pat as it used to be because of the increase in pension fund money, an indicator that serves as a confirmer of major market turns is the mutual fund cash ratio, a measurement of the percentage of cash to total assets as announced once a month by virtually all mutual funds. Mutual fund figures are released, usually around the twentieth of each month, and published in *The Wall Street Journal*. (Similar information from other institutions like banks and pension funds has become available, but not so readily obtained, so the concentration on what the mutual funds are doing remains an important indicator.) As shown on the chart, the low points of available cash come at or very close to market tops; spikes at the top of the chart, when the funds have lots of buying power, are indicative of important bottoms. In large part this is because as the market rises, more cash is tossed in; it has not paid to stay in cash, nor to sit on fresh cash that is coming in from the public *to be invested*. The managers are being paid to do, not sit, and so they do. Late in a market rise, almost like a rite of passage, these managers start spending more money on stocks than is coming into their funds, causing the ratio to decline. At the same time, the other half of the ratio—the level of the Dow and S & P 500 averages—is still rising. The result is a low reading near the top; approaching 6 percent cash has consistently been a reliable clue to a forthcoming major market top. (Statistics for pension fund activity lack sufficient history, but even lower levels of cash are being seen at important tops, due to the widespread requirement of being 100 percent long.) But we hasten to add that the ratio is a *warning* indicator, not a precise timing vehicle; nor should one await an absolute mathematical number. The very direction of falling, and then falling some more, until the cash available is minimal gives you the help you want in telling you when to sell.

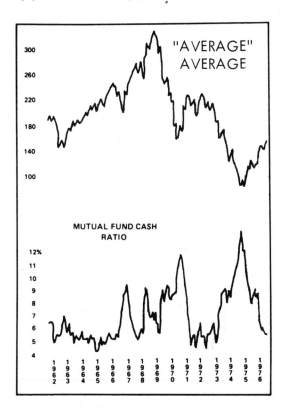

Even after the market has convincingly plunged, fund managers do what seems to be an absurdly small amount of selling. They keep waiting for a rally to get out; they hope it'll be just a correction and not a genuine bear market. But as the market keeps declining, and they begin to understand *why*, their selling picks up.

Combined with the shrinkage in their assets due to a falling market, such selling—plus a considerable dumping late in the decline—eventually produces a relatively high reading at bottoms: ranging from 12 percent, as in 1970, to as much as nearly 16 percent in 1974. The bulk of portfolios will remain invested in equities during an entire market collapse. That's not a good advertisement for professional management when they should be conserving your capital, but for our purposes, it's a usefully consistent indicator message.

The Advance/Decline Line

Many of our most valuable indicators are available in regular newspapers every day: we use both *The New York Times* and *The Wall Street Journal*, and sometimes the *Investor's Business Daily*. *Barron's* reprints the important daily numbers in their weekly edition. In these statistical sections you can find a record of highs and lows, as well as the number of stocks advancing, declining, and remaining unchanged in each day's trading. From these basic market statistics you can construct two different indicators: the cumulative advance/decline line and the advance/decline ratio. The advance/decline line is the most important of all the divergence indicators (although the high/low indicators have a better timing record) because of its report on market breadth. This line is a simple running total of the net difference each day between advances and declines (ignoring the unchanged stocks). Like the high/low differential, this indicator is in gear with the rising averages during healthy markets, when the broad list of stocks is actually doing what the Dow proclaims, but will diverge when the trend is shaping up for a change. Here again, as the advance starts to falter, more and more issues will lag, fewer and fewer will advance as they should on days when the Dow is up. Brokers around the country will hear bewildered customers complaining, "The Dow's up, so why aren't my stocks going up too?" The natural sequence of shifting from a broad, robust rally to a narrower, tired rally is available for anyone to see.

This indicator, too, will take only a few seconds of your time each day. You can start at any time with any arbitrary number (even zero) and then merely add or subtract the day's net difference, keeping a running total. Here's the way this indicator acted in the early seventies, as illustrated on the accompanying charts.

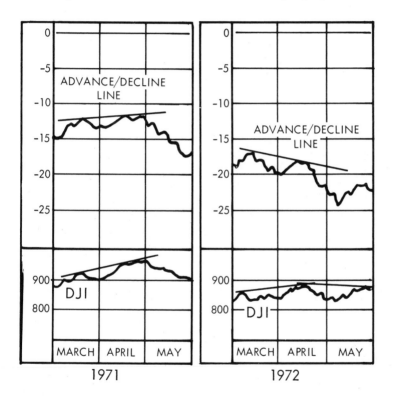

We've drawn a trend line for March 1971, matched against the Dow's action. You can see the divergence: the Dow shot up to higher highs while the advance/decline line held fairly steady. The divergence warned of a loss of market momentum and an impending change in the intermediate trend. The reason it was not a particularly drastic divergence was that this intermediate-term top came relatively early in a primary bull market. A few months later, in August 1971, another significant divergence occurred when, following the Nixon "Phase I" rally, the DJI exceeded its July rally peak of 905 and shot up to 925. But the A/D line emphatically refused to confirm the alleged strength by falling far short of its own July peak. Next, note how extreme the divergence was nearly one year later, as another intermediate-term top rolled around. The A/D line was totally incapable of reaching its March peak even though the Dow was then busting on ahead. By the end of April 1972, the A/D line had smashed below its March reaction low and was heading down. The Dow at that time was still well above its March lows, leading those who watched only the blue-chip average to believe that nothing particularly significant on the downside was in progress. Instead, it was the beginning of the end.

Here, indeed, were three successive warnings of impending sharp market declines: March-April 1971, again in August of that year, and March-April 1972. In each instance, although the Dow made the market look secure, the A/D line was diverging. *Individual stocks that someone may have owned had become increasingly likely to decline even though the Dow was comforting.* What's more, the third instance came at a time when the A/D line was writing finis to its own rise—*that* was its high point, and was followed by an immense drop over the next two and a half years. So the pronouncement was not only of an intermediate-term top but, as it turned out, of a change in the primary trend. Add these sell messages to those of the high/low differential and you can see just how valuable it can be to take a few seconds each day with the newspaper and a pencil.

The rule of thumb that applies to divergence indicators such as the A/D line is: *Intermediate-term tops are made on bad rallies.* Sooner or later, although many investors will be convinced that it's just another normal correction on the way to the end of the rainbow, the ensuing rally will be feeble, less broad and less powerful. Strength in a few Dow stocks uplifting that average will hide the underlying weakness from the public, a few leaping popular names will encourage them to buy some more, but divergences will disclose that the rally is a bad one. The blight will not go away, will not be erased and replaced with a healthy rally again, not until the price is paid. The best example of a rally so weak that *its weakness was the warning* took place in September 1987.

Bear in mind that it takes time for the market to roll over. With a little experience in spotting divergences, you'll probably be early as you see the first signs of deterioration. This can be turned to your advantage since these leading signals will give you the opportunity to sell *into* the remaining strength of the rally. Remember that the best time to sell is when others are clamoring for what you have; failing rallies have a habit of looking "best" near their end, so observing developing divergences can help you keep your head—selling instead of meekly waiting until weakness more blatantly sets in. Such signals, therefore, can get you out near the top, at the best possible prices, and while there is someone to sell to.

The Advance/Decline Ratio

*T*ry to convince those who rely on fundamentals that technical analysis is effective and the reply often is that it didn't work on such and such a day. Because it seems so magical to them, they expect it to be perfect, and since it is not, they reject it out of hand. And yet they use much of its lingo, particularly the terms overbought and oversold. (The word "over" implies, in both instances, that the move has gone so far so furiously that it has passed normal bounds and gone to an excess.) These words are commonly abused by those who write about the market without knowing very much; as facile descriptions, they are used to explain any sort of unaccounted-for-movement, or to justify what the writers hope to do. That is, if they've missed the rally and need to see a dip so they can buy, they'll call the market overbought to justify why they are waiting instead of buying. Thus they apply these phrases subjectively rather than objectively, often much sooner than they should, and in regard to much smaller swings than are warranted. Without being perfect—for, indeed, what is overbought in one type of climate, or at one point in a trend, is not necessarily overbought in another—there is a way, via technical analysis, to come up with a specific measurement of these two concepts.

One can use the advance/decline ratio, otherwise known as the "Overbought-Oversold Oscillator." There are a few different ways to track this indicator. Some technicians track a combination of upside/downside volume and the breadth numbers, but besides being more complex, and more abstract, this so-called "Arms" or "TRIN" indicator has been considerably distorted by the vast number of newly listed (in the early '90s) financial equities that all move in the same direction at the same time. We use a simpler measure: the identical figure already computed for the advance/decline line—the net difference between advances and declines for the day—but instead of a running total (as for the cumulative line), we want a ten-day moving average. Simply add up the latest ten entries and divide by ten for the ratio. (The ease of the math makes a ten-day better than those who fiddle with nine-day or thirteen-day readings, and we have never found any material difference in the way this indicator works.) After the next day's trading, you add the latest differential while dropping the eleventh day. The resulting chart will "oscillate."

The advance/decline ratio has certain peculiarities you should know about. First, in the early stages of a rally it shoots up quite high, so that it actually reaches an overbought extreme very quickly. You are dropping the dreadful minus days of the last phase of the preceding decline and substituting the plus days of a new rally. Hence, if this initial rally is vigorous enough to produce extra big pluses, as it really ought to do to be significant, you can get a powerful new reading; it will look like an overbought extreme, and indeed it is, but that early strength is the message. The averages will dip for a few days to alleviate the overboughtness, but such a whopping overbought reading immediately *after* a big intermediate correction or bear-market low is consistently a message that the rise is just beginning and that it is going to be powerful: *do not sell.* In the first edition, we cited three examples—December 1971, October 1974 (which was the actual bear market bottom) and January 1975 when the entire new secular bull market began. More recently, such major signals of a powerful rally being heralded by an immediate and extreme overbought oscillator reading have been seen in August 1982 and in January 1991 (as Desert Storm was launched).

Spectacular examples come as new bull markets are beginning. Bears dismiss the rally as just "a technical move." Traders take their quick profits. This oscillator retreats back toward the "zero" line, and the proverbial "wall of worry" has been erected. Prices resume their rise in more stolid, less dramatic, fashion. As this new bull market runs its course, there will be intermediate-sized corrections and fresh bottoms; as the advance/decline ratio is a swinger with intermediate moves, there will be sharp rises from oversold to overbought upon reversals from those corrections, indicating a renewal of the major uptrend. Eventually, of course, a genuine reversal will, nevertheless, occur late in a bull trend; *that* overboughtness won't look much different than previous ones so you have to watch a bevy of indicators to put it into context. There is a big difference between the market's situation after a bear market—as in January '75, or January 1991—than late in an uptrend, as was the case in December 1972, or October 1993. Early in a new bull market, divergences and lessening overbought readings will foretell a correction, so you can not only take some profits but get ready to buy back in. The later it becomes, however, the more you must respect failures in other indicators so that you will be prepared for trouble when this A/D ratio identifies the days when the rally is taking the market to just about as overbought a reading as it is likely to produce. It gives you the chance to sell while there are still buyers around.

Thus we would classify the advance/decline ratio as the *timing* instrument most able to pinpoint. While not being as much of a divergence indicator as the cumulative A/D line and the H/L differential, we have increasingly begun to heed the degree to which it can, and does, give a a somewhat similar message—that is, upon each successive short-term swing up within a rally (or down, in a market selloff) successive oscillator readings tend to *diminish*, almost always is no better than or is actually less than the previous swing, while the Dow is usually higher. In this way, the oscillator speaks of a waning momentum to each market move—the best leg is the initial move, and then, as breadth narrows, each successive leg lessens: fewer stocks participate, and folks start muttering "the easy money has been made." But the averages keep rising. Often, there are three swings, sometimes four, with bouts of short-term profit-taking dips in between. Naturally, the second swing up, while not approaching the initial *extreme* reading, still has some vigor to it, while subsequent swings will increasingly reflect late-in-the-move narrowness. (Similarly, this sequence of lessening "oversold" oscillations also develop when the market is in the midst of an intermediate-sized decline, as more and more stocks start to hold while the averages keep going down.) Thus you can *generally* tell where the market is in its overall rise; successively lower readings bespeak waning, as if the market has been climbing the stairs of the Old North Church, tired it has become, and ready to hang out the warning lanterns.

By then other aspects you watch should also be creating concern—you have a pile of increasingly struggling and even toppy individual stock charts, you can see that the number of new highs has begun to lag, etc. But the day-to-day trend has been upward and you want to stick with your own holdings as long as the rally can be sustained (especially since the last few days of a rise often produce sharp emotional gains, boosted by panicked short covering). When, exactly, do you sell? When the market becomes just about as overbought as it can become—and that's what this ratio can measure statistically. We want to sell *into* the last bits of strength—so there'll be someone to sell to. (This *timing* is particularly helpful in options trading.)

Our personal refinement, therefore, is to pay particular attention to the actual sequence of numbers already registered; by observing the magnitude of the numbers which are going to be dropped from the Moving Average, you can estimate in advance just about which day is going to roll the ratio over. At this very moment, as we write this, we are looking at a string of five minus numbers that will be dropped over the next five trading days, and those five are followed by five plus numbers. So we can reason that if the market continues its rise over the next five days, we will have (a) taken it to about as overbought a reading as seems feasible (dropping the minus, adding in the plus) and (b) our moving average will then have ten straight plus readings, which would (c) suggest that an ensuing downturn could go from overbought to oversold rather quickly—i.e., the potential is there for a sharp decline once this rally peters out, and it looks as if the rally will last no longer than the next five trading days.

The specificity of our original example may help you visualize this, using the May 1972 overbought reading as an example, since it proved to have been an important time to get out of stocks. On May 18, a net difference of +466 replaces the eleventh prior day's -84; on May 19, +511 replaces +131; on May 22, +177 replaces -530; and on May 23, even though there are 113 more declines than advances, the number being dropped from the Moving Average that day is a whopping -1,200. The ratio has continued to advance toward an overbought condition even though the rally has begun to falter. And now, counting backward, you can see that the next figures to be dropped are +492, +412, and +573. There's no way for a faltering rally to surpass such big positive numbers and keep the oscillator moving upward. So you can quickly come to a useful conclusion: (1) the market is about as overbought as it's going to be; and (2) considering the other negative signals that were then around, you'd better do some selling right then and there. In this particular instance, the DJIA actually advanced three more days—replacing those three big plus numbers while the oscillator staggered around—thus providing ample time to sell into the still seemingly advancing market, far better than waiting to dump after the market has already started down. Sometimes, however, weaker markets, poorer rises, will die a day or two prematurely. It is not the role of this oscillator to be brilliant to the moment but, rather, to tell you, as no other indicator can do so well, how near you are to the end.

However, do not be misled into thinking that a steeply oversold reading means that the worst is over and it is now safe to hold. Just as a huge overbought reading on an initial rally means there is much more upside action to come, a drop to an extremely oversold level, coming on an *initial* slide, can be quite negative; such markets often *stay* oversold for a while. Replacing big minus numbers with smaller minus numbers may cause an oscillation back up toward the zero line, but that, you'll quickly realize, is purely mathematical. A simple example is the initial slide in August of 1990 (the "Kuwaiti" bear market). The averages went lower in October, and had another big sell-off in November and December. A handful of the best stocks made their lows on the August slide (which proved to be the left shoulder of a head-and-shoulders bottom) so you'll want to watch for those issues that hold above their lows while the averages go lower—that kind of relative strength is what buyers are always searching for. But you don't know which ones they are; you only know that there'll be more selling after such a deep slide has its oversold bounce. For capital protection purposes you should sell the recovery. Let a genuine bottom form—whenever and wherever it will—instead of hoping, without any objective evidence, that your portfolio has survived.

In a bear market, this oscillator is likely to stay oversold even on attempts to rebound. An example of this behavior came in October 1976, when the Dow finally broke below a prolonged narrow trading range. The oversold reading got about as low as it had been in over five years, a signal not that the decline was over but that it had begun. The Dow rebounded in mediocre fashion, and the 1977 bear market followed. Oversold readings on this indicator must literally *dwindle* on each succeeding move down before you can even begin to think of returning to the long side of the market.

In sum, the advance/decline ratio helps determine when to act, provided you are already alert to the need. If it has no message, that's a message in itself that the market is unlikely to move decisively in one direction or the other for a while. An initial move from one extreme to the other is a message of "early" in a changed trend. And when it is "ready," it will let you time the lesser swings within the intermediate trend. Put more colorfully, its prime function in trading the intermediate term is to pinpoint the wave that is going to break on the shoals already detected by divergence.

The Odd-Lot Index and
Odd-Lot Short Sales Ratio

*A*t this juncture in the original edition of *When To Sell*, we
went into detail about the odd-lot statistics. Even then, "the
odd-lotters," we wrote, "have become a diminishing factor in the
marketplace." The statistics are still published, both on the "broad
tape" not long after the market opens each morning and the next
day in the *Journal*, but now that use of derivative products has become widespread, these odd-lot statistics are scarcely worth fussing about. Almost all of those who would formerly have traded in
lots of less than 100 shares now will buy a few puts or calls for the
same money.

Thus we don't track these indicators any more, although we
confess to glancing at the odd-lot short selling figures after the
market has been falling for a while *because their best message is
when odd-lot short-selling finally increases sharply.* The principle remains the same: intensified odd-lot short-selling takes place
just before a steep decline is on the verge of climaxing, but
changes in the ratio (odd-lot short-selling to total odd-lot selling)
are no longer extremist enough to be relied upon. We sure do
miss this indicator because the put/call ratios, which have taken its
place, are vaguer and often blander, are much more and much too
short-term in nature, and are considerably and increasingly distorted by hedging usage. It was the purity of the odd-lotter that
made that indicator work, but options are used for many different,
often quite sophisticated, reasons.

We track the figures for both the CBOE in Chicago—for individual stocks—and their concoction known as the OEX, which is
an average of 100 leading stocks designed to reflect the swings in
the market itself. (The narrower "average" developed at the American Stock Exchange was intended to more closely mirror the Dow
Industrials, but doesn't trade actively enough for our purposes.
Ditto for all those other things around—you can make a career of
watching everything, but we've learned they add little, and when
you might want to know what they're saying, eyeballing them is

usually good enough.) Our method of calculation is simple: dividing the number of puts by the number of calls. And yes, there is much else to track: prices, expirations, and when it comes to the options on the futures, even open interest, etc. Computers make tracking all this extra stuff easier, of course, but in our experience even the basic statistics themselves are not so terrific, and not so precise, as to make it worth doing all that extra work. What we are in desperate need of is what the odd-lot statistics provided: what's the little guy doing? because he's apt to be wrong at important, and emotional, turning points. Put/call ratios provide a partial albeit flawed answer, and might be said to measure sentiment generally. As long as it is a ratio, whatever it measures has a message when it changes.

There's the raw data itself. (If you do your work in the evenings, you can get the statistics from Chicago via a recorded message.) *Extreme readings typically cap moves.* A CBOE put/call ratio over 1.00 is an extreme, and you don't need to or want to sell when such a reading is reported—the decline has become overdone, and if you panic you'll be joining the crowd. An OEX extreme is rather more vague—high readings in the 1.40 area would count. Because options on such averages are much used as hedging tools by money managers, their kind of big order can distort the statistics, and represent a "reason" which is often contra-speculative, when it is the emotions of speculation that we are trying to measure. And because they think they are being sophisticated, they'll often use spreads and further out options as well; one "reason," for example, can be to lock in their profits for the year; another, for those who are required to be fully invested, may more simply be to protect those positions with put "insurance." Thus spasmodic days of extreme OEX ratios can occur; we prefer to consider an emotional extreme when it features a dramatically higher CBOE reading as well.

Naturally, this works at the other end of the spectrum as well. *Low readings are "sell" messages.* They are likely to coincide with an already-getting-overbought oscillator, toppy and perhaps already failing stocks, and other troublesome indicators. Ratios in the 50s for the CBOE, in the 70s for the OEX, are to be treated

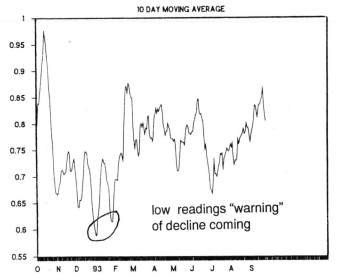

CBOE PUT/CALL RATIO

10 DAY MOVING AVERAGE

low readings "warning"
of decline coming

with respect. (One exception is during triple witching week, with its attendant distortions.) Two or three rising-Dow-days in which the ratios get progressively lower are often the way the message unfolds. We keep both statistics on a ten-day moving average basis because this gets away from the very-short-term raw data readings and into a much more desirable *intermediate-term* perspective. If you do this for awhile, you will begin to see *areas* at the top of the chart page (high readings—too much bearishness and put buying) from which rallies usually begin, and *areas* at the bottom of the chart (low readings—too much optimism and call buying) from which declines usually begin. Thus *the put/call ratios are basically contrary indicators* just as the odd-lot short-sellers were— you want to do the opposite of what option players are doing when they are doing it to an extreme extent.

Believing the Indicators

*T*he foregoing are simple indicators to keep, requiring very little time each day. It is better to keep your own statistics and charts, rather than relying on outside services, because when the answer is right there at your fingertips you are a lot more likely to see it, and believe in it. Very few take the time. The typical shareholder is busy making excuses: the Dow is up, so his stocks will surely follow sooner or later, or, the Dow is down but it will soon rise again in some inexorable fashion. The typical broker is busy calling clients: the market is up and going higher, so he wants to get 'em to do some more buying. But the astute seller must learn to follow his own calculations rather than the forecasts of experts or the deceptive action of the Dow. Doing your own calculations and keeping your own charts will actively provide the objective answer to "What's the market doing?" rather than the sound-bite answer that doesn't help at all. (Being old-fashioned, we continue to keep these statistics by hand in a notebook. Recording them in your computer will take little longer, while providing several advantages: doesn't make careless math mistakes; can simultaneously prepare the material for you to see in graph form; and the game of "What if?" can be played, especially for those indicators based on moving averages.) To be sure, there will still be the burden of making a decision *and* acting on it. Warnings are easily dismissed as being too vague, imperfect, premature, or, even, too ominous to accept. But in the stock market an indicator that cries wolf on occasion is better than a system that remains silent while the lambs are being slaughtered.

These indicators are not the concoctions of alchemists, nor do they have the faintest resemblance to tea leaves. They develop from the market's internal action, and *objectively*—because they are what they are—illustrate what is going on beneath the headlines. They don't tell you why (and it's often better that you don't know), but do demonstrate what, and that "what" is useful enough. We must also add that it is possible to extract from such a plethora of statistics umpteen different indicators, or to twist simple measurements into pretzel-like devices. We knew one investor who decided, he told us, that a nine-day Moving Average works better than a ten-day, and to this we respond "So what?" A ten-day calculation makes the arithmetic vastly easier; and nothing is so precise that the difference of a day will matter, unless you are on the floor trading options or futures, and in that case you ought to be watching a minute-by-minute or tick-by-tick chart rather than the day itself. If nine days works sometimes, so will eleven or eight at other times. Similarly, there are those who place absolute credence in minuscule differences: if the A/D line makes a new high by +2, they are delighted at the signal. To us, it is mathematically trivial; we want decisive readings. And then there are others who see what the indicators are saying, but when they don't want to believe the message, they rationalize, finding six other obscure indicators that say otherwise, or preferring a rumor or arcane interpretation that "explains" the undesired reading; they believe it'll change tomorrow, or it won't matter that much in terms of price or time or both, so that they can keep their feet up on the desk without having to do anything. It's hard work believing in simple indicators; it can be exhausting, and risky, to have to act. For our money, when you see that everything is in gear, according to your statistics and charts, you can put your broker on hold and have patience; as soon as divergences begin to appear, move to the edge of your chair. You are seeing the first warnings of a change in trend, well ahead of top time.

But don't expect them to shout off the page at an exact moment. They are guidelines, tools to help you grasp objectively what is going on in the marketplace. They may not be perfect (premature; a bit wishy-washy; full of whipsaws; even inaccurate once in a while), but that's why you want to watch several of them rather than just one. Then you can see what the weight of the evidence suggests. This is important to understand because other sources will be trying to push you in other directions. The headlines and write-ups, and in particular the seductive flow of commentary on CNBC, will be surface summations of what the Dow and a few fancy stocks are doing, plus superficial and/or standard technical commentaries that prove the truth of the old expression about "a little knowledge is a dangerous thing." And your own broker will be phoning you with (what else can he say?) a mass of tales and firm-proffered and promoted recommendations. By delineating tendencies and revealing shifts, technical indicators measure with objectivity what the market's underlying condition is; then it is up to you to decide what steps to take. When it comes to potential tops, the indicators serve to alert investors to impending trouble, like a medical exam that reveals too much cholesterol, high blood pressure, or other danger signs. Sure, the patient may survive, may just have a setback and recover, may even last longer than the prognosis suggests, but the odds are against him unless protective measures are taken promptly. So too in the market: symptoms warn, "Better safe than sorry."

The financially healthy investor, of course, doesn't wait for the indicators to jump up and grab him by the lapels, any more than the person careful about his physical well-being waits for unbearable pain to begin. There are always questions to be asked about the market—suspicious, cynical, paranoid questions, if you will— and the answers just might give you an advantage. "Why did Westinghouse go down on a day the DJI rallied 10 points?" (When there's no ready answer, the action is apt to be more serious, and earlier, than if there's a readily available explanation.) "Why is the list of new lows full of machine-tool stocks when everyone says cyclicals are the place to be?" "Why did all those glamour stocks close at their lows for the day, even though they were up?" Such questions not only help keep you alert, they provide you with a sense of whether the market is all it is supposed to be. The indicators themselves, dealing with specific data and specific sectors, are ways to objectify such questions.

It's taken you far longer to read this than it will to keep up with these statistics each day. We repeat: Don't rely on someone else to do what will take you so little time. You'll find you get a much better feel for what is actually happening by keeping your own hand and mind in. This chapter has presented a few major indicators: two divergence measures (the cumulative advance/decline line and the high/low differential); one timing guide (the advance/decline ratio that serves as an overbought/oversold oscillator); and a sentiment indicator replacing the odd-lotters of old (the put/call ratios). Each are based on statistics to be found in the daily newspaper tables, plus one monthly reading (the mutual fund cash ratio), which reports on broader sentiment within the longer-term trend. Other indicators with good records, whose statistics appear once a week or once a month, will be discussed next, so you will have a suitable array for identifying turns. Rarely will one indicator act in isolation; usually many will be saying "sell" in various tones at just about the same time. Don't expect a bell to go off; but when they are "speaking" about the same troubles, believe them.

Chapter Six

When to Sell (II)

With indicators, as with love making, there is one essential goal; a few interesting variations reliably achieve this goal, while a host of others work only sporadically. Only the obsessed try them all. At a meeting of the Wall Street Technicians we once attended, a brokerage-house analyst proudly described ninety-seven different market indicators that he maintained on a regular basis. That gave him the appearance of being an expert's expert, but finally someone asked: "What are those indicators telling us now?" And the analyst was forced to admit: "I'm not sure." Some were bullish, some were unfavorable, still others were meandering around saying nothing of use. So how could he decide?

Obviously, one can overload the circuitry. There is no good purpose served by trying to track so many indicators that the ultimate answer is obscured. And yet, folks adore computerized systems that'll put up four charts at once on the screen. Not only can so much lead to too little, some individual indicators yield data that is too inconsistent to rely on, or too short-term in nature. Two changes in the last decade have combined to turn not only the technical indicators but the investors' point of view toward the very short-term: the development of the computer and the development of derivative products. Computer software shows RSI and stochastics in nine-day chunks; stock charts that the machines put up on the screen are often no more than six months in duration, and in some cases are accompanied by five and fifteen-day moving average lines. There is an unstated but pervasive goal of "what's going to happen right now?" so that, in search of instant gratification, the user can buy a put or call or trade the futures or options on the futures or whatever arcane combination the computer can calculate. The market, however, does not care about such things, nor can it read a calendar; it is so broad, so diverse, that it cannot be hugged by a computer—although, of course, it can be used, as a gigolo might use a wealthy woman, for program trading purposes...perhaps the most extreme of all momentary-trading devices.

The ability of the computer to calculate has made "money flow" statistics much more precise than they were at the time of our first edition. They still are too inconsistent for our purposes and lack timing, but we've found that when—*after*—we have begun to focus on an individual stock chart that is developing a serious top, deteriorating money flow is useful information in proceeding to act. It, and other computer-generated and now very popular indicators such as RSI and stochastics, work as divergence messengers—stock going up, while the stochastic level is rolling over. We would dub all such computer-generated material as confirmers, hand-holders, *and* warn you to understand that they are much more short-term oriented than you are or the market is. (The exception is money flow, which can be more intermediate-term in nature, and more reliable as well.) You can, of course, put some of our old-fashioned indicators on the computer to your advantage: the chart they'll show will make the message more vivid.

Through the years, a handful of other measurements also have proved themselves consistent enough and perceptive enough to be included in this technical approach to timing—well, it isn't timing so much any more as *forecasting.* We will leave timing to those who want to buy a call at the exact moment the stock is about to rise, and concentrate our efforts on trying to anticipate when market, and individual stock, trends are *about to* change. In the fifteen years since the first edition, some have become trivial (the odd-lot statistics); others consistently work (the advance/decline line and ratio, and the high/low stuff); still others, as we shall see, have had their parameters altered. Those basic indicators, as described in the previous chapter, should keep you alert to what is going on regarding the intermediate-term trend. But a few other special weapons should be added to your arsenal to further improve your ability to anticipate trend changes.

An "Average" Average

*T*he Dow, as we've already pointed out, represents only thirty supposedly blue-chip, old-line stocks, many out of fashion, others mummified, and in the calculation of its "average" so distorted by stock splits and replacement names that it has become a mathematical freak—its so-called divisor has become a multiplier. More and more frequently, thanks to games played with derivatives, this average can be up (or down) when the rest of the market chalks up a "down" (or up) number. And market history shows the occasions when the DJIA, like a chicken with its head cut off, runs wild long after the market has stopped rising, as the grand finale top of January 1973 or the pre-crash summer of 1987 exemplify. That's why we use it to measure our divergences.

The other widely used averages are the New York Stock Exchange composite and the Standard & Poor's 500. Both are heavily weighted in favor of large capitalization, which causes its own form of distortion. Both are calculated by multiplying a stock's price by the number of shares outstanding. Thus, large capitalized companies exert an extra influence on the apparent action of these averages. The higher and longer a particular stock group rises, as the oils did in 1979 and 1980, the more the action of those stocks begins to dominate the achievements of these broad averages because they become, increasingly, the biggest of the "big-cap" stocks. As it happens, those are the stocks institutions favor because of their liquidity—they can be readily bought and sold in large quantities. (When something goes wrong, you want to be able to get out quickly.) Because they concentrate on such issues, their buying has a self-fulfilling prophecy to it, causing the averages to go up. In early 1973, the market looked much better than it actually was, due to strong gains in "the Nifty Fifty" stocks favored by institutions. At one point, the S & P composite was up some 5 percent, and that gain was accounted for by a mere fifteen stocks! The other 485 were actually down during that time span.

The way to avoid being deceived by this sort of flimflammery is to have your own market average. Here's how, using the statistics furnished on the Quotron desk-top interrogation machine (QCHA for the NYSE; QACH for the American Stock Exchange). *Barron's* conveniently carries this information each week in its statistical pages, so that the calculating for an average of your own can be done once a week in just a few minutes. (The Automatic Data system, which we sit in front of in our current office, uses the symbol MKCN with similar results.) What QCHA provides is the collective percentage price change for all NYSE common stocks at any given moment, as it relates to the previous day's close. A reading of, say, +.50 means that the average percentage change from the day before for all common stocks is a gain of one half of 1 percent. That is the average percentage change for the average stock. Unlike the weighted averages or the Dow Industrials, it tells you what the entire list is actually doing. As a simple illustration, if the DJI were up 30 points from 3300 to 3330, for a gain of 1 percent, and QCHA reported the gain for the average stock as being +.50, you'd know the Dow had been twice as "strong" as the rest of the market. When that happens in the course of a rally, it can be a sign of deterioration and of narrowing. Divergence is rearing its dangerous head again, and it is time to consider selling.

Much of this can be seen at a glance by comparing the two statistics. Times when QCHA leads will be times of broad participation and lively action in smaller stocks. And there are times when the Dow is up and QCHA is actually down for the day—a sign of an awful rally no matter what the media says. Learning about these distinctions can be important over a longer period of time, too, so you should keep your own "average" average yourself along with the other statistics being described in this book. To begin, simply start at an arbitrary number (100 is easiest) and multiply it by the closing percentage change. A gain is then added to the base number; a loss is subtracted. Do this each day, by multiplying the preceding day's result by the new percentage change, and you've got a computer-based, totally unweighted, all-inclusive average. This "average" average is what your own portfolio should be compared to for relative performance, because it is as close to a true picture of the overall market trend as you can get.

Obviously, the single closing figure will produce a simple line chart, rather than the conventional bar chart with its high, low, and close. But that's okay; if you let your computer keep this statistic for you (doesn't make math mistakes, remember), it'll also let you play with the proper scale for its chart. This should make it easier to read precisely where key highs and lows occurred in the past. You'll find that its look will be reasonably similar to the cumulative advance/decline line; any deviation is likely to be caused by a single sector—again, useful information for your overall understanding.

It is also a good idea to keep a Moving Average of your "average" average. Moving Averages, as noted previously, smooth out the distortions that can occur in a day-to-day or week-to-week chart. So short-term oriented has the market become since the crash that many people use brief time spans for their moving averages. While a ten-day M.A. is helpful for many indicators, when it comes to market averages a much longer time span is used to smooth out the picture of the primary market trend. Commonly used thirty- or fifty-day moving averages seem to us full of whipsaws, crossings back and forth to no avail, and other distracting and deceptive looks. As traditionalists, we vote for a 200-day Moving Average, which is essentially forty weeks, or a 150-day (thirty weeks). Your computer can make these calculations for you. Plot the Moving Average on the same chart as the "average" average to see how the trend is shaping up and to get signals. Most of us tend to be impatient and to make too much of minor jiggles; the M.A. gives us some much needed perspective. An up trend which continues for a long time without the M.A. being crossed becomes increasingly important. Not until the rising M.A. stops going up, rolls over and starts down, *and* is intersected by the daily unweighted average's action, can it be considered definitive that a major change in trend is underway. (Of course, if an individual stock goes through that reversal sequence you'd start selling it independently of what the market was doing.) Similarly, long-term bottom buying clues can come from the reversal of the Moving Average as it coincides with turns in price action. The M.A.'s inviolate downtrend should help you refrain from buying until the bottom is established. Otherwise, you will, at best, be painfully and unnecessarily early.

CHART A

1969 – 1970 BEAR MARKET

30 – Week Moving Average

NYSE "Average" Average

1969   1970
JAN. APR. JUL. OCT. JAN. APR. JUL. OCT.

Two examples of applying this to stock-market reality are shown on the accompanying charts. In chart A, a thirty-week Moving Average has been plotted along with an "average" average. Notice in the upper-left-hand corner that, at the start of 1969, both warnings happened almost simultaneously: the "average" average broke through the Moving Average, and the M.A. itself arced over and headed down. This came virtually at the top of the market for all common stocks in early 1969. The M.A. then contained the entire decline—keeping you out of stocks until the reverse took place in the fall of 1970. (Remember that Moving Averages are mathematical: they don't roll over until you are replacing higher numbers with lower numbers.)

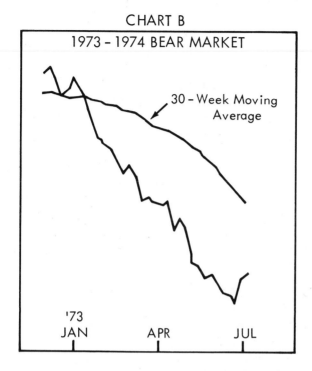

CHART B
1973 - 1974 BEAR MARKET
30 - Week Moving Average
'73
JAN   APR   JUL

A similar top signal is shown in chart B. The breakdown through the Moving Average line occurred in January 1973, a few days after the Dow made its then all time high over 1,000. With the M.A. heading downward, it was a signal to sell all your stocks at virtually the exact top. Now look at July 1973, when a powerful rally was about to begin. You'll notice that it was then a huge distance away from a still sharply *declining* Moving Average, a sure clue to beware of the bear. The chart was telling you that there was room for a rally, but it was far too early to expect a major trend reversal. *That* came more than a year later, when the Moving Average was much closer, and thus capable of being penetrated earlier in the rally. Even then—and this is the nature of bottoms—it took two lows months apart to make the turn full-fledged.

While this discussion centers on applying a Moving Average to the "average" average, we have developed, through the years, these guidelines: (a) when an M.A. wanders *through* the price action (of a stock or average), a subsequent crossing should be considered of little consequence; (b) when the M.A. has contained the entire price action through several short-term swings, a subsequent crossing is not only clear but also decisive; and (c) if the M.A. is still heading upward (or downward, when awaiting some kind of bottom opportunity) it is still *early*. It takes time for a moving average to turn, and you are deliberately using a longer-term average so as to get a longer-term message of turning; you will find yourself being early enough if you wait patiently for the M.A. to start arcing.

Indicators Using Other Averages

As one version of a very broad average, this unweighted "average" average can be helpful in itself, as well as serving as an antidote to the deceptions of the Dow Industrial average. Just making the comparison on a day when the DJIA has had an exceptional move can provide a useful check. (In 1993-1994, we've been particularly aware of how many down or up days the Dow has had by itself—while QCHA at a glance was "saying" the rest of the market was actually doing the opposite.) But there is another average that also can be used effectively in this regard: the Dow Utility average. Because the DJU represents a sector of the market peculiarly influenced by such factors as money rates and industrial activity, it is a technically useful barometer, even for those who are such swingers that they'd never buy supposedly staid utility stocks. Periods when the Utilities and the Industrials are moving in the same direction (are "in gear") are the norm, to be expected. But on several different, and vital, occasions such as 1965, 1973, and 1993, the DJU has *led* the rest of the market, by topping out and heading down before any such behavior in the

DJIA or S & P 500. (Similarly, it can serve as a leading indicator when first to bottom and head up, as it did in mid-1982 and the summer of 1974.) It's a simple matter to track this indicator since it and the DJI are charted one under the other in *The Wall Street Journal* every day. When the Utility Average refuses to participate in a rally, not just for one or two days, but for a couple of weeks or more, its divergence becomes significant, warning of potential trouble for the rest of the list. It's hard to believe, because the other averages are still bubbling, but simple in concept because such a divergence is the forerunner of a major change in the direction of interest rates.

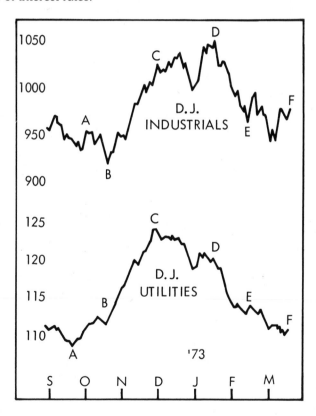

The chart on the previous page shows the leading nature of the DJU at work. Note how, in 1972 (A & B), the rising DJU vs. the falling DJI forecast a rally for the market, with the Industrials then shooting up over 1,000. But in December 1972, the DJU began to warn that something was seriously amiss. It kept sliding in conspicuously divergent fashion while the DJI was continuing up (C & D). As if that weren't enough, when the DJI was struggling to firm up in March 1973 and the "bargain" hunters were already at work, the DJU stubbornly refused to go along, producing a radical divergence at E & F; that continued divergence warned that the market was still heading downward. As a rule, *what doesn't make sense is doubly important*, and Dow Utility divergences are one of the most significant illustrations of that truism.

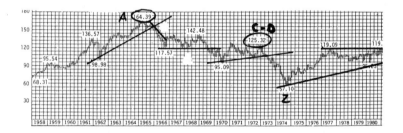

Such negative divergences can have long-term significance as well. After being the market leaders for nearly three years, utility stocks began to falter in the spring of 1965; the DJU failed to make a new high and began to decline even though the Industrials were still going up, for warning number one. A 10% DJIA correction followed a few weeks thereafter. The Industrials then rallied while the Utilities *persisted* on their downward course for warning number two, a powerful message that the rally was doomed to failure; the FRB raised the discount rate, and a few weeks thereafter the 1966 bear market began. A look at the long-term trend shows that the Dow Utility Average declined for *nine* years (A to Z) after that initial negative divergence—although there were several intervening rises of some magnitude (including the major divergence at C-D depicted in close-up on the previous page), not one was able to go to a higher high. The downtrend continued until the summer of 1974—for a total haircut of 67 percent!—until a positive divergence (DJU starting to rise while the Industrials were still going down) developed. There have been bear (and bull) markets without such a Utility warning of a reversal coming, but to the best of our knowledge every negative divergence has been followed by a serious market decline, and every decline thus forewarned has ultimately also had a positive divergence signal that the entire bear was over.

A more recent example (not yet completed as we write) appeared in October 1993. Although that was a period when naive investors were "taking more risk to get more yield," the Dow Utility average was collapsing! Answers to "Who was selling?" and "Why?" didn't matter, compared to the "doubly important" divergence that was taking place. Charts of the individual electric utility components of that average showed that the declines were widespread across the country; sophisticated and experienced investors had ceased buying and begun to sell, even though the high price of the thirty-year Treasury Bond had put yields at their lowest levels in over a decade, and while the Dow Industrial average was making several successive new highs. Because this particular negative divergence of the DJU was so glaring—noticed, yet unbelieved—we reprinted the chart shown on page 139 in our weekly *Letter*, while adding similar C and D points to the 1993 action of the Utilities, Industrials, and Treasury Bonds (see page 142). The Utility divergence proved once again to be one of the very best

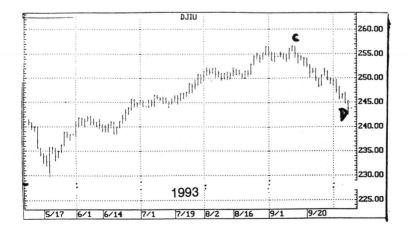

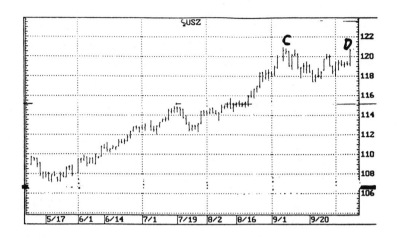

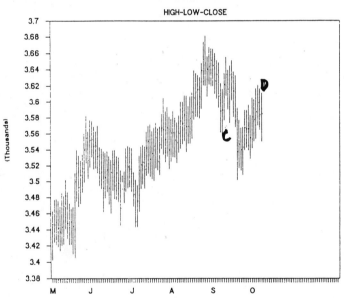

DOW JONES INDUSTRIAL AVERAGE

leading indicators; in mid-October '93, bond prices peaked and began to decline. The divergence signal was clear, not only anticipating the end of the long-term T-Bond rise, but also usefully well in advance of the major Industrial peak at the end of January '94. You have to perceive this behavior while the DJIA is still bubbling, *and* believe in it.

One other "divergent" use of the Dow averages is the venerable Dow Theory. The subject has been amply discussed elsewhere, but briefly put, this theory revolves around the relationship between the Dow Industrials and the transportation issues. Both should be in sync; when one makes a new high which remains unconfirmed by the other, that sort of divergence foretells a trend reversal. Folks may talk about "giving the lagging average more time to catch up," but that's because they are squeamish about admitting to the problem that has been created. Such failures to confirm are much more reliable Dow Theory messages than the ultimate case which takes place after the market is on its way down, when a drop to a lower low by *both* averages becomes the confirmation of a new bear trend. The latter, as you can see, comes much later; the former kind of divergence is therefore much more helpful. Indeed, the Dow Theory has an increasingly erratic history in that "confirmation" signals often come so late in market swings that the market is becoming oversold, and thus the signal is too quickly followed by action that goes against the message. A good example of the problem was the lower lows that both the Industrials and Transports made together—"confirming" a new bear market—that came exactly at the bottom of the decline on October 5, 1992. At first glance, it seemed like a perfect illustration of the Theory signalling "sell," but proved instead to be a very important *low* and reversal point, perhaps abetted by the manner in which the Dow Theory signal helped keep many observers bearish into the ensuing rally. Divergences, as always, work better, and are more significant, than confirmations.

At this point in the original text, we also wrote about using point-and-figure charts of the averages. It's true that such a style of charting compacts the action so that support and resistance areas can be easily identified in a small area on the page, but through the years we have become increasingly disinterested in these charts. Those who have grown used to them are welcome to them; no more would we try to dissuade anyone from eating peas with a fork and knife instead of a spoon. But to keep point & figure charts accurately requires access to intraday swings during a volatile market; lacks any relationship whatsoever to time or to the ongoing nature of the auction market; is a blunt instrument, requiring point changes, when useful nuances can lie in fractional numbers; and tends to be awkward (and often late) in its trendlines. Point-and-figure charting is an abstraction thrice removed from the actual ticks taking place; in our dotage we have become increasingly convinced that time spans—the length of time it takes a stock to do something—have significance that requires its existence on the chart...but then, we've also been using semi-log charts so long we get aggravated at arithmetic scales, too.

One of the ways we try to create even more subtle messages of supply and demand in the Dow averages is by keeping line charts of the hourly changes as reported each day in the *Wall Street Journal*. The computer can do this easily and print these charts clearly, thus providing a different perspective; many useful *shorter-term* trendlines materialize for traders. And you should, of course, view daily bar charts for the various averages—NASDAQ, the S & P 500 and MidCap, the Russell 2000, and so on—going back a year or more. And make sure you have at hand *longer-term* weekly charts which extend back in time far enough to at a minimum portray the entire bull or bear trend currently in play, and probably the previous primary move as well. At least thus far, there has not been a message of divergence between NASDAQ or these other averages and the DJIA of any particular market *timing* significance. However, tracking a genuine *small stock* index—the Russell 2000 is the one we've begun to use—does help distinguish between big cap and small cap interests and that's important to know. (You should be able to discern some of this by studying the kind of names on the daily new high and new low lists.) There've been periods of great small-stock outperformance, but for the most part, we've found that the stock's industry is more important than its size. Lastly, as you look at the charts keep in mind that averages do *not* make big patterned tops in the manner of individual stocks—their tops are smaller, and their end comes more abruptly. Watching trendlines and moving average lines for potential breaks is better than searching for, and awaiting, a definable pattern. Head-and-shoulders patterns may be perceived in the Dow but become too obvious to matter; indeed, the nature of bull market endings is that investors begin to look for "one more rally" to create a more convincing top, so the market, in its perversity, doesn't wait.

Volume Indicators

A long with the averages, newspapers report daily volume (the number of shares traded in a day). Those papers printing a chart of an average typically print total volume in bar form underneath. Tradition has it that increasing volume on rallies and decreasing volume on declines are signs of a healthy situation, but often that is not the case. Sluggish markets can be deadly, and the wildest volume fling of a rally often occurs right at the momentum top (while subsequent narrowing rallies that take the averages higher also show negative volume divergences). Don't accept conventional wisdom unquestioningly; consider the significance behind the statistics.

To be favorable, volume must continue to expand over the previous rally, and not merely in comparison with a low-keyed correction. Peak volume is usually seen around the middle of a market move; even though "heavy" volume materializes later, and reporters make a big deal of such "heavy" activity, when you look back for a comparison you'll find that it isn't as high as it had been as a previous rally was ending. The problem with that kind of observation is its dependence on hindsight. Later failures on what seems like high volume should have a different characteristic: the former has prices advancing, the latter will show much more churning, with narrowing breadth and high/low differentials. Upside volume will fail to exceed the pace of previous rallies even though the Dow will have gone on to a new high, and even though commentators talk about "very active trading." This is often an early warning sign of a tiring market, and can be seen, if plotted against the averages on a chart, as a negative divergence.

On the upside, beware of incredibly busy tapes. Modern technology has now been able to speed up the ticker so as to virtually eliminate the need for such old, helpful, messages as Flash Prices—if we ever see that again, it'll be at the climax of a dreadful decline. But very active trading that is due to an increase in smaller transactions rather than institutional blocks is a sign that the rally is becoming exhausted and about to reverse. One of the anomalies of such seemingly heavy volume is volume's relationship to the action of individual stocks: a stock that has already made what *seems* like a top, and *seems* to have rolled over, will take those tentative "seems" out of the sentence if and when *and as* it rebounds on much lower volume. Often, that occurs under cover of heavy overall activity (which is another useful perception stemming from posting one's own charts). While others may feel that they've been saved because the price recovers, meager trading volume that takes a stock back up to its overhead resistance level and downtrend line is perhaps the single most important—and most readily observable—message that you should be selling into such a rally rather than relaxing.

Low volume pullbacks are fine to see in the *early* stages of a new bull market, since it indicates (a) that sellers are sold out while a base is forming; and (b) that even after an upturn begins, there is very little pressure during a "normal" correction. *You want to own a stock that is "hard to buy."* That is, when a stock starts going up, and doesn't dip back down enough in price or in time or on enough volume to let investors get in on those dips, it is worth reaching up to take the offer because such action is a sign of a stock very early in a longer-term uptrend. One of the most valid of all Wall Street adages is a must for you to remember: "It takes buying to put stocks up, but they can fall of their own weight." Wall-of-worry gripers will say the rise is over, but if volume dries up during a pullback (often coming back down to the upside breakout point), that's a confirmation that you are on the right track; as sellers peter out, buyers will have to lift their bids, and you'll see a successful test (a higher low) of the correction's initial lows during which volume will be low on the downside and then immediately pick up as the stock starts rising again. Many folks make the mistake of trying to get the "ideal" price on such pullbacks, and thus let the stock get away from them on the upside all over again. Forget price; buy the stock that acts well even if you have to pay up.

However, all of that changes *late* in that bull market, and *early in a new bear trend*. The wall-of-worriers have long since been convinced, so when you hear or read that the correction is not worrisome because it is occurring on low volume—*you* worry. Such comments stem from over-confidence which, in turn, stems from the fact that prices have been rising a long way already. In a bear trend even a 1,000-share order "to sell at the market" might knock the price down whereas a similarly sized buy order won't lift the stock up at all. Low volume declines as the underlying trend is rolling over are mostly due to (a) a lack of concern and/or (b) a lack of bids underneath to sell to.

Thus what seems like routine and desultory selling, easily dismissed by the optimists, can become damaging. The absence of active buyers is evidence that every bull has already bought. Those who have their eyes on the tired and dying uptrend, expecting a leap up again, are deceived by such low volume, thinking it a virtue, when, in fact, it represents a dwindling lack of interest and an increasing willingness to sell if only there were someone to sell to. Since they still feel as if the uptrend is intact, their sell orders are "on a scale up." They sit there overhead, hoping someone will come along and take their shares—thus limiting rallies, and, as you can see, making any such rally a low volume one. But soon one or two holders become anxious and turn into "hit the bid" sellers. Whereas a still-bullish stock's correction looks like a stair-step down in orderly fashion, tops form in a rounding manner as shares are distributed. Prices droop, recover on low volume, then erode, and then break and launch a slide. It is only in the *later* stages of the decline when the optimists begin to panic and bargain-hunters are finally willing to appear, that heavier volume finally comes out. In sum, low volume in the early stages of a decline can be far more bearish than is commonly believed.

Every little piece of information can be helpful, so you'll occasionally want to know what the volume was during a particular portion of the trading day. Was it heavy on the upside on the opening because of news, but once that burst of reactive trading was over, did volume dry up? not a good sign. Nor is late-in-the-day selling after a desultory day's trading. Intervening (against the trend) intraday moves should see less volume. Where, you should ask, is the life of the market? on the upside or the down?

Certain conscientious financial pages also separate the volume for advancing stocks and the volume for those stocks which ended the day on the minus side, and that frequently can be a helpful distinction. For example, upside/downside volume proved to be the best timing clue to the May 1970 bottom. The DJI, continuing a collapse, closed on a Tuesday evening off 10 points to yet another new bear-market low. But a glance at this statistic showed that upside volume had equaled downside—indicating that buyers were busier than the Dow's then drastic decline suggested. The same kind of volume message often appears at important top areas, providing evidence of a rotting market. The averages may be going up, but when you track volume, you'll see too much downside trading in evidence. This indicates that a lot of selling is taking place under cover of the rally, selling which should not be ignored, for it is another instance of divergence telling the tale. There are those who convert such volume statistics into a more complex overbought-oversold indicator by setting up a ratio between upside over downside volume divided by advances over declines. That is, if advancing stocks have the same proportion of upside volume that declining stocks have, proportionately to downside volume, this ratio would be at 1.00. (This is sometimes called the Arms ratio, named after its originator.) It's kind of interesting to see, but we've always felt that trying to combine two factors, each of which is already a summary, contains the built-in possibility of a distortion caused when a particular sector is moving spectacularly and persistently in one direction or the other although the rest of the market is not. In the '92-'94 period, for example, the movement of financial stocks, being so *en masse*, conveyed messages of persistent overboughtness that were not reflective of the way other stocks were declining, and then, when financial stocks turned troublesome, the reverse occurred, with many days featuring more downside volume than upside, producing a persistent oversoldness that did not help catch rebounds elsewhere, and eventually making for a massive oversold extreme reading which greatly exaggerated the extent of the market's decline. Thus we've always maintained these statistics separately, keeping a chart of upside/downside volume on a ten-day moving average basis just as we keep the advance/decline ratio, and similarly looking for failures and divergences, both positive and negative. A series of lower highs, for example, vs. a rising DJI would likely occur along with other negative divergences and serve as a confirming volume factor to that message.

In the initial edition, we wrote here of the relationship of Big Board to Amex activity, known as the speculation index. But nowadays the American Stock Exchange has a diminished role— options are its main life—and any such comparison should be made with NASDAQ, the over-the-counter market, to measure degrees of speculation. A heated-up NASDAQ market due to action in smaller, unseasoned, "hot-tip-type" stocks is supposed to smack of trouble to come. Thus some folks comment when NASDAQ volume exceeds that of the NYSE, but to us that is a distinction without a difference, for it is more likely to be based on a big increase in activity in NASDAQ's big stocks such as Microsoft or Intel instead. Given the growth of public companies, this is not likely to be a reliable indicator. But we do need something that'll report on excessive speculation; for that, read the most active lists.

Indicators Based on the Most-Active List

You really do need a daily newspaper which publishes the most-active lists on a daily basis...and the percentage and/or point gainers and losers, too, plus, of course, the lists of individual new highs and lows. Each is a handy at-a-glance reference guide to where the life of the market has been. First, of course, you should scan the names, to determine the quality of those in the forefront and the degree to which they've experienced price changes, or are not doing what the averages did that day, as well as which groups are doing what, while asking yourself such cynical questions as: Is the list filling up with lower-priced, more speculative, and often unfamiliar, names? are stocks that had been going up, or were supposedly very popular, down on a day when the averages say the market was up? are individual stocks trading down on good news? are they opening up to make a new high on such news, but then closing lower and perhaps even down on the day? These are like the warming-up scales for a concert pianist: they loosen your mind up for the big event. We've seen so-called technicians "read" the daily newspaper and skip right over names—to us the life blood of the market—while caring only about their top-down calculations. Why, we wonder, why?

Healthy markets have an active list of companies of substance going up to an "ooh, isn't that nice" degree. A seemingly big up day in the Dow accompanied by an active list of (a) unfamiliar names; or (b) familiar names only up an 1/8 or 1/4; and/or (c) a starkly negative advance/decline ratio of those fifteen (or twenty) names listed) for such an up day in the averages—are all messages of deterioration. Thus when the most-active list becomes increasingly speculative and low-priced, watch out! the upside is late and exhausted. And we've seen days when the Dow was up mega-points but the list itself read, for example, five up (with three of those only up an 1/8 or 1/4, and the other two on news), seven down, and three unchanged. A day the Dow goes up in continuance of a rally while the most-active list shows more stocks on the downside at the close is a sign of an exhausted upswing; traders can expect imminent trouble. Beware when the stocks that were up big, making the market look exciting, are names you'd never heard of, or are highly speculative low-priced issues; or, more subtly, are the only names up big. We've often called this "the Hupp Corp. syndrome" because in the old days when H could be seen all over the tape, and Hupp Corp. made the active list, it rang a bell that even the froth was maxing out.

If you take that short-term factor into account over a longer period of time, you can create a miniature advance/decline line from the most-active list. The principle is the same. Good rallies find the stocks most in demand charging up right along. Toward the end, though, you'll find deterioration: the Dow up 10 points, but the most-active list showing seven up, six down, and two unchanged. When that persists in this mini-a/d line vs. a rising Dow, you're getting a reliable divergence signal of a change in trend. If the stocks showing the most market interest can't go up, failure for the whole ball game is near at hand.

You can also construct an indicator based on the *volume* of these most-actives to reveal when markets are heating up. A chart illustrating this is published regularly in the *Mansfield Chart Service*. It shows that peak volume readings come at market highs—a message of overheated-ness—while low levels of most-active stock activity mark market bottoms.

Other Useful Indicators

So much for daily exercises. We have come to believe in the importance of what we've dubbed "the dog that didn't bark" signals, in honor of the Sherlock Holmes story—a crossing, a divergence, a bell ringing that *should have happened but didn't* is often as important a message as an actual signal. What the market is *not* "saying" is to be heeded. An investor searching for details may want to expand on the number of indicators kept, as experience dictates and as the stock hobby captivates, but our belief is to keep matters simple. It is the responsibility of indicators to restrain emotional excesses and to provide an objective view of what the market is actually doing. They serve as a check on what is happening, not only to "the market" in general, but also on individual stocks. *That doesn't work if you are keeping so many in-*

dicators you are "sure" to find one or two giving you the opinion you want to hear.

Make sure, when you scan the actual stock tables for the price activity of your stocks, that you don't get carried away by visions of triplings. If you can hear yourself boasting—sell! Keep in mind that Wall Street couplet: "When you're laughing, you should be selling." (The counterpart is "When you're crying, you should be buying.") Constantly lead with cynicism. Ask yourself questions: why didn't it close on its high? how was the volume compared to yesterday? how far is it to overhead resistance? how are other stocks in the group doing? and the like. In the end, though, the primary requisite remains the ability to do, to act decisively, to have the guts to sell in the face of whatever yearnings and opposing sentiment (and natural reluctance to take a loss) may abound. Toward this end, indicators can provide the objective shove to act, so here are a few other tried-and-true indicators to track. These will involve, at the most, another fifteen minutes of work on the weekend, using a financial publication such as *Barron's* whose weekly statistical roundup provides the data.

First and foremost comes the need to find out what the professionals are doing. The most readily available information, and by far the most useful, are statistics on short-selling by exchange members—in particular, the specialists, standing on the floor of the exchange and handling the auction market in those stocks specifically allocated to them. Most of their shorting is a routine of the marketplace; they have no choice but to sell short when there are no nearby public sell orders in the stocks they handle and when they themselves have no more long stock to parcel out from their own account. The only leeway specialists can exercise is the degree to which they actually do go short, whether enough to meet the requirements of maintaining an orderly market, or by being a more aggressive seller. Another group of members, the floor traders, have more freedom, both of stock selection and trading direction; they roam the floor in search of quick trades. For the privilege of initiating their orders on the floor, they have to put up a considerable sum and agree to abide by certain restrictive rules. Those who don't want to, or who have other things to do during the day besides trade stocks, or whose feet can't stand standing up all day, turn to off-floor trading. Rules apply to these traders too, but not as many or as restrictive. These off-floor traders watch the same desktop machine inputs as the rest of us, but have the advantage, of course, of playing the game at less commission cost, and the bigger advantage of being there every day because it is their profession, and thus gaining the experience of readily making constant decisions that to others would seem like a big deal. They are, to use a tennis term, constantly "match fit."

Each of these three segments of exchange membership is required to report its trading activity to the exchange, so that its dealings can be monitored to ensure that the rules are being respected. Weekly tabulations must be filed by the Friday of the following week. The exchange then compiles the data and releases them to the SEC and the financial press by the next Friday. Accordingly, the statistics that appear in *Barron's* that weekend and in the *Wall Street Journal* on Mondays relate to the trading activity of two weeks previous. (Statistics are also available for the Amex, too, but we've never been able to derive anything from the ASE statistics that say anything materially different from what can be gleaned from the Big Board data.) This two-week delay in learning the "answer" is *not* generally a problem. When tops are forming, the end does not occur in an instant but, rather, over time; high specialist short-selling activity—the signal—is usually given in ample time, and is often repeated for another week or two or three to make sure you get the message. Besides, if you do your selling in the top area, you'll be winner enough. (Bottoming readings, however, are more usually coincident with the market's bottomings and are more likely to be one-time-only clearly low readings.)

The most consistently useful of these statistics continues to be the specialist short-sales ratio—calculated by dividing the number of shares sold short by specialists by the total number of shares sold short that week. There was persistent high shorting at the 1968 top, and at the 1971 significant intermediate-term top; it then continued at a high level going into the major top at the end of 1972. However, the arrival of derivative products has changed parameters on many indicators, none more glaringly so than this one. It has also, to some extent, changed the nature of specialist activity: they now have a separate place to lay off their positions. The result: a squished kind of indicator, with peak readings—extreme specialist short selling—scarcely over 50, and often enough rendering a sell message in the upper 40s. What has happened is that specialists use the options market for hedging; their "normal" function of having to sell short is still there but is muted. We've found that the way to "read" these statistics is to use the general areas as significant enough extremes—low 30s for buy signals, upper 40s for sell signals. But what has become more important now is the trend itself: a reading that remains in the middle—that is, neutral and non-messaging—which then (in keeping with a rise in the Dow) rises up out of that neutral zone, is a negative signal enough although it may lack pinpoint timing. For example: 39-43 readings for a prolonged period, with the market mostly in an uptrend, should be read as neutral/passive; but then, as the DJIA rises to a higher high for its entire move, if the specialist short selling statistic is reported at 46 percent, and the next report comes in at 48 percent, you are seeing a shift in tone that tells the tale. (Short selling ratios in the low 30s, or even down to 29, have been more precise parameters—identifying potential bottoms and warning against agressive short selling—then those we've gotten in the '90s on the sell side, where toppy markets have sometimes lacked definitive signals entirely.) *You are not looking for a bell to go off, but for a tendency to begin to develop, so that you, too, can be on the sell side.* High readings are not to be ignored, because when the specialists have been unloading their long positions and are now starting to sell short in addition, it's time for you to be on their side.

It is also particularly effective to match this indicator with the previously discussed batch of divergent indicators. As you'll recall, we've done a lot of measuring of deterioration. In such circumstances, and knowing that individual stocks top out at their own pace and in their own style, you want to start selling any of your holdings that have become suspicious—charts that haven't done very much wrong, but aren't very far from doing a lot of things wrong, *and seem* to have lost their ability to go up much any more. But what of those that are part of the dwindling band still showing strength? You want to hang on to them as long as possible, don't you? well, yes and no. You *do* want to continue to hold the best-acting stocks, but when our internal indicators are showing divergences, and high specialist short-selling readings are materializing, the market has become much more vulnerable. It is time to take advantage of the fact that there are still buyers around...and give 'em your shares. One of the mind-boggling but typical patterns of market behavior is how what had seemed to be "okay to hold" becomes victim to a market downturn the indicators had been warning about. When the breakdown comes, stocks go "far enough down to make you glad you've sold." What else do you need to know?

At the same time you are calculating the specialist ratio, only a few fingertip touches on your calculator will provide the long-division answer to the member short-sales ratio as well. Here you are including not only the specialists but also the activity of those professionals who act exclusively on their own. This indicator used to work very well in identifying tops, but the ability to use options and futures when trading has changed its nature. Such pros tend *to buy* individual stocks but to *short* the market itself—that is, selling S & P futures contracts and often buying OEX puts when they think the market is going down. As a result, their trading is skewed; the parameters for member short selling have changed so that readings in the mid- to upper 70s are as high as it gets nowadays. (We have a hunch, too, that such traders are more *coincident* with the market action on the short side—puts can be bought virtually instantaneously with a market turndown.) We continue to track member short-selling to see if it is confirming—reinforcing—what the specialists are doing, and besides, the numbers are sitting right there on the page anyhow.

If you've got another few seconds you can also subtract the total of member shorting that you've just used from the total of all shorting and you've got the amount of shorting the public did during that particular week. Divide that amount by the week's volume and you get what is known as the public short-sales ratio. This indicator reveals that small round-lot traders are just as apt to be wrong at important tops as the odd-lotter; both virtually cease all short-side activity just as the market rally is coming to an end.

Another secondary indicator derived from the back pages of *Barron's* is the amount of big blocks traded during the week. But the manner in which institutions dispose of large positions has become so varied, and often so ongoing, that this information is a lot less viable than the potential gold mine of clues that it seems to be. If you want to delve into the statistics, keep in mind that what you are looking for is blocks sold—that is, a trade which takes place at a lower price than the previous *different* price (someone anxious to get out)—as compared to those bought (at a price higher than the last different price). Over a period of time you might very well see some subtle changes begin to appear—but they will tend to confirm what you already "know" from the more basic indicators.

The same can be said for tracking the number of secondaries for the week—secondaries being a substantial number of shares sold by announcement and pre-arrangement, done through brokers who charge no commission. That's the lure to get the public to buy (while the brokers are compensated by the sellers themselves for getting them out). This is an example of how stocks are often distributed from strong to weak hands. Thus an increase in secondary distributions tends to come after the market has been up a lot; it takes a market that looks "terrific" to lure unsophisticated buyers. (You certainly want to be leery of a broker who calls you up with such buy ideas, using the "no commission" line as bait.)

More important—and much more dramatic—is the new issues market. These initial public offerings—a company issuing shares for the first time—also require the fertile soil of a bubbling lively "gotta own 'em" kind of marketplace. When the climate becomes ripe—that is, when there is ample investment money around, much of it in the hands of relatively sophisticated professional money managers—companies truly in need of capital to grow past their infancies will come public. At first you can't get any of those newly issued shares—usually you'll never even hear about them until they open for trading at substantial premiums above the offering price. The more that happens, the more the appetite grows for more such initial public offerings, the more frothy that niche becomes. Two guys in a rented garage with an idea for a new product, or one lady with three small clothing stores that gets called a chain, become well advertised new issues…until the IPO market becomes a bubble waiting to burst. So you, too, become an indicator! When, after the good ones have been issued and have leapt, and brokers start calling you up to "let you in on a hot one," you know the end is near. Ordinary bear markets typically begin for other reasons; the culmination of an IPO frenzy consistently comes at major tops because it takes the over-confidence born of a prolonged bull move to suck all that money into untried and highly speculative companies. The action represents an excess of cash being flung at paper, cash which has been diverted from buying other, more established, stocks, or, as was the case in 1994, money taken from the safe havens of certificates of deposit to the high-risk sphere of "emerging" markets. Clues of an impending end are the descending quality of new issues, when John Q. can get some shares in a new issue, but most spectacularly when a highly visible IPO flops—*that's* a sign of exhaustion.

In situations like these, remember the old IBM motto: "Think." Why, for example does the seller of a big block of stock have to offer the dealer twice the normal commission to get it sold? Why is that supposedly hot new issue available to you all of a sudden? How come a "bargain" is sitting down near its lows for such a long time, and what makes you think it's a big bargain when no one else seems to care? A few suspicious questions on your part, plus some cynical answers (remember: no one is about to do you a favor), will keep you aware of important tops being formed. The market is subtle in its myriad distinctions, but is blunt about one thing: *when something happens that shouldn't happen, the trend is changing.*

Indicators Based on Fundamentals

*T*he pages of *Barron's* also supply, for the benefit of tinkerers, data on bond/stock yields, dividend ratios, or how much of a dividend a dollar's worth of the Dow obtains. Such fundamental data is not our turf; there is, of course, a relationship to stocks, but not necessarily to stock trends. Much has been made, for example, of the price to dividend ratio because it has soared in recent years. It was often cited in 1987 as a message of stock market overvaluation when it got "too" high (35 or 36 times) or when the yield on the S & P 500 got down under 3 percent, but neither facet seemed to get in the way of the market's climb in 1993. Too much money available, and a change in viewing such valuations because of much lower interest rates, proved to be just a rationalization that lasted until buyers were finally exhausted. It might be said that the very definition of an extreme is "that's far enough." We sometimes only half-jokingly call it an "excessive extreme." But while markets are able to, and invariably do, go to extremes, there is no timing to such calculations, nor is there any assurance to the readings. What might be an extreme in a high-interest rate environment, might not be so much, or might be greater, when rates are low. Or, the extreme reading itself might last and last and last. Or, there is an emotional extreme attached to such high readings that needs to be exhausted before the bell will toll. But consider why that might be: widespread awareness of "overvaluation" tends to cause anxiety on the part of fundamentalists; that, in turn, skews the market's sentiment readings so that our indicators remain somewhat below *their* extremes. *The true definition of an emotional extreme is not in measuring such fundamental valuations but when even those valuations are thrown to the wind in the enthusiasm to buy stocks.* The operative phrase becomes "this market is never going down again."

Lest you think economic, fiscal, and monetary matters should be dodged entirely, here's what we think you should know. First, drop a note to the Federal Reserve Bank of St. Louis and ask to be put on their mailing list. Each week they'll send a booklet free of charge that charts several important monetary statistics, giving you charts of money supply and the monetary base, among several important items. If you read the weekly Fed release itself as reprinted on Friday mornings in the *Journal* and the *Times*, you can often get a sense of direction, and then a change in that direction, yourself, even without particularly knowing what the numbers "mean." You don't need to be able to explain such matters brilliantly at a dinner party to perceive whether the Federal Reserve Board is making money easier or tightening it, and of course it is better to see for yourself than to rely on other people's guesses. Stocks have continued to rise while tightening begins—classically, there is a switch out of financials and into economically sensitive names—but not for ever, or even, for long.

We've found, though, that while the conventional analyst waits for readings in the area of money supply, cannier analysts use two other statistics to understand the trends in monetary policy: the monetary base, which tends to lead money-supply statistics, and net-free (or net-borrowed) reserves. The Federal Reserve Board releases its data after the market's close each week on Thursday afternoons so that it appears in Friday morning's major newspapers. It is *the trend* that matters. Although less vital to follow during recent years, the reserve statistics are worth understanding. Net-free reserves obtain when banks hold more money in reserve than they have borrowed from the Fed. When conditions get tighter, how

Bank Net Free and Net Borrowed Reserves

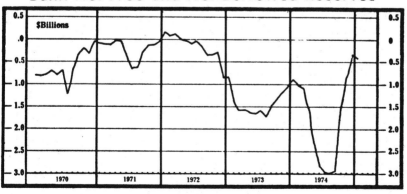

ever, they are compelled to borrow more and more at the Fed window, producing a net-borrowed reserves figure. On the chart, you can see the downward trend throughout 1972, warning of tightening and thus of deep trouble ahead. But *ahead of* the market's major bottom in late 1974, conditions loosened and the trend changed toward "free."

We also wrote, in the first edition, of another indicator that provides no timing but does give a useful overview of monetary conditions: the ratio between the yields of corporate AAA bonds and short-term treasury bills. As the ratio narrows, the situation becomes more hostile to stocks. For example, in late December 1972 the ratio fell for the first time under its 1.4 warning level and stayed negative until it came back up across that level in early October 1974, which was the Dow's first bottom at the end of that major bear market. Because of the decline in rates, and the positive yield curve from 1982 to 1993, these parameters haven't been as precise in more recent years, but they are certainly worth noticing along the way. Any trend change in the relationship between long and short rates does matter.

A similar relationship that can be calculated at a glance is the TED spread—the three-month T-bill contract vs. the equivalent EuroDollar contract. Here, too, a significant change is more important than the number itself. This indicator gave a warning message in the spring of 1984, for what it is warning about is a banking crisis. (In 1984, Continental Bank was in jeopardy due to the collapse of a small German bank.) The TED spread widens as "insiders" start acting in fear of such a crisis. Prior to the 1987 crash the number expanded enormously.

Monetary statistics are reports on fundamentals, but technical analysis requires knowing more than just the narrow world of the stock market, especially since monetary policy is so basic to the economy itself. But the same guidelines apply as for any other indicator: the trend matters more than the raw number; waiting to be "sure" can be too late; and being suspicious of whatever the consensus is saying is vital.

Three Monthly Indicators

*L*et's move on to three monthly statistics worth watching. We discussed the mutual-fund cash ratio in the previous chapter. Upon release, these once-a-month figures are usually buried somewhere in *The Wall Street Journal*. To refresh your memory, the experts responsible for running those vast sums of money have just about spent it all when a top is arriving. Liquidity gets down under 6 percent of assets. Don't quibble about a tenth of 1 percent; the more content they are to be bought up, the warier you should be. But here again, it's the trend: is the percentage trending downward? What's more, are they using up their buying power but having little or no effect on the stock market? *That* churning was the case in late 1993 through early 1994 when the grand influx of public money appeared to make little difference to the typical individual stock. Keep in mind that a rising Dow is one part of the ratio that can cause the percentage to decrease; combine that with a flat or lessening inflow of fund investors and the confidence that the money can be or ought to be readily invested, and you can begin to anticipate a trend toward a lessening percentage.

A vast increase in pension funds has made that investment sector a similarly important source of buying power to be watched. These numbers (from *Indata*) are not readily available, however, but they are known so you should watch for mention of them in your readings. Low percentages are warnings.

The second monthly indicator noted in *When To Sell*'s prior edition is the short interest ratio. It used to matter; it is now beset by the advent of derivative products, and an enormous increase in short positions used for hedging purposes. As a result, this indicator has lost its potency. The headlines, the brief newspaper write-ups, and your own scanning of the particular statistics are enough, nowadays, to know, so great has the distortion become.

The third item, margin debt, is truly long-term trend-defining. It takes a long time to turn the direction of margin debt around; several months of rounding under and starting to increase mark major bottoms, as those who trade on margin keep stepping up the pace of tossing their money and all they can borrow into the game. It has, in the past, topped out and begun to turn down coincident with important tops, but in market climates beset with group rotation (as in the early '90s) it can be somewhat late since it'll be measuring an overall attitude. When margin debt stops growing, it is usually a sign that enough losses have begun to mount for such traders to begin to temper their enthusiasm. When it does turn down, even if late, it can be a significant signal of a major change in direction.

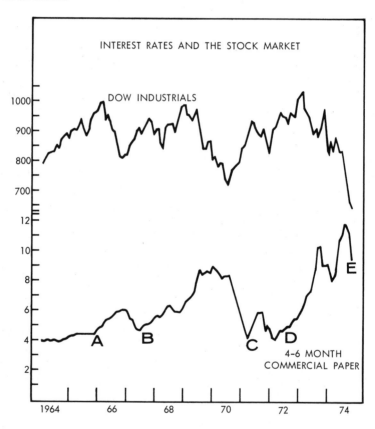

Lest you think that indicators always work, here's an indicator to remind you that nothing is perfect in the stock market. This chart comes from a respected and eminently worthwhile advisory service and is meant to illustrate a theory that the trend of interest rates (as represented, in this case, by commercial paper) can predict the stock market's course. One can readily see how yield levels were reversing in relationship to stock market turns. But try to forecast stock movements consistently from this chart. There was a rise in rates (A) which heralded the 1966 top and the ensuing bear market. But if you had been scared away when a similar rise set in in 1967 (B), you'd have missed a whopping gain: the Dow went up, while the "average" average soared to an all-time peak. In 1971 (C), a rise in interest rates caught a sharp intermediate-term sell-off, while the rise in D spelled doom indeed—but look how early it was. And, talking about early, note the twin downturns in interest rates at E. The first was drastically deceptive, but even the second came a good four months and 170 Dow points too soon. Obviously, although the overall relationship is clearly there, the sharpness we need to help us make stock market decisions is missing. Such indicators are like pats on the back: encouraging when you're already doing well; frustratingly useless when you need support.

Examples abound; nothing's perfect! Sometimes a particular statistic becomes so closely and publicly watched it can become a red herring; be cynical about something everyone is talking about. But the indicators we've discussed in the past two chapters are basic. They are summaries of what is going on rather than abstractions or mathematical concepts—and in their simplicity have good track records. Using them will provide a good balance of (1) primary indicators that can be warnings; (2) intermediate-term trend indicators announcing that the rally is (a) deteriorating and (b) about to reverse into a sharp correction; and (3) timing indicators that tell you more precisely when to sell. When you get those signals, put all thought of "getting that last 1/8 of a point" out of your head; don't fret if the momentum of one of the stocks you've sold carries it still higher; ignore the people rushing about buying stocks as if they will go up forever; take a vacation if you need to, to keep from getting emotionally involved all over again; move your money into safe short-term money-market instruments (such as Treasury Bills or "money market" funds); and have the patience to wait out a sliding stock market. The "profit" that you make by giving up the opportunity for a higher yield or further stock rise comes from having the buying power to accumulate stocks at the start of the next bull market.

There is no perfect forecasting system, and even if there were, the grand rush to embrace it would be self-defeating. Instead, there is a form of reality: in summary and objective form, the indicators add to the body of knowledge we possess about the stock market and its potential future course. Applied properly, with sensitivity gained through experience, they can help us win the battle with our emotions. They should be evaluated collectively, their evidence weighed in bulk to determine the urgency of the message. Anyone who knows what they are saying—high specialist shorting, a divergence in the advance/decline line, fewer new highs vs. a higher Dow, margin debt beginning to slacken, and so on—and yet goes blithely ahead to buy another stock in the hope of making a fast buck is hopeless. Any one who gets those messages and excuses them, saying "not yet, not yet" is a fool.

"Oh no, not me," you say. But those indicators warning you of trouble ahead will not pick up your phone and dial your broker. That's something you have to learn to do yourself.

Chapter Seven

The Specialists

*T*he specialist system, the basis for the way the New York Stock Exchange functions, is what it always has been, except that the generation of men of stature, standing at their posts and stemming declines, is gone. Their sons and grandsons and former clerks made partners, and machines, are now in place. Many of the changes introduced have been designed to improve market functionings: to speed up executions, to make them more efficient, faster, and fairer. Such changes in the system do not concern us to any great degree. In the old days, when the printing of prices on the ticker tape lagged badly, we would see FLASH prices appear as a means of keeping traders informed; this was a powerful message of climactic panic. But now the tape can chug along fast enough—helped by computerized means of deleting characters—that the limitation is our eye, not the mechanics. Nor is the tape itself even a particularly important matter any more, although it does count as the traditional means of officially recording transactions. Many brokerage offices don't even have ticker tapes on their walls any more, and anyone can keep up with the action simply by punching the keyboard on the ubiquitous desktop machine or by watching television at home. But the specialist system endures.

On the floor of the New York Stock Exchange, the heart of capitalism, there is scarcely any competition. Each specialist unit—comprised of a number of partners—has a virtual franchise for a number of different listed stocks. The problem with competition is that either it works, and the better specialist takes more and more business away from its rival until the competitor quits or asks to merge, or it is evaded, with brokerage firms deciding to do business with one competitor for six months and with the other for the next six months. What competition there was gradually disappeared and was gone by the end of the sixties. Nor are there any isolated individual specialists any more. The need for substantial capital has led to the formation of specialist firms of several partners, and even specialist units of two or more firms working together. These units handle a number of different listed stocks at a particular trading post. Although individual partners concentrate on a few stocks, or, in some cases only one particularly active stock, they are always able to take over the partner's issues when he is unavailable.

Thus, when we talk about the specialist we mean both the individual and the unit. The specialist wears two hats: the staid bowler of the broker who simply functions as an agent for those orders left with him, and the jaunty derby of the dealer who gets into the fray with his own money. As a broker the specialist maintains a once real, now mostly theoretical "book," a long thin ledger wherein is recorded all limited price orders in a particular stock which are away from the current market. When orders in the book become capable of execution, whether moments or months later, the specialist simply represents them in the marketplace at the designated price. As a dealer, on the other hand, the specialist assumes the responsibility for maintaining a "fair and orderly market" in that particular stock, and does so by buying or selling for his own account whenever necessary, that is, when there are no other buyers or sellers around.

It is that dual hat of broker and of dealer that we need to understand. Although many changes have taken place over the last decade that require revisions to this chapter, perhaps the most significant relates to the size of orders—even a simple "retail" (public as compared to institutional) order from a doctor or dentist has increased in size from a couple of hundred shares to one or two thousand. The introduction of the DOT system for rapid transmission and execution of straightforward orders has had a major effect on how business is done on the floor. But at the risk of describing something old-fashioned and perhaps already on the verge of becoming out-moded, we think you should be able to picture, and hence understand, the underlying principles of a transaction that ultimately can affect the way the stock's chart looks.

Let us suppose that various brokerage firms have received limited price orders in XYZ from their customers and given them to the specialist for execution. In the absence of such orders—over the years, his "book" has dwindled drastically—the specialist must step forward to buy or sell for his own account. The highest-priced order to buy XYZ is at 50, and the lowest-priced offer to sell is at 51, with the last sale price having been at 50 1/2. A Merrill Lynch broker then crosses the exchange floor with a piece of paper in his hand, representing a customer's order which has just been entered "upstairs" and transmitted to the firm's array of clerks on the floor. Although the broker knows that the order is to buy 1,000 shares, he doesn't disclose this to the specialist when he approaches and asks: "How's XYZ?"

Although the "real" market of orders in hand would be 50-51, the specialist realizes that's too wide, so he replies: "50 1/4-50 3/4," telling the broker the bid price first and the offer second. This quotation is firm, having been made publicly. The specialist can't change his mind suddenly and withdraw the quote if he doesn't like what the broker is anxious to do (nor will the broker try to blindside him); shares must trade at or within that quoted range. The specialist often adds—and certainly will announce if asked—the "size" in the market for the stock; that is, how many shares are being bid for at that price and how many are offered, i.e., "ten by five" (meaning 1,000 shares bid for at 50 1/4, 500 shares offered for sale at 50 3/4). He cannot, however, reveal any other orders on the book. Only the best bid and the best offer are the "known" market (although he will, of course, discuss with a broker how to facilitate the execution of a larger order so that it won't disrupt the market).

The broker instantaneously absorbs this information and responds, "A half for two thousand," meaning that he is making a bid to fill his order at 50 1/2, the last sale price, thus trying to do better for his customer. If he were representing a sell order, he'd say: "Two thousand at a half," noting first the amount of shares he was willing to sell and then the price he'd accept.

Another floor broker might be standing at the same trading post "working an order" and thus would be willing to sell stock at that price, but in this example let's suppose the specialist replies "A half to three-quarters," indicating that the quotation has now changed, the Merrill broker having produced the higher bid. That order is now the quoted bid price while the offer remains the same. This terse response also tells the broker that he has failed to get an execution for the order he has in his hand, while the previously quoted size of 500 shares for sale at 50 3/4 tells him he can't "fill" his entire order by simply taking the offer. His attempt to buy at a better price for his customer has turned out to be futile, albeit worth trying. If the broker has been handling an order to buy "at the market," meaning that he immediately has to buy at whatever price is available, his next step would be to take the offered shares at 50 3/4; the specialist, in turn, now knowing the size of the buy order and being unwilling to sell more than 500 shares for his own account at 50 3/4, would probably inform the broker that he could fill the rest of his order at 51. The broker cannot risk loitering at the trading post to see if a lower-priced sell order shows up because, if another broker darted in and grabbed the shares offered ahead of him, he would thus fail to buy "at the market" and would thereby become liable for an execution. In this case, however, our broker turns over the scrap of paper in his hand to show the specialist that his buy order had, in fact, been limited to 50 1/2 and that he can bid no higher. Having business to transact elsewhere, he leaves the order with the specialist, who enters it in his book at that price. The specialist now becomes the broker representing that order in the marketplace, and he collects the floor broker's commission for the task. Meanwhile, the specialist has made known the new quotation (50 1/2-51) so that it can be fed into the computer, thus making it instantly available to brokerage offices via those desk-top interrogation devices. If you happened to be watching, you'd see the quote change to 50 1/2 bid for 2,000 shares, even though no transaction had yet taken place.

Let's brood for a moment. Suppose the order has a 51 limit instead. Suppose the stock trades at 51. Suppose this occurs at the end of the trading day: the stock then closes at 51 and the newspaper table reads: "+1/2." Here is a stock that hasn't done anything all day, selling between the bid and the offer, selling around 50 1/2, its previous day's close—and one modest order whether for 200 or 2,000 shares that "takes" the offer makes the stock look "strong"—up half a point. If there happened to be no interest in XYZ the next morning, except for a small and random sell order, the stock might open at the bid of 50 1/2, down a half point, and look "weak" when, in reality, it hasn't gone anywhere at all. (OTC trading between the bid and offer displays this, sometimes egregiously.) *Before you can use an adjective about a stock's price changes, you must know the quoted bid and asked, and the volume of transactions.* It is what someone will pay or will sell at on the *next* transaction that matters.

The other aspect to reflect on is the specialist's behavior. The bid, and the offer, and the price the stock trades at, are all public, readily available, knowledge. Anyone sitting in front of a desktop interrogation machine can keep constant track of those important bits of information, and professional traders do. But we have to write a script to try to relate to what the specialist has in mind. He might be reluctant to sell shares—for his own account as a dealer, in the absence of other orders—simply because he has already built up a substantial short position, and the damn stock keeps going up. On the other hand, he might be long, and an earnest believer in owning the shares, and thus would feed out the shares he owns with some reluctance, sticking only to what he feels he is required to do to maintain that fair and orderly market. He's human, can have the same emotional responses, but is kept "on the right side" by the market action.

The most likely sequence goes like this: XYZ declines, and so there are times, during the trading day, when an absence of nearby bidders compels the specialist to be the buyer. If there are times when there is an absence of sellers, he offers his own "long" position, and may very well spend a lucrative day buying at 50

1/4 and 3/8, selling at 5/8 and 3/4. The numbers may be narrower, the opportunities may be more or less, but he is there as a potential buyer on the bid, seller on the offer. Of course, the really good, really experienced, specialist develops the ability to sense (or very quickly respond to) changes in what the market is doing. Suddenly, sensing that the market wants to go up—the noise of the ticker tape speeding up is often a clue—he'll be willing to buy at 1/2 and then 5/8. The nuance of bidding a little bit higher, or selling a little bit lower if he doesn't like what the market seems to be doing, is about the only expression of free will he has, or needs to have, in order to make a buck.

Much of what happens, including his own profits and/or losses from what he is compelled to do in his dealer account, is determined by what the next broker coming across the exchange floor has an order to do, except that nowadays we have to add other determining factors: (a) what flows through the DOT system; (b) what program trade is being hatched by the discount or excessive premium that develops in the S & P futures contract. Old days or new days, one thing hasn't changed yet (although it will, as the exchange works toward giving bigger institutions "direct access" to the floor). But at least for now, it is still the specialist's domain to ensure the fair and orderly market in each stock, and in the course of so doing to accumulate a short position—selling when there is no other seller and he has no long position of his own left—or a long position, by being the buyer of last resort and therefore accumulating shares as the stock declines. Of course, he will try to keep his dealer position where he'd like it to be, whether short, long, or even, but sometimes the market's course of action will not give him a chance. He can get trapped against the tide and lose megabucks in a matter of hours, and yet, *because the market fluctuates,* even what he didn't want to do, was forced to do so as to meet his responsibilities, enables him to consistently rack up profits. At least on that tick-by-tick trading basis, by doing what at that moment seems most scary to do is what often turns out to be most profitable.

Good News, Bad News

A great example of how going against the crowd pays off for the specialist is worth repeating from the earlier edition. It concerns the action on August 16, 1971, the day after then-President Nixon announced a drastic new game plan to cure the country's economic ills. That Monday morning, public and institutional orders to buy poured into the NYSE floor for what turned out to be one of the most dramatic openings in the history of the exchange. It made no difference to a specialist whether he agreed with Nixon's schemes or not; he had no choice about what to do. His job is not to interpret but rather to respond to how *other* people think, and the avalanche of buy orders was already dictating his task. Each specialist, arriving at his trading post, quickly realized he was going to have to sell, and sell short, to the limits of his capital. He wouldn't be able to buy even if he thought that buying was the smart thing to do, as so many others obviously did.

It was an extraordinarily emotional situation. In their eagerness and excitement, the morning's investors failed to play devil's advocate with themselves and ask one basic question: *Should they be selling instead?* Because the specialist has no choice, he can be far cooler than the people who have eagerly tossed their buy orders into the boiling pot. So the question to keep in mind is: *Should you be selling, along with the specialist, when everyone else is avid to buy?*

The market, you see, is a different world than the headlines, and often a perverse one. Over at Post 2, where Chrysler traded on that fateful morning, the specialist firm had a tradition of opening Chrysler each day as soon as possible, but the flood of buy orders made that impossible; rather, the challenge was to open Chrysler by the closing bell. The Nixon formula had provided particular aid to the then-sagging automobile industry and the Chrysler specialist was swamped under a tidal wave of buy orders.

Chrysler had closed the previous Friday at 26 3/8. Orders to buy Chrysler at the market (that is, at any price) or at a limit of 31 (the buyer willing to go that high but no higher) totalled 670,000 shares; offers to sell, however, amounted to only 269,000 shares at a price of 31 or lower. Thus even, if the specialist were to open Chrysler at 31—17 percent higher than Friday's closing price—he would have had to be able to supply over 400,000 shares from somewhere just to match opening supply with opening demand.

Faced with such an overwhelming disparity, a simple solution would have been to raise the potential opening price higher and higher until it reached a level at which many buyers would have withdrawn and an increasing number of sellers would have come forth, so that the orders could be matched. That would have been entirely plausible within an auction market governed by the law of supply and demand. But the law of the Stock Exchange scowls on such drastic jumps in price, and 31 was considered high enough. Anyone who complained about how high the actual opening price turned out to be should consider how high it might have been were supply and demand the only force in effect. Obviously, to keep within reason, the specialist would have to sell from his own account.

But 400,000 shares? even if his firm had the capital resources needed ($12.5 million), he couldn't afford to tie it all up in one stock, since he and his partners would need to meet the demands, as market makers, in more than a dozen other important stocks they also had responsibility for. The specialist fortunately happened to have a few thousand shares in his dealer account, paltry compared to what was needed, but better than being caught empty-handed or short, as some specialists were in other stocks.

In extreme situations like this, the first step is to get formal permission from a floor official to delay the opening. Such approval is always required when, due to an imbalance of orders, a stock can't be opened within half an hour. Next, the specialist instructs the various floor brokers to notify their firms that the stock is going to open substantially higher, in the hope that more sellers might be encouraged to offer stock if they realized they could get a higher price, and that some buyers, perhaps calming down somewhat, would cancel their orders when they learned they were going to be hit with a huge markup.

By the time the first half hour had passed, easier-to-open stocks were already streaming across the ticker tape at sharply higher prices. Brokers who handled orders for institutions were combing the floor in search of blocks of stocks to buy; as far as they were concerned, *any* block in any stock would do. The tiny patch of floor space where the Chrysler specialist held the fort remained bedlam. Partners had to shout in each other's ear as they conferred, exchange officials hovered nearby, and the beleaguered clerks struggled to keep the pile of orders under control. In such circumstances, once the opening picture becomes clearer, a specialist will usually announce a preliminary indication of the possible opening price range. Thus, emerging from the day's madness, the Chrysler specialist was finally able to lift his head up and declare: "It looks like 30 to 32." It was a bold announcement, for sufficient sellers had yet to be found. Upstairs, in the block-trading departments of many member firms, salesmen were busy scouring the portfolios of mutual funds and other institutions for holders of large amounts of Chrysler stock.

Finally, late in the trading day, an institutional holder was found who was willing to sell nearly 325,000 shares at 31. Only one big-block holder had the intelligence and fortitude to disregard the torrent of unquestioning optimism and overwhelming enthusiasm pervading the Street that day! Yet here was a unique opportunity to sell a very large block of stock all at once at a price spectacularly higher than the day before. But, alas, money managers can be as emotional as the man in the street, and they are creatures of habit as well, often waiting until a stock turns down, when it finally dawns on them something's wrong, and then hastening to dump the block on the market when there are few if any buyers around.

The offering of that big block reduced the disparity between buyers and sellers to about 75,000 shares, still leaving more than $2.3 million to go on the offering side. In a voice scarcely heard in the din, the specialist told anxious floor officials that he was willing to supply that amount by selling 75,000 shares short in his dealer account to get the stock open. (At the same time, he was also risking another $1.3 million to sell Chrysler warrants short in conjunction with the opening of the common.) Considering the unabated bullishness that still raged on the floor and in board rooms, and the fact that General Motors was nowhere near opening, and so could not guide his own relative risk, this was a remarkable step. Another wave of buyers might surge in, sweeping Chrysler higher and, of course, creating a potentially catastrophic loss in the specialist's short position. The very survival of the firm was being placed on the line just to get Chrysler open by the closing bell, making it the only auto stock to print on the tape that day.

Three months later, Chrysler was selling at 25.

As a rule of thumb, forget your own reaction to news, ignore the stampeding emotional herd, and ask yourself what the specialist's reaction is going to have to be. If we can learn a healthy market approach from the specialist, we can also learn the penalties of obstinacy and daydreaming from the fund managers who were so busy buying that they couldn't and wouldn't consider selling. Within two days of that opening at 31, the total daily volume in Chrysler had dropped to less than half the shares of that one institutional block alone! Selling into lower volume was far more difficult and costly, which is exactly what happened to one large-block holder of General Motors in essentially the same circumstances. Disdaining the chance to get 85 for 395,000 shares of GM, which wasn't even able to open at that price until Tuesday, one institutional money manager waited two months and finally settled for 82 for the same block, $12 million less than if he had seized the moment on August 16. The moral: One of the best times to sell is when buyers are pleading for your stock. And that goes for 100 or 1,000 shares as well as for 100,000. It is not a time to be coy.

Specialists and THE Crash

A more recent, but equally dramatic, illustration of the usefulness of knowing which side of the market the specialists are going to be on took place during the Crash of '87...actually, at *the* exact bottom of the crash. You'll recall Black Monday, surely, but the bottom occurred midday on Terrifying Tuesday. Overnight, share prices had recovered; whispers spread through Wall Street that IBM had traded 25 points higher in Switzerland, and the very same salesmen who had ignored our "bearish" warnings that summer (as published in our Special Report entitled "The Philosophy of Tops") met us at the office door with pleas not to say anything negative. (No need, of course, for such concern, because it should be instinctive to start looking for a bottom when everyone else is terrified.) But the averages actually opened higher that Tuesday morning, and that's *never* a sign of a bottom (you want a big down opening, instead). Premature bargain-hunters were bagged, and prices quickly began to sag again.

What was different that Tuesday morning was that the selling pressure, once resumed, had a grimmer tone. On Black Monday the failure of "portfolio insurance" to actually insure against loss, but to, rather, feed the flames, caused those who were being burned to dump big blocks of big cap stocks. Thus, as soon as it was perceived that the rout was resuming, a substantial amount of selling reached the exchange floor in a very short period of time, causing—what else?—many specialists to seek, and to get, permission to halt trading in their premier issues. Word spread throughout the investment world that trading had been halted in Merck, in Philip Morris, in Telephone, and so on... Some big names were added to the rumor as anxiety intensified, but for the most part 'it was true—trading in individual stocks had been halted all over the floor due to an influx of sell orders. That they couldn't get out made most investors want to sell all the more. Yet the halt in trading *marked the bottom.*

How could that be? consider the reality, rather than the emotion. Trading's been halted, so that in the specialist's sweaty palm is clasped a flood of sell orders, and no buy orders. *Virtually everyone who had panicked and wanted to sell had entered their sell orders.* When the specialist re-opened the stock—whenever that was to be, and at whatever price would be determined as fair under the circumstances—*all of the sell orders* were going to be cleaned up, executed, sold! Simple reasoning said then—says at any time—that when the sellers are being taken out of their positions, a vacuum will be left overhead—no sellers around any more because they've all sold—one simple buy order coming along thereafter can start the stock rallying. The specialist has got to be, in such situations, on the buy side, cleaning up all those sellers. As it turned out, of course, the sharply lower re-opening prices, during the New York lunch hour, proved to be a classic buying opportunity at "sold out" prices. Thus the best guide for *not panicking* is to put yourself in the specialist's shoes and wallet.

This kind of situation also exists in particular individual stocks when they "blow off" on good news. Big "up" openings, with so many buy orders causing a delay, are invariably followed by declines; typically, the stock's literal top is made at such times. If you are lucky enough to own such a stock, you must wrench your excited emotions around to the sell side.

Using the Book

*T*he suspicion that the specialist has an unfair advantage because of his knowledge of where limited price orders are entered (and kept in his "book") has faded away. It never was anything more than a trivial advantage, far less important to his financial well-being than his years of experience at the trading post. What he has learned by direct observation is that being compelled to go against the crowd provides the real advantage.

In any event, specialist "books" have become thinner and thinner—almost as much of an anachronism as an appendix is. The use of options and futures products to hedge, to offset, to trade more easily, has changed what he "knows." Nevertheless, the old Wall Street saying that "stocks move in the direction of the book" is still valid—only now that there is really little or no "book," it is a philosophical guide rather than an actual one. Consider the origins: if someone wants to buy a block of shares, he can sit there on the bid side of the market for however long it takes to fill that order. But if the motivation to buy has more imminence, more eagerness to it, then he must consider reaching up to take the shares offered. But that is only worth doing when there is actually enough stock available to buy on the offer—that is, not just the specialist's need to make a market in the stock, but also limited price orders for sale at or just above the current market price. When a buyer *takes* the offered price, he causes the stock to trade at a higher price, or at a price unchanged from what has previously been a higher price. The more shares offered, the more willing the broker would be to complete his order by buying them. But when there is little or none to buy, he must wait, instead of reaching and thus driving the price up further. But how long can he hang around? If he leaves his order with the specialist to represent, in the hope that a seller will come along, the "book" fills in on the bid side, and thus if that seller comes in to hit his bid, the price will decline in that direction. As you can see, orders to buy are best filled when there are actual sell orders available; the price, therefore, must move upward in the direction of the sell side of the "book" (whether actually written down, kept in the specialist's palm, or made known to him informally as available "in case a buyer shows up").

Two useful things stem from this theory. First, if you are reading the data on a desktop publishing machine, a sizable offer is positive—and not to be interpreted as "oh oh, someone wants to sell a big piece, I better get out." Second, from this is derived the very valuable Specialist Short Selling Ratio (as discussed earlier), all of which is connected with the ability of the specialists to profit from going against the crowd *and* having to take the place of absent public orders. Eager buyers drive the price up in the direction of the book but then the orders on the book—that is, available sellers—are exhausted. It is at this turning point that the specialist must take their place, being required, under the rules, to sell his own shares, or to sell short in the absence of other sellers. At the same time, other buyers, not willing to pay up, but wanting to buy, are entering limited-price orders on the bid side of the book, so that the weight of, the direction of, the book is now toward lower prices. Obviously, that retracement back down gives the specialist, in a brief time span, a profit on the shares he has just sold. And when this kind of sequence is both widespread and continuing, you can see that stocks moving in the direction of the "book" is the precursor of an increase around the floor of specialist short selling, thereby resulting in a higher and higher ratio. When the specialists dominate short selling, other sellers have been used up, and when no one's left to sell, stocks are about to turn down toward where the bid orders are.

Back to Chrysler

*B*eing a seller on August 16, 1971, the side of the market that public enthusiasm has forced on the specialists, proved to be the right tactic. Just one month later, 45 percent of listed NYSE stocks were substantially lower than their opening price, and the majority of these had never even traded higher than that opening price. An additional 25 percent sold at prices sharply lower than their openings within the first week, before gradually recovering that lost ground. Less than one third were higher a month later. In sum, after twenty trading days, with the DJI *up* 80 points in that span, buyers on that explosive opening failed to show a profit or suffered sizable losses in about 70 percent of all NYSE stocks. Similar scrutiny of the twenty-five most widely held stocks yields much the same answer. One month later, thirteen of these were not only lower than their massive Monday opening prices but were actually selling below the preceding Friday's close before the speech! Another four were down from their opening prices. Only eight of the twenty-five went higher in the next four weeks (again, less than one third) even though the averages had advanced. Thus, no matter what stock you bought, the odds of showing a profit after what was then the grandest opening fling in market history were a whopping seven to three against you, and, of course, in favor of the specialist who was forced to sell. Clearly, determining which side of the market the specialist would be on would have pointed the way to the proper decision. *Selling along with the specialist is a sound policy.* (Fifteen years after having written those words, and with a lot more experience in a lot of different markets, we remain convinced that the principle behind that policy is sound—*you always want to be on the opposite side of an emotional eruption.*)

Let's return to the situation in Chrysler to carry this study further. As soon as the specialist has bridged the gap between supply and demand, having opened the stock up 17 percent, there is a brand-new ball game, and one side or the other now has to commit itself. Will it come from the buy side? A massive number of buyers have already expressed their willingness to pay 31; that includes all those who were willing to buy at whatever the arranged price was, so no one is left after that opening who wants to pay more—i.e., no one in the U.S.A. or on the stock exchange floor is interested in bidding the stock up any further although, of course, many having bought now are hoping someone else will. What's more, having bought, they can take to the sidelines to wait and see; other stocks are also providing fireworks. There does remain an untold number of potential buyers at lower prices—those whose specified limits excluded them from the opening at 31. This pile of unexecuted buy orders is in the hands of the specialist firm and its clerks, awaiting *lower* prices.

So what about the sell side? Here, too, the specialist has some leftover limited-price orders from would-be sellers who had insisted that they get more than 31—albeit far fewer than those on the buy side. At first glance it would seem that just about any potential seller who was willing to take 31 would already have entered his order before the well-publicized and long-delayed opening. But there is one difference between buyers and sellers; sellers already own the stock. While the potential buyer is perhaps awed by the excitement, intrigued by watching other stocks trade, the potential seller is anxious, feeling the need to make an important decision again and again. Thus, there is a critical distinction between sellers and buyers, which is then given an emotional goose by seeing the actual price print on the ticker tape. "If I had known the stock was going to open that high," a typical reaction goes, "I would have sold." One or two little downticks and this reaction is not only typical but becomes more and more prevalent if/as the stock does not immediately shoot up toward the moon.

It only takes a few, now uncomfortable, holders deciding to sell to ease Chrysler downward. The tape shows a few prints at 30 7/8, inspiring a few nervous holders to finally make a decision they'd been hesitant about. Seeing 30 3/4, with the bid down to 5/8 even as they talk to their brokers, a few of those sellers who had greedily wanted even more than 31 now hasten to cash in, too. At the same time, the specialist is now in the enviable position of being able—profitably—to take the place of any absent buyers, covering a portion of his 75,000-share hitherto scary short position by buying stock from these latecoming sellers. In the few minutes of trading remaining on that day, about 90,000 more shares of Chrysler changed hands, much of it finding the specialist on the buy side, making sure that the decline was orderly.

We do not want to proclaim that every mob-fed opening price will be the perfect price (sometimes emotional buying makes the "left shoulder" of a head & shoulders top rather than the "head') but if the price you get isn't the all-time peak, it's going to be near enough to be satisfactory. There is *no way* to measure the cumulative extreme of mob emotions. Chrysler, for example, received a new, albeit momentary, lease on life the very next day, when General Motors finally opened up 8 1/4 points. Although less of a percentage gain than Chrysler's opening had been—enthusiasm typically is measured in points, not percentages—the big jump renewed the buying spark in C and the stock shot up to 32 3/4. Sellers, being a greedy lot, might have wished they'd waited. But when that secondary, slightly higher, peak unfolds there is no way to identify the perfect moment to sell in the manner in which an opening price serves so conveniently and decisively. On Wednesday, Chrysler started sliding again, and within a few more days, it had dropped under 30. It's far tougher to sell under those circumstances; eking out a higher price once again is illusory...but tempting. Once that clear-cut opportunity to sell, the temptation to wait usually leads to not selling at all, as the price dwindles. To repeat: it is far less nerve-racking and emotion-deceiving, far easier and far more objective to join the specialist on his side of the market.

This guideline is particularly vital when the news comes late in the cycle. With various signs among the indicators telling you the rise has gotten past middle age, headline announcements are selling opportunities. That's important to remember, because invariably the most enticing news comes right near the top, when optimism is pervasive, and when even those who have begun to become concerned can be seduced into holding, or even buying some more. "Good news comes at tops" is more than just cocktail party conversation; it's a truism that's true. To keep your head under such circumstances, you don't really need to know the literal significance of the news, nor do you need the advice of an expert. In the old days, reports available from the exchange floor before the opening of "Buyers" or "Sellers" served to identify the direction of that day's market opening. Now, though, we have a more convenient and perhaps more accurate measure: trading activity in Europe flows through the news wires and is followed by trading in the S & P futures contracts and the Amex's Major Market Index *beforehand*. The greater the extremity of their chiefly emotional trading, the greater the warning. Think contrary. If your reaction is delighted anticipation of the forthcoming higher price, realize that puts you squarely in the middle of the emotional crowd. Turn your emotions around to grumpiness. The market's moments of generosity are few, but news-induced optimism rewards cynics for being cynical.

Chapter Eight

A Basic Selling Strategy

Success in the stock market is nothing more than mastering a game of probabilities. The more efficiently you play the probable course, using the odds instead of betting on a long shot, the more successful you will be year in and year out. One rule, as we've just discussed, is to react to news by being on the side of the exchange specialist. How do you know in advance that such opportunities exist? You don't, but then, neither does the specialist. But while you may never know just which side of the market the specialist is going to be on during the trading day, there is one time each day that you do have a chance to relate to the specialist's activity, and that's the opening transaction. Let's see why selling at the opening is more likely to be selling when the odds are in your favor, both emotionally and objectively.

In the first edition—boy! does this bring back memories—we used the example of a trader who owned 1,000 shares of Technicolor (bought at 28 on a hot tip just before going away on vacation). It took a while for TK to get rolling, but then, late one Friday afternoon, he got an excited call from his broker: Technicolor was running away on the upside: 32 1/2...32 3/4...33 all over the tape. He rushed for the newspaper at the country store the next morning and saw that the stock had closed at 33 1/2, its high for the day. Contemplating that $5,000 was an eminently satisfactory profit, he decided to sell. But on Monday morning he took his hand back off the phone, deciding that since it was a long-distance call he'd wait until after the stock had opened, to see how it was doing before placing a specific sell order. "Opened at 35," the broker told him, "but it's backing down a bit now." How much? "Oh, just normal profit-taking. It's 34…no, wait, here it is now on the tape at 33 3/4."

He confessed to the broker that he'd been thinking of selling, but, well, too bad, he'd missed the chance. Vacillation had set in; on Sunday he was going to sell; by Monday he was only thinking about it. Yet, you'll notice, had he simply said "sell," he could have hit the bid at that moment of 33 1/2, achieving the same price he'd been delighted with on Friday's close. But TK had been up to 35 and that changed the way it looked in his mind. Emotion had interfered twice: in wanting to see what was going to happen on Monday morning before acting, and then in permitting what actually did happen to alter the decision he'd already made.

In turn, the broker, not wanting the responsibility for advice that might turn out to be wrong, was silent for a moment, and then asked, "Should I watch it and call you back if it rallies?" "No," was the response, but, with renewed resolve, the trader added, "I decided to sell, so I'm going to." Notice how he thinks he's not being greedy, but decisive. "It's bound to bounce back up again, so enter an order to sell at 34 1/2."

It would be nice to report that he was saved, or lucky, but then there'd be nothing more to write about. The market is not kind to the naive. TK did bounce back, albeit momentarily, correcting the initial reversal, but only traded one tick at 34 3/8. And from there the path was steadily downward to an ultimately serious loss. Yet our trader had not only decided to sell but had actually put an order in. How could the situation have been botched so badly, even though the profits were there and the right decision had been made? You'll notice, for one thing, that an absurdly petty extraneous item was involved: the notion of a long-distance phone call…although we suspect that he'd have hesitated anyhow, wanting to see the opening even though a decision seemingly already had been made. Often there is some such irrational or irrelevant impediment to be found in the history of market mistakes. As they say: "shoulda, woulda, coulda." But besides that, two things could have been—should have been—done differently. First, the order should have been entered before the market opened; and second, having made up his mind to sell, having actually given his broker the sell order, he should have used an "at the market" order rather than specifying a limit price. Let's examine these two aspects in detail, because they are basic to an intelligent approach to selling.

The Market Order

NYSE Rule 13 defines a market order as "an order to buy or sell a stated amount of a security at the most advantageous price obtainable after the order is represented in the Trading Crowd." This means that, not only must the floor broker try to obtain the best price he can when he gets to the post where the specialist stands (the "trading crowd"), but he is also responsible for making the deal immediately (in floor language, he must not "miss the market") in order to ensure that he has, indeed, gotten the most advantageous price possible at that moment. He can't shilly-shally around trying to do better for you or he risks another broker coming in and doing business ahead of him. If that happens, you're entitled to an adjustment to the price you should have received.

The best reason to use a market order when selling is to be sure of getting an execution. Accordingly, certain variations have arisen for those who desperately need an execution but want to play games with the market beforehand. One variation is to enter an order which becomes a market order at a specific time, such as 12:30 P.M., a patently absurd gimmick, since the clock has no relationship to an intelligent selling decision. More frequently the game is played by overextended traders who are obliged to sell a position by the end of the business day to pay for something else they've bought (or simply because they want to ensure going home without any position whatsoever). In an attempt to do better under such pressure, they enter what is known as an "at the close" order, which is defined in Rule 13 as "a market order which is to be executed at or as near to the close as practicable." In its most common guise, such an order is entered as either sell at X (a hoped-for limited price above the current price) or at the market at the close. If the upside limit is not reached, and the stock remains unsold near the close, the specialist will cancel the limited-price part and sell the stock at the market as near to the closing bell as possible, though it need not be the very last trade of the day.

Perhaps you can see how absurd that is. Such an order entices you into holding on in the hope that maybe you'll do better. Hope does not have a very high batting average, and leads to one of the most deceptive thoughts in the market. It violates a basic principle that, when a stock is hard to sell (i.e., there aren't enough buyers around to take it up to your limit), it should be sold promptly. If it's not rising, buyers are scarce and other sellers may be in the way. Don't wait; sell! Remember that at the close, the stock will be sold to the best bid in the market. Suppose the stock is 25 bid, offered at 25 1/2, last sale at 25 1/4; already you are getting a down price (at 25). What's more, the specialist knows your order is in there to sell at the close. If, due to an absence of public bids, he realizes he's the one who's going to have to buy your stock, he's less apt to take a stand. Why buy a lot at 25, and yours too, when he can ease the bid down from trade to trade? Similarly, knowing he's going to be handed your shares at the close, he can trade against them by selling short, for example, at 25 3/8, thus keeping the stock from reaching the limit you were hoping for), and covering by buying your shares at the 25 bid at the close. It isn't so much that an order to sell at the close is theoretically wrong; it's that no one should ever put himself in a position that, on a practical basis, necessitates using it. Traders who do so are confessing to letting the market take control of their options and decisions.

But our basic guideline is to make our own decisions and to do so objectively, without the pressures of moment-to-moment occurrences. To repeat a point worth repeating, it is only an opportunity lost to miss a chance on the buy side if you limit your order to a specific price, because you can always buy another stock. In a climate truly ripe for buying, professionals know there will be many stocks worth grabbing, each as promising as the other, since there's no way to know in advance which the big winner will be.

(A paucity of buy ideas is, in its own way, a negative indicator.) But when it comes to selling, there's no such leeway. You already own the shares, and if the time has come to sell, failure to do so could be costly—fractions if you play the game of at the close, but potentially immense if you wait for your "perfect" price. It's hard enough deciding when to sell, without compounding the issue by also trying to decide at what exact price. There are exceptions, to be sure (and we'll discuss them later), but by and large, selling at the market is a sound practice. Every day profits have turned into losses because the shareholder pursued one more 1/8. "I put in market orders," one off-floor member-trader said, explaining how he trades for his firm's account, "for the speed and to make sure I get an execution." Decisiveness has a much better batting average than hope. It frees one's mind to get on with the next decision.

Many amateurs are reluctant to enter a market order, because they fear the specialist will somehow take advantage of it. Scalping did exist in the very old days, but the consciously bad execution is now extremely rare. You may, rather, get an inadvertently delayed execution, such as can happen if the floor broker who is to handle your order happens to be far away from the booth where his clerk receives your order, has to hoof back to get it, and then has to re-cross the floor to reach the trading post. Another broker can reach the post seconds ahead of yours and hit the bid, driving the price down. (The increasingly automated systems in place obviate almost all of these carpings nowadays.) A much more significant problem may be you yourself (often on the phone in combination with your broker). Whereas a single tick on the tape may ring a bell in the professional trader's head, the public trader often watches an entire sequence, 1/4, 1/4, 1/4, 1/8, 0, 0, then bingo, up he jumps, ordering the broker to sell him out, having been unable to stand the sequence of falling prices any longer. When such a market order reaches the floor and gets executed, the price may already be down near the low for the day. It is never a good idea to finally panic out in obvious company with sellers; but it is often a lovely idea to toss a sell order into the midst of a pot boiling over with buyers, on the repeatedly useful principle that when a lot of people are clamoring for your shares it is a good time to oblige them. You might want to post a couple of bad rhymes on your machine or phone: "When you're laughin', you should be sellin'; when you're cryin', you should be buyin'."

Specialists on both the NYSE and the Amex have confirmed our long-held suspicion that the public often has matters backward. The typical public trader fires a buy order to the floor in a volatile stock and thinks a market order is sensible in order to be sure of an execution. But after buying willy-nilly at the market, near the top of rallies, the same trader will then turn around and enter a limited-price order on the sell side, now trying to play it safe and cagey. But when it comes to getting out, especially in a volatile stock, the risk of not selling could leave you locked into a stock while it tumbles. Trying to pick the intraday price you want may seem like careful behavior, but it is really endangering your capital, waiving certainty for the sake of engaging in a battle of wits.

Do it the other way around, the specialists on the floor advise. We emphatically agree. Use limit orders when trying to accumulate stocks—that is, buy carefully, and don't chase them—but once you've decided to get out, avoid the unnecessary risk of not selling. Use a market order.

Limited-Price and Other Types of Orders

*T*here is one exception to this dictum of "sell, and be out." (It is *not*, however, selling a partial position. Although that may seem like a good compromise to indecision, we've found that once a partial position has been sold, the holder becomes overly relaxed about the remaining shares where losses can mount unattended because he thinks he's already done his selling job.) Our exception is, rather, that if you have a particular upside target in mind, realistically determined beforehand, and based on objective factors (not simply because that's a gain you'll settle for), such as an overhead supply area and technical pattern measurements that confirm the target near resistance, you can enter a limited-price order and let it sit on the specialist's book until executed. Some brokers, on behalf of some customers, think it is enough to plug such a target number into their machine which can remind them that the price has been reached. This doesn't work psychologically—see our friend with his TK profit—because it too often induces waiting to see one tick more, and then another, and another. We are in search of decisiveness without the compunction to be brilliant.

Such a limited-price order can be combined with an either/or order effectively. Here you aim for a higher price, say, where you can see formidable resistance overhead, while wanting to protect yourself in case the trap door falls open. You can then enter an order such as "Sell at 26 limit or on stop at 22 7/8." This is a sound way to sell objectively, no matter what happens—the objectivity coming from having the order entered before emotions enter the picture; the emotions coming from muttering "Oh my god, I don't want to sell down here" or "Look how strong that stock is, I'll just raise my limit a couple of points."

Thus there is a virtue to using a GTC order (good till canceled), rather than a day order which expires if unexecuted that day. The GTC order can go along with any type of limited-price order, such as the simple limit or the more complex either/or. As you can see, the day order necessitates revving yourself up again each day to be objective; that psychological struggle can turn out to be a formidable stumbling block, often abetted by the notion that it didn't go off yesterday so "I'll just watch it today," instead of putting the order back in. What could happen to make the situation different? your emotions may change, that's what! If the stock seemed a sound sale on Monday, why would it be different on Tuesday? maybe you feel more greedy, maybe more scared. The only thing that is likely to have changed is your hopes, rather than the reality.

To its practical advantage, too, any GTC order retains its time priority on the specialist's book, while the day order, if re-entered, must start again at the bottom of the list of orders awaiting execution. Your broker, needless to say, should remind you from time to time that you have a GTC order entered; months later, you really are entitled to reconsider your original objective decision.

What we like about the GTC order is that chance to sell into strength at an objectively determined target price. "Five minutes after buying," one professional off-floor trader remarked, "I have a GTC order in to sell at a limit price." His objectivity may be much narrower in scope than yours, but when you see quite clearly on a chart just about where a stock should be sold—when you "know" at the time of making the buy decision whether the price target is worth the buying—the use of a GTC order can be appropriate. Our experience over the years is that a measured target that coincides with a recognizable resistance area has a high degree of leading to a successful sale. Just don't let the limit become a pipe dream; it may be "bad luck" to raise a sell limit—it's actually a sign of greediness—but you must always be willing to admit along the way that the stock isn't doing as well as you'd expected.

While on the subject of limited-price orders, it's worth noting that the public has a habit of dispensing such an order and then, scared that they won't get an execution for being so pettily restrictive, tacking on the phrase "an extra 1/8 discretion" or "or better." Such added fillips are useless. When a floor broker has received a limited-price order, he must try to get you the best price available when he reaches the trading post, whether or not you ask him to do better. If you specify an extra 1/8 leeway, that simply changes the limit you've established; if you say, "Sell at 12 1/2 limit, with an extra 1/8 discretion," the broker effectively has a sell limit of 12 3/8 to play with. And then, if he misses the market, and the stock sells down from 12 1/4, which you could have gotten, to 6, you'll feel foolish for having set any sort of limit when selling "at the market" would have gotten you out decisively. A fraction of a point can look trivial compared to an ultimate loss. Put limits in on the upside when you are in a position to make that sort of objective decision about a target ahead of time; sell at the market otherwise.

There are a variety of other limited-price orders, each with a peculiar twist. "Immediate or cancel" is a limit order which is canceled on the spot if at that time it cannot be executed at or within the limit set. It has its trading uses, but the virtues are entirely on the buy side. On the sell side, you run the grave risk of having an order canceled which ought to be executed—or why the "immediate?" The same holds true for two cousins of the "immediate or cancel" order, the "fill or kill" and the "all or none." Shun them on the sell side. They introduce non-market factors to the decision-making process.

Lastly, it is necessary to add a few words about decisions to sell (or buy, for that matter) over-the-counter stocks. NASDAQ, as a form of "exchange," has made a big deal out of its maturity; growth in substance and solidity may very well be true, and there are lots of times when we will want to buy and subsequently sell o-t-c stocks. But it is a different marketplace: not the auction situation you may be used to from Big Board experiences, more insular, less accessible and less flexible. Typically, many different firms make a market in the stock you are interested in and yet that doesn't seem to be as satisfactory a situation as having a central specialist. Of course, sizable orders on behalf of institutions (mutual funds, pension funds, and the like) are "worked" by a trader at the firm to which that order has been given in much the same manner that a floor broker might station himself by the post on the NYSE floor. But for others, it is *extremely difficult to get an execution of an order between the bid and asked prices.* That means, as a practical matter, that using a limited price order to try to do better, or to expect the over-the-counter trader at the firm with which you have placed your order to accomplish that on your behalf, is frustratingly unlikely. If you want to sell, and the best bid is an 1/8 better somewhere else unknown to you...well, you'll never know. For various reasons, many of which sound reasonable when explained to you, you just don't happen to get an execution. You are really going to pay the offer if you buy, and accept the bid price if you sell. That wouldn't be so bad if some of the spreads weren't so wide; *you* pay for the OTC's trader's timidity and fear of volatility and, in a very real sense, greed (for after all, the trader is sitting there buying on the bid and selling on the offer). Accordingly, using a limit with an over-the-counter order is mostly a matter of making you feel better that you'll do no worse than what you are supposed to get. You might just as well use a market order in fatalistic fashion.

Entering the Order Before the Opening

*P*receding chapters have discussed the importance of guarding against loss. It's folly to allow a losing situation of a stock not behaving as expected to become a disaster. The use of stop-loss orders is sound protection for locking in profits, too. But since stops are triggered on declines, and since we now know how to identify certain signs of impending market weakness, it is preferable to take our profits by selling into strength during advances. A stop-loss order is a good defense, but as the saying goes, the best defense is a good offense. Better to let avid buyers have our shares at higher prices than to wait, as a subsequent decline stops us out, or paralyzes those who haven't utilized that protection. As you can see, however (refer back to the man holding Technicolor), this requires other skills: specifically, an order entered to sell at the market, plus, we believe, a means of eliminating any potentially interfering emotion.

Easier said than done, of course. The first hurdle is in recognizing that no stock—even the one you are riding to fortune—goes up forever. Indeed, the best sell signal of all may be sounded whenever some rapturous voice inside your head exults: "Have I got a big winner!" If, somehow, science could hook up an investor's brain with electrodes which would transmit a sell order to the exchange floor whenever this sort of self-congratulatory attitude becomes excessively enthusiastic, the complexities of selling would be solved.

What is more apt to happen is that we become so fond of our beautiful choice that we don't notice wrinkles developing, the aching back, the flab. We're turned on by good news that revives the glamour, or by the heights the stock has reached, or by the Dow's own continuing highs. The most dangerous reaction to owning a stock that goes up is to fall in love with it and swear that you two will never part. Not long ago we overheard one man boasting to another about an Amex stock which had gone up from 8 to 20, and no one, he said (yet how did it get from 8 to 20?) realized how huge the earnings were going to be. Without knowing anything about that stock, we muttered: "A sure sell signal," and sure enough, it was down to 15 within two weeks. And then, the consoling phrase becomes: "It's just a correction." The more selling becomes inconceivable, the closer to a top the stock is.

There must be a way to avoid the penchant to hang on, to see "one more tick" or "one more day." We first observed the answer many years ago in the behavior of an off-floor trader. This gentleman, having retired from a prosperous business, had treated himself to his own seat on the exchange. Not the least bit interested in sitting in front of the tape all day every day, he would invariably march into the brokerage firm office that handled his bookkeeping about fifteen minutes before the market closed and, without taking his coat off, would study the tape for a few minutes and buy any especially active stock that was about to close on its high for the day. The name of the company didn't matter, or what business it was in, or its earnings, or its future prospects. And, having bought, he would simply leave behind an order to sell his position at the opening the next morning. No fuss, no muss; just sell at the market at the opening, thank you. (Compare this sequence with those who utilize computer software programs to study the market overnight; theoretically, and often in reality, their computer-generated buy decisions cause them to buy from the trader who had anticipated such a next-day opening.) Strength at the close almost always ensures a higher opening the next trading day, even though that opening may turn out to be the peak for the day, or, as with Technicolor, for the whole move. Indeed, if there is no follow-through strength on the next day's opening, something may be wrong, and one is best sold out anyhow.

Higher openings may stem from a news item, boosting the stock when it appears on the Dow Jones news ticker during the day and then inducing added buying from those who read the news in the morning paper. Often, the strength precedes the actual announcement—who knows in advance, eh? guessers or leakers? Or it may be that the strong performance itself catches the attention of other investors. Perhaps salesmen are pushing a new recommendation from their firm's research department and word of such a recommendation did seep out ahead of time. Very late in a trend, when exhaustion exists, such action may not last more than the very next morning, but there is undoubtedly some law operative in the market akin to the momentum of an object once set in motion. It's better not to know the reason, because then you might want to hold on a bit longer to "see," when it is best to sell at the opening.

How the Opening Is Arranged

While the specialist's assigned duty is to maintain a fair and orderly market throughout the trading day, it is at each morning's opening that this task receives extra emphasis. Buy and sell orders have accumulated overnight, creating a fresh battle between supply and demand. Gone is the randomness, for just this one time each day the specialist must resolve any disparity and determine a fair opening price. We've already shown how you can benefit by putting yourself in the specialist's shoes when events are about to cause an extreme opening. Opening prices up, on news or hysterical eagerness to buy for whatever reason, should be viewed as selling opportunities. (However, big openings down on bad news are not the clean-outs they used to be: less bottom-fishing buyers, more and more potential sellers who want out at any cost. The result has been brief ineffectual bounces and a return to the downside to prices lower than the arranged opening. Accordingly, buying into such emotional down openings is *not* the mirror image of selling into emotional up openings. The difficult decision of whether one should join the sellers when bad news strikes a stock you own will be confronted below.) But first let's see how the way the specialist handles routine openings can also work in your favor.

In what are now accurately described as "the old days," openings were hectic and not nearly as fair as they are now. The specialist was then just another face in the exchange crowd. Each broker represented his own firm's order, and when the opening bell rang, every one began to shout at once what he wanted to do: buy or sell, at what price, and how many shares. From the wild scene that ensued, reminiscent of the homesteading scrambles of the West, a split opening often ensued, and a stock could actually open at different prices at the same time.

Split openings have long since gone the way of downtick short selling. When volume began to perk up after World War II, brokers from larger firms found that they couldn't properly fill all their opening orders, since that would have required them to be at several different trading posts at the same time. So the rule was changed, and now the broker dashes around the floor beforehand, dropping off the pre-opening orders from his firm's customers with the various specialists involved (or they are directed in computerized fashion through the system to the proper post). Because this made the task of arranging a fair opening price more convenient, the specialist was willing to wave the usual floor brokerage fee that would be charged for handling the order, and thus the originating broker keeps the commission (his fee is included in the overall commission the investor pays). Obviously, the broker is delighted to get the execution gratis. The result is that such opening order came to be known as love orders, equating the granting of monetary favors with an act of affection.

As we've said, the practical effect of permitting love orders at openings is to eliminate the random sequence and frantic scene that would otherwise take place. With virtually all orders in his hand, the specialist's task is much easier, dependent not on an unpredictable flow of orders one after the other but on the actual supply and demand at that time. If, after the orders have been sorted, a discrepancy between buyers and sellers remains, the specialist would then meet his obligation to get the stock open by trading for his own dealer account. In so doing, he can't go against the functioning of supply and demand; if there are more buyers than sellers, the stock obviously should open higher. Specialist selling that would cause a lower price instead is not permissible.

When it comes to determining the opening price, the specialist takes all available information into consideration: the orders left with him for love's sake on both sides of the market, his own dealer position or lack of one, limited-price orders previously entered on the book away from the closing price, any additional orders brokers in the crowd may be representing themselves, and whatever a floor trader hanging around might be tempted to do. Before coming to a decision, he's likely to consider the overall market, too, and what overnight trading overseas in both U.S. stocks and the thirty-year Treasury Bond have been like. But in the end, the decision must be justified on the basis of the market's law of supply and demand: how many orders to buy, how many to sell, how many are transactable at a given price related to the previous closing price. The preponderance of one side over the other determines the tilt, and then, if necessary to get the stock open, the specialist will deal for his own account. Because the specialist thus, in effect, decides on a fair price for you, and often for himself as well, our belief is that *openings generally provide the soundest selling opportunity.*

The SEC, in a special study of the securities markets conducted in the early 1960s, determined that "the opening price of an issue is probably the single most important price of the day." (Subsequently, of course, the newspaper stock tables were redesigned to eliminate this "important price" in exchange for the treacherously misleading item of price/earnings ratios!) While other moments are random—they might prove satisfactory, but could just as well be disadvantageous; might be lucky, or unlucky depending on whether one is buying or selling—the opening is the time when (1) there is most apt to be an excess of buyers over sellers, and (2) the specialist is able to produce the most objectively calculated (least random) price of the day. The most important reason of all: *entering your order before the market opens is the single best way not to be influenced by emotional factors.*

Why You Can Get a Better Price

*I*n hindsight, it certainly would have been sensible to have entered that sell order in Technicolor before the opening; such big ups at the close often *culminate* in a big up opening the next day. However, the opening can be beneficial as well in mundane situations and in run-of-the-mill stocks. Let's say you own 100 shares of XYZ, which you thought was going to be marvelous but wasn't, so you decide to sell, figuring that it's better to put the money to work elsewhere: a strong stock is more apt to go up for you than waiting for a weak one to come back up. You phone your broker that afternoon and are told that XYZ's last sale was at 20 and, the broker adds, punching his desktop interrogation machine, the current quotation is 19 3/4 bid, while the best offer is 20 1/4. Noticing that the quote exactly straddles the last sale, and that the size is 500 bid for, 500 offered, you surmise that no one is particularly interested in the stock and that the specialist himself may be on one or both sides of the market just to keep things alive.

Perhaps your reaction is: "What the hell, it's going nowhere fast; let's get rid of it right now and find some action elsewhere." In this case, if your broker sends a market sell order to the floor before the close of trading, you'd wind up getting the bid price, 19 3/4. If you try to be cute about it and enter a limit order at the same price as the last sale (20), as many public players are tempted to do, you may wind up without an execution at all, unless, by chance, a buyer drifts in before the closing bell. But you are risking, in that game, another seller hitting the bid at 19 3/4 ahead of you and thereby dropping the price even more. Oh, you hope, maybe that buyer will meander in and take the offer.

So you hem and haw, and finally tell your broker you're going to think about it overnight. After a restless sleep, you decide that, with the market growing toppy according to the indicators and with XYZ going sideways, you are right to want to sell out. The emotions bred by an on-going ticker tape are absent; without further hesitation, having made an objective decision based on what you actually do know (and unaffected by wondering what the market is going to do next), you phone your broker immediately after breakfast and direct him to sell at the market, at whatever the opening price is destined to be. How simple! No worrying about what the next tick will prove, no dreams of pots of gold blinding your judgment, no prayer that it will bounce back up to where you should have sold it, no need to cling to the phone or haunt a brokerage office all day. You are going to accept whatever the specialist decides is a fair opening price, and kiss the stock goodbye.

XYZ will open either up, unchanged, or down, but it will open, because your market order must be executed. According to Rule 13, a market order has precedence over a limited-price order and must be executed even if the stock opens at exactly the price of the limit. (The limited-price order will get an execution only if there is another buyer around to match the limit order.) Thus you can go about your real business for the rest of the day, secure in the knowledge that you've made a decision as unemotionally as possible and that you're assured of an execution. The phone is not going to ring with your broker at the other end of the line hysterically crying out, "You missed it! What do you want to do now?"

Ponder for a moment how impossible it is to make a rational decision with your broker whining like that. "Dump!" is he implying? or "Wait!" He's sitting there, watching. Should you rush to turn on CNBC? get off the other phone with your boss? What's the Dow doing? does it matter? Why doesn't he give you some information to make the next decision sensibly? What *is* that magical information? Let's go back to see, in practical terms, just how that "sell at the market at the opening" would work out instead.

First, suppose someone else in this vast country has decided to buy 100 shares of XYZ at the market, and likewise, a man who lives across the street from the company's accountant wants to acquire 500 shares. (We're making this example as simple as possible, using a very small number of shares to illustrate the point; you can add zeros if you wish.) When the specialist arrives at his trading post, his clerk informs him that XYZ has 600 shares to buy, and 100 shares (yours) at the market to sell. He ruffles through his book, and notes that there are 500 shares entered to sell at 20 1/4 "good till canceled," the same shares that were being offered as part of the quotation the afternoon before. This situation is strictly procedural. He simply takes the 600 shares to buy, matches them with 600 shares to sell, and opens the stock at the price at which he can do so as the agent, without involving his own account as dealer—specifically, at 20 1/4. Even if the limit order were not there to sell, and he had to supply stock from his own account (selling long, if he had any shares, or selling short if need be) he could still properly open the stock at 20 1/4, up 1/4 from the previous closing price, since a disparity between buyers and sellers (in this case 600 to 100 shares) calls for an opening price which fairly represents the weight of supply and demand; 20 1/4 would be fair enough. Note that although the opening price was up only 1/4 of a point from the previous close, you've actually gotten half a point more than you would have received had you sold at the market the previous afternoon to the then-prevailing bid at 19 3/4. That's an extra $50 in your pocket, a reward for making your decision away from the pressures of broker and ticker tape.

But suppose the situation isn't that convenient. The specialist himself may have a long position that he wants to whittle down, thus, for whatever his reasons, agreeing with you that XYZ is better sold than held. With the weight of orders on the buy side and the opportunity to do some selling of his own, he could legitimately open the stock an 1/8 higher, at 20 1/8, or could even open XYZ unchanged, which is what most specialists would do especially if they intended to continue to sell later on. In this case, he'd be saying: "I'm the professional right on the floor. I own the same stock as you, and I also want to sell it now." And you'd still be doing better than you would have the previous afternoon (by $25), while guaranteeing yourself an execution by making it a market rather than a limited-price sell order. The specialist, in joining you, has not held off to see if he can do better later on, and neither should you.

This scenario is predicated on buyers having drifted in overnight. If only 100 shares to buy came in, to match yours, the stock would open at 20 (again, $25 more for you). But let's make it worse. If no buyers have come in before the opening, you'd be back to the situation that prevailed the afternoon before. Your 100 shares to sell, and no buyers would call for an opening price of 19 3/4. In keeping with the rules requiring a "fair and orderly" market, the specialist couldn't permit a variation on a mere 100 shares of more than that 1/4 of a point from the previous closing price (in fact, in the nineties that probably holds true for 1,000 shares). So you wouldn't have lost anything by waiting for the opening, and you still have the possibility of doing better. What's more, that possibility is nurtured in reality, rather than in sheer hope, for the odds favor getting more for your shares, even if the specialist decides to open the stock unchanged.

Finally, take the worst possible situation. Suppose orders coming in overnight turn out to be on the sell side instead: let's make it 2,000 shares to sell, plus of course your 100 shares. Now the stock can't open higher at all. Too bad, it seems, and yet there is a virtue here, too. Although the specialist might be willing to reaffirm his bid at 19 3/4, that may be a bit more than he may want to absorb in such a thin, relatively inactive stock. He could decide to open the stock at 19 1/2 (where he may have other bidders on his book apart from his own account taking all the risk). This lower opening costs you that 1/4 of point from what you'd have gotten the previous afternoon. But it has also told you that your decision to sell was sound, since the balance of supply and demand has shifted. The seller or sellers may have an innocent reason, or a more knowledgeable one, and, indeed, there may be more shares for sale behind that piece. So you've gained one other advantage. Instead of being on the phone with your broker a few minutes after the opening—the quotation on his machine is now announcing, 19 1/4 bid, offered at 19 3/4—desperately trying to decide what to do now that the stock has opened lower, and the bid side of the market is even lower, you are already, peacefully, out on the opening.

Meanwhile, your broker is on the other line with an investor who hesitated, who wanted to see one more tick, who wanted to wait to see how the market opening was going to be. Now there's trouble, temporary perhaps, but the startled holder confronted with a crisis has to decide quickly. "Any news on the broad tape?" the broker shouts across the room. The Dow has opened down, too. "They"—whoever they may be—didn't like this or that news item. But perhaps it's only temporary; there's an uptick; he feels relieved...or should he take it as a selling opportunity? Another downtick, an even lower bid...should he just settle for whatever he can get? The lull before the storm can be quiet, or a consolidation of forces. Another barrage of selling and XYZ is down to 19 before the investor on the other line has made a decision, and then the decision, all too often, is "Oh, sell the damn thing if it rallies back to 20." And it doesn't, and he's still holding down near 10. No thanks! not least among the virtues of selling at the market at the opening is that you relieve yourself of these enormously dangerous, and draining, conversations with your broker while the tape is running.

But Suppose There *Is* News

Despite the smug awareness and constant reiteration that both the market and individual stocks discount news in advance, news inevitably has an immediate effect on behavior. Somehow there is always a flock of sheep streaming into buy when headlines or TV announcers proclaim a favorable news item, or to rush, like lemmings, out of a stock on what sounds like bad news. This has been fed by the arrival on the scene of instant news: CNBC, as the "market channel," tells all, and breathlessly, as if every item is of equal importance; while the market is open, a ticker tape runs along the bottom of the screen on CNN's Headline News channel, with regular verbal updates similar to those presented every half hour on radio all-news stations. Instant news is provided on every broker's desktop machine via Dow Jones or Reuters. Everything is accessible to everyone at once. The sequential learning of the news, and a sequential reaction to it has changed to an instant reaction to this instant knowledge—an instant *emotional* reaction, we should say. Much has changed, and yet little of substance has changed.

We are here discussing a variety of different kinds of news: (1) the hype the media creates in anticipation of an "all-important" economic number—it used to be money supply; then trade deficits mattered; more recently, it became the monthly employment statistic, until that gave way to the drama of the Producer Price

Index; (2) individual stock earnings and/or product announcements, sometimes causing drastic and "unexpected" reactions; (3)
non-economic news such as the Russian coup. Put another way:
(1) what's worried about beforehand; (2) what matches or fails to
match market expectations; and (3) what surprises.

Economic statistical data always has an emotional tint. The
human animal needs something that seems rational, understandable, as if there is something that will soothe, or justify, one's anxiety, and it is precisely that yearning for the rational which creates
emotional reactions. The media, in its need to sound all-knowing
as it reports statistics, feeds those emotions. Every announcer on
CNBC will refer to the "next number." Every interviewee will haz-
ard a forecast; they're worried, they're bullish because of it, or
bearish. "All bets are off if it comes in at…" is a common excuse
heard from those who are supposed to "know," but are terrified to
"anticipate." Inevitably, the stage is set for an emotional reaction.
It may be a big letdown, that "the number" is unchanged, means
little. You may get angry, if it's different than you expected, or
from what the experts had led you to expect. *But then comes the
real test:* how is the market responding to this "all-important"
number? And next, how are *you* supposed to respond to the emotional response you've already had? buy, sell, or hold? or curse
yourself, for not having done something in the market the afternoon before? And by then, the announcers are now already talking about "the next number." That's the nature of market news
nowadays: it's so damnably instantaneous that it doesn't last.

At the risk of being a bit repetitious, there are certain rules to
promulgate. First, as it applies to individual stocks, and the stock
market generally: (1) Good news comes out at tops; the more euphoric a response, the better the sale. (2) Good news in a stock
that has already been making what looks like a top on its chart—
and which, the pre-opening indications tell us, will not open at a
new high—should be viewed as an opportunity to sell. (3) *Only* if
the stock has been trending sideways and is going to open up on a
big gap into new high territory, can such good news be considered
an on-going positive. (4) Good news that comes out after a decline
has been taking place will cause a rebound, but not a reversal. (5)

If the pre-opening indications for a stock delayed due to good news start to diminish on the offer side—indicating that more sellers have come in—that is all the more reason to sell.

Second, as it applies to economic and other fundamental statistics: (6) Most "magic number" news has been anticipated so much that it is "in the market." Profit-taking by those who were right in their anticipation is usually the underlying reason why the market may respond to the announced news in what seems like a perverse way. (7) If the market action in response to news reverses fifteen minutes after the opening, this reversal is likely to be the meaningful direction. (8) If the news is startling beyond expectation, and there is no reversal thereafter, the direction taken is likely to have intermediate-term duration.

Third, if the individual stock news is negative: (9) There is often one last "negative" news item very early in a stock's upside breakout—"wall of worry" stuff can cause a quick sharp selloff to scare folks away. (10) When already deep into a downtrend, bad news has usually been long since anticipated. A price decline from 16 to 9, followed by an announcement of a quarterly earnings loss, should not exactly come as a surprise, should it? (11) However— we're thinking of a real life example—if the stock has recently recovered from that 9 low back up to 12, it has become re-vulnerable to a negative surprise (since, obviously, recent buyers have been lulled into believing everything is okay/cheap). Negative news is occasionally a literal surprise. (12) Often, in cases of a prior extensive decline, a putative left shoulder of a head & shoulders bottom can be seen, followed by a bounce, so that the bad news comes along to make a lower low which turns out to be the "head" of such a bottom. This is tricky but discernible; you don't want to be panicked out at the absolute low of a "head" so check for lessened volume even though this spate of negative news may seem to be worse than the dumping that came during the "left shoulder" sell off. (See the Kuwaiti bear market sequence for an example in the DJIA itself.) (13) Many times, what seems like "surprise" negative news occurs in a stock that has been in a major rising trend. Even though the daily chart may have been revealing faltering action—the negative news may be a big surprise to the marketplace. The pre-opening indication will show just how surprising the news is.

We would take such indications seriously. In the old days, news travelled much more sequentially, and decisions were not made so instantaneously. Nowadays, however, the market often looks like an ocean liner in which everyone rushes to one side of the ship, so that it lists badly. Thus the speeded-up and more helpful information that has become the norm in the nineties can enable us to learn, before the stock opens, the emotional reactions of others. Broker desktop machines will carry opening indications, and these will be repeated on, for example, CNBC, and will be updated, if necessary, before the stock actually opens for trading. Note that word indication; it is a message from the floor of what the opening might look like; thus it can, and frequently does, change as additional orders are entered and reach the post at which the stock is traded. Read these changing indications as a "conversation" with you as to how others have reacted, first to the news itself, and then, subsequently, to the indicated bid and offer. "Ah, I'll sell at that price," they might think, and rush some more sell orders to the floor. Then the next indication would show a lower quote. At other times, "Cheap at that price" is the reaction, and buy orders come in, causing the bid side of the quote to rise. *The direction of these changing indications has become an important, and not quite so contrary, guide in the nineties: buyers come in, not so bad; additional sellers, something seriously wrong.* That tendency to rush to one side or the other should be "read" as a message as to the seriousness of the news.

If you happen to be stuck in a stock subject to a "surprise" negative announcement, there are two factors to confront when using the pre-opening indications. The first is whether or not such an opening is going to do damage to the stock's chart—often such openings will gap down under the stock's uptrend line, or below what had looked like a major support level. When the chart itself is going to be ruined, the hell with fussing—just get out. The second factor to consider is the potential for a post-opening bounce as a better opportunity to get out than on the opening itself. We hate to give such advice because holders tend *not* to sell even though they intended to. One method of protection, once you've decided to sell, is to use an either/or order, trying to snag the bounce with a limit order on the upside just under the previously indicated offer, or on stop 1/8 under the opening price. Let's say your stock opens at 18 1/2, midway in its announced "indication only" range. You reason that the upper limit of 19 1/2 is a maximum expectation; being trapped, you don't want to fuss over a fraction of a point, so you enter your order: "Sell at 19 1/4 limit or on stop at 18 3/8." In that way, if the stock resumes its weakness, you'll be sold out promptly without having to wait for that panicky phone call from your broker.

The problem has become one in which there is now so much stock for sale, in a market so dominated by institutions who just want out, that the first bounce is usually feeble, the stock then goes to a lower low, and it is the second bounce that one has to have the patience to wait to sell into. Here are some alternatives to consider: (a) If the bid side is lifting during the pre-opening indi- cations, consider *that* a bounce in itself, and sell on the opening. (See, for example, the chart in Levitz that we're reproducing from the first edition, wherein an opening indication of 43-49 (last sale 59 1/2) was literally the lowest; buyers poured in, and the bid side rose so strongly that it became clear the specialist was going to be able to open the stock at a price level at which he wasn't going to have to be a buyer but might even be compelled to be a seller. That oddity—a gift, if you will—suggested being on the sell side, too, if you'd been stuck. LEV opened at 49, went to 49 1/8, and eventually fell to 1 1/2. The moral, as always: pay attention to shifting nuances; the market has no absolutes. (b) If the stock opens near the low end of its indication, the *first* bounce will be trivial, and laggard sellers typically come in to take the stock lower; (c) The subsequent bounce will carry back up above the opening price, *but no further than the indication's offering price.* One last comment: the word "temporary"—as in "it's just a one-quarter problem"—should serve as a red flag. Nine times out of ten it proves to be an on-going problem.

We are, of course, here tinkering with what is spilt milk al- ready...so what's a little more? Experience has convinced us of two "rules of thumb:" First, that losses are made back faster by switching to strong stocks than in waiting for a now-weak stock to come back. And second, that a bull trend may be survivable (although rule one still applies), but when the market is in a bear trend, hanging onto a stock that has been impacted by negative news can be a disaster.

Your responsibility, in theory, is not to get caught in such situations. Nuances begin to make a chart "uncomfortable" but only in hindsight do they become an overt message. It's excusable to say, "I saw it, but it wasn't enough to act upon." But there are instances in which enough shows up to serve as a valid warning— again, a good reason to keep one's own charts. "Something's wrong" should be more than just musing: a trend line broken, a second lower high on lower volume—that is, a second or third failure is taking place. You may even decide to sell "on the next rally." In the old days we would have relied on a protective stop order, but nowadays so much of this "penny light" negative earnings news comes overnight that even a properly placed stop order doesn't save you because the stock opens on such a big gap below that price, breaking all sorts of trendlines and support *afterwards*. Now you know it's serious stuff, but the damage has already been done before you had a chance to act because it occurred overnight. The market teaches hard lessons: cynicism and suspicion is better than being blinded by love and longer-term devotion.

An old, but straightforward, example of this sort of situation developed in Campbell Soup. The stock had already been sagging when unexpected news struck: an allegation of botulism in their cans made the headlines. With Campbell trading in the mid-30s before the news, the initial indication from the floor before the opening was "31-33." It was, therefore, a situation in which an already weak stock assumed added vulnerability. No one knew how widespread incidents of potentially deadly cans might become. Hanging on to the stock in such circumstances seemed to many to be too risky; but the opening was going to be sharply lower. Thus the notion of trying to catch the bounce after the delayed opening seemed sensible, if only to protect capital. CPB opened at 32, exactly in the middle of the indicated range, rallied back up to 32

3/4, and got no higher, thus illustrating two common happenings: it failed under the upper limit of the announced range, and also under a round number. Here an either/or order would have been sensible, to catch the quick rebound if possible, but with protection 1/8 under the opening price, so that if the decline were to resume before the bounce got to your limit order (as it actually would have in this case, sliding on down into the 20s), you'd get stopped out before it had a chance to accelerate. Don't worry about the other half of the order; if it is designated either/or, the unexecuted portion is automatically canceled.

Such selling decisions are, as we've said, among the most difficult of all, because of the added pressure of the company of other sellers. In sum, our guidelines should be: Was it beginning to look like a possible sale before the news struck? Is the potential opening price going to spoil the technical chart picture for a long time to come (break important support, plunge below a trend line or moving average line, etc.)? Has it already had a substantial slide, discounting the impact of this news? Or is it the kind of bad news that simply has the effect of shaking out nervous traders before an already strong rise resumes? A first rumor can be shrugged off, but we wouldn't ignore repeated messages—not after we saw how that sequence took place in Philip Morris before it collapsed in 1993. Any "normal" rise is allowed at least one, and probably two "normal" corrections, even if news induced. In fact, one final question to ask yourself ought to be: if I didn't know what this stock was, or what the news might be, how would its chart "read?"

Above all, keep your wits about you. If it's time to sell, it's time to sell, whether the news is good or bad—in your definition, or the market's. Here's an example we'll never forget of the value of perspective, considering the market as a whole. President Eisenhower's heart attack came in the late stages of a prolonged intermediate-term rally, which was getting tired and beginning to emanate toppy clues. Thus, the startling and totally unexpected news struck a market which had already become vulnerable; many stocks were unable to open until that day's closing bell, when one transaction was printed on the tape. The bounce lasted the entire next day, and no further; it paid to sell into that rebound, given the market situation, for a full scale intermediate correction ensued. On the other hand, Ike's ileitis attack came after a severe several-weeks-long decline. The market trembled for about an hour, but after the news had shaken out a last bevy of nervous holders, prices began to rebound strongly and a new uptrend was actually launched on the news. It is almost as if the market has its own rhythms regardless of human headlines.

We've jabbered on here about news, but one additional reality needs to be pointed out: *non-economic news, no matter how scary, is transient; news that has an economic impact is what counts.* A Russian coup can send prices tumbling...temporarily. The Iraqi attack on Kuwait, and its material effect on oil prices, was a more lasting crisis (although then, too, it was only a five-week decline, and a five-month re-basing period). The fact is that economic changes are not news; they take place gradually over time, and thus can be observed in the behavior of the marketplace. Thus, "how was the stock acting beforehand?"—its perspective—and "what is the specialist going to have to do for his own account?"—its imminence—are the basis for evaluating individual stock situations.

The Professional's Pet

The stock market mirrors America, and one of the peripheral images it reflects is that of the affluent society. One of the astonishing changes from the mid-seventies to this rewriting in 1993-94 is how the typical public order involved 100 shares, or maybe 200 or 300, whereas that has increased tenfold—a 1,000 or 2,000 share order is the norm nowadays. Thanks to stock splits, many investors have accumulated tidy blocks of stock: 10,000 or even 25,000 shares of a particular issue. In the abstract, the holder can calculate the value of the block at the latest closing price; in reality, it's worth is what he can get for it, and the more shares offered for sale, the more it will adversely affect the price. Sometimes we recommend *scaling out*—small chunks into every rally as the chart shows the stock beginning to fail. But when a decision is made to sell the entire block, it is wise to use the type of order professionals use to get out of *their* big positions: the not-held order.

The not-held order provides the same sort of advantages as selling at the opening, with the added one that it can take away some of the randomness of executions during the trading day. It is not suited to the modest transaction, but the more you have to liquidate, the better an order it can be. In some firms, if the size of the order is substantial enough it can move the handling of the sale from the retail order desk over to the institutional. The more you have to liquidate, the better this kind of order can be (and it can't be any worse than trying to mastermind it yourself, and is usually better). What you get is the attention and experience of the broker on the floor. The market can be tested for interest on the other side; often, a report back from the floor will help you focus on a price limit, or a time limit. The floor broker's experienced input may be just the added nuance you need so you won't be flying blind.

You'll recall that the floor broker handling a market order is responsible for not missing the market, and must get the best price available to him on reaching the trading crowd. Since the basis of record is the ticker tape itself, the term "held" denotes that the broker is literally bound to the sequence of prints on the tape as they appear. As a result, when a broker has a market order to sell, he'll march to the post, ask for the quotation, try an offer a little better than what he could otherwise get by hitting the bid at once, and in the end, if he must, will settle for selling to the best price available as promptly thereafter as possible because he is "held" to the tape which will print the next transaction in timed sequence.

In contrast, by marking the order "not-held," the customer is, in effect, saying "disregard tape," or "take time," thus excusing the floor broker from being held to the tape sequence. Via this order shorthand, he is telling the broker to use his own judgment: that he won't get angry if, in hindsight, it seems that the broker has missed a good price—for whatever reason, bad luck, butchering, or what seemed like the sensible decision at the time. Thus a not-held sell order, which can be either at the market or with a limit prescribing the price below which the customer does not want to go, gives the floor broker discretion to handle the order as he feels best, based on his intimate vantage point. Whether or not to place a limit on the order depends on the number of shares involved and how active the stock is. Using a limit initially can be in the form of the kind of question one bridge partner asks another via the bidding: "Can I get my limit if you take your time and handle the order on a not-held basis?" or "Does the situation at the post look as if we should fold right now?"

The more experienced the floor broker is, the wiser it is to give him his head. But it is always sensible to let him know in advance what it is you have in mind: the key is communication. In addition to specifying that the order is not-held, some of the phrases institutions add to such orders are "no hurry," or "go along with the market" (meaning, ride the tides and don't buck them), or "don't initiate" (which tells the broker not to make a trade at a new price, but if someone else does it first, join in). [However, the phrase "an extra 1/8" is nothing more than changing the limit.]

For example, you may spot a huge head-and-shoulders top (see next chapter) forming in a stock you've nursed upward for years, so that you now have a substantial portion of your net worth at stake in a stock that may be finished rising. You want to sell, but because the stock hasn't actually broken down as yet, you have some time to let the floor broker distribute the block, via a "not held" order, at the best prices he can get. Another example would occur after the stock has broken down and you want to sell the entire block into the pullback rally. Since you're in no position to know how far the rally can carry before dying—not privy to the nuances on the floor, nor having the time to spend watching every tick—you use the "not-held" order to turn the problem over to the broker on floor, who is being told to sell whenever he feels he should (giving him a price limit and a time limit as well would probably help in this kind of situation). Don't be surprised if, upon entering such an order, the floor broker comes back to you with the information that he can get such-and-such a price for the entire block at once. The decision is yours once again, but it is the sort of information you wished you had, isn't it?

As might be expected, floor brokers are decidedly more edgy when handling a sell order than a buy order, fearing that the price could tumble rapidly on them while they wait. They confess to feeling they can safely hold back with a buy order, even allowing the stock to get away, because they are confident it will fluctuate toward support again—and that you will, by raising your limit, inform them if you want to attack. But a sell order is handled more aggressively to be sure of an execution. Often prices can ebb on an absence of bidders—and they might learn from the specialist when such is the case—so they'll want to take advantage of a buyer's presence while they can. (That's a good reason to let the broker know the entire amount you want to sell; he needs to know the amount of buying he has to locate, and he wants to be able to assure the buyer that more isn't going to get dumped on him immediately after he buys some.) Oddly enough (or not so oddly, given the psychology of selling), while the floor broker instinctively wants to persist in selling instead of tinkering with the order, the institutional money manager upstairs is more likely to try to mastermind the sell order by placing limits but to let the buy order go to the floor at the market. Again, they've got it backwards, just as the public has when trying to sell a volatile stock at a set price while buying recklessly at whatever price they can. The pain of reckoning is never in the buying.

Back to Basics

*F*or those with grey hair, even now the morning of August 16, 1971—the day after Nixon announced his economic game plan—is remembered as a bullish day. After all, it was a then-record rise on then-record volume. Actually, it presented a clear call to sell. It was just a simple matter of being on the same side as the specialist and selling at the opening. It is obvious in retrospect, and should have been obvious at the time, that the correct deci-

214 When to Sell

sion was to sell. But of course you have to make the decisions, and without hindsight's benefit. And it's made even harder when a dramatic instance isn't handy, when you have to "read" the indicators (fewer new highs than the day before, for example) and decide, rather defiantly, that the time has come to sell, even as the market looks exciting.

We hope we've convinced you that it is better, far better, to make such decisions while the tape is still. Take a few moments to concentrate on each stock you hold. What are your feelings about the stock? sorry you bought it, or too comfortable to even give it that needed thought? sorry you haven't sold it already, or dreaming of riches? Once you make up your mind to sell, stick by that decision, and simplify its execution by entering the order before the opening. You could garner a fractionally better price than if you were compelled to hit the prevailing bid the afternoon before, but if the stock is too weak, you'll at least be out before the situation deteriorates further. You certainly don't want to add to the emotional burden of selling at a loss by having to make the decision during the turmoil of the market's trading day. Any random uptick might lure you into delaying; any downtick could be a further distortion.

And don't spoil the decision at the very end by entering your sell order with a limit price attached—that can be like deciding to sell while not doing it. Knowing that the opening is the most advantageous time to sell, harness this unique market moment, which occurs but once a day, by utilizing at-the-market orders. Let the specialist himself determine a fair opening price, while getting your own emotions out of the way. When he balances the overnight gathering of orders on both sides of the market, a limited-price order fights his options. If you limit your sell order to a supposedly desirable price (desired by you, for extraneous reasons, but not necessarily by anyone else), the stock might open just below your set figure not out of any manipulation, but simply because the specialist may be able to balance the opening without you. What's more, when the specialist matches the orders in hand before the opening, a market order has precedence over a limit order. The stock actually could open at the price of your limit order without your getting an execution because the market orders balanced at that price, shutting you out. You'd feel pretty foolish, and a lot poorer, if the stock tumbled while you still owned it, even though you'd picked the exact opening price to get out at. That would be the ultimate in making sure you get punished by the market: the perfect decision, and still the loser.

As Simple As Selling Can Get

As the author of the book named "When To Sell" the question is often asked as to "when" that is. This question typically comes up *after* the market has had a substantial decline—and "when" it may very well be too late. Indeed, those media phone calls can be a sentiment signal that it is "too late to sell" because the decline has finally become widely recognized. The question really is: "when" do you sell in the ordinary course of events? We have tried in the preceding chapters to outline the market aspects—grasping when market action and our indicators have become negative, because a market decline can pull even the most beloved of stocks down; how to deal with the emotional impediments to selling; and how to use the various tools available to execute a sell order. But when it comes to specific stock selling, the answer is in one simple/complex word: failure. Identifying when to sell a stock requires failure. A stock should not be sold until it does something wrong, or fails to do something expected. The better it has done, the more failures should be required. No apologies or excuses are permitted; failure is failure, objectively seen. In the next chapters we are going to discuss various situations, as we "read" those charts for the first edition of this book, and with amendments and additions based on subsequent experience. Keep in mind most of all that the recognition of failures is not like eating salted peanuts—waiting for one more and then another failure before acting is precisely what we are trying to avoid as we learn to say "now" to the question of "When to Sell?"

Chapter Nine

Individual Stocks

We've been discussing the market in general terms, setting up the background against which stocks rise and fall. Intelligent selling depends on knowing, and relating to, the market's overall trend. But when it comes right down to it, your selling decisions, even though influenced by those general market factors, must be made stock by stock. It's not the dignified Dow, or the high/low differential, but each individual issue that will make your fortune or break your bank. International Business Machines has been a great example of a stock that persisted in going down even while market behavior was positive. You must be able to sell an individual holding whenever it's time to sell, regardless of the market.

In this chapter we'll discuss various ways you can tell when a stock is ripe for selling. For the most part, that information is contained in the what of a stock's chart action, even though you may not know the why. It's not difficult, it's not exotic, but it does require that you be able to view charts of the stocks in your portfolio. You can keep them yourself, as you should be keeping those few indicators we've already discussed, or you can purchase them from a number of sources. Despite the advent of computer programs that will put a stock chart up on the monitor, we believe fervently in the "feel," the sensitivity of posting one's own charts. Such computer look-sees are transitory, sometimes have scales that distort what you are seeing, and are too short-term, often showing only the last few months. Because we are in the business of knowing what a lot of stocks are doing, we keep several hundred *daily* charts, posting them with a sharpened pencil; the computer helps because it can be programmed to plug into Dow Jones News Retrieval (or a similar service) to obtain a printout of the high, low, close and volume of each stock in our pile, so that we can post each chart's action without having to search for the name in the newspaper tables. Our associate in the office uses the desktop machine to obtain the needed information almost as rapidly. After a few weeks of getting used to doing such postings, two charts per minute is a snap.

However, no one should try to post more charts than can be kept without getting behind in the effort. In our experience, the best compromise between the amount of time and effort needed to track a lot of different stocks and doing more than needed is to keep daily charts on a handful of market leaders (GM, IBM, etc.) plus the stocks you actually hold (starting charts upon any purchase) while subscribing to a published chart service. We use *Mansfield Chart Service* because (a) it provides a weekly, rather than a daily, chart—for a much needed longer-term perspective—and (b) it covers all listed NYSE stocks. (This is not something you need to receive *every* single week.) We also subscribe to the *Daily Graph* services (both NYSE and OTC books) so as to have a handy reference for daily action in individual stocks we don't chart ourselves. This will give you the past history for stocks you are directly interested in, as well as provide the chance to study the whole market, thus uncovering new groups and stocks as they emerge as buying or selling candidates. As a rule, watch (or chart) only what you can watch closely; if you try to do too much, you'll find that mistakes are happening before you can catch up.

Keep in mind that the charts don't reveal the future. They show exactly what has been happening up to that moment, and that's all. They provide an *objective* picture of the past, so you won't have to make a subjective judgment and emotional decision. Now let's learn how to read such charts so that we can make intelligent sales.

Analyzing Rally Action

*T*here are two ways to botch the sale of a stock that has risen: selling too soon in the move, or waiting too long and selling after the decline has set in. Let's discuss the problem of premature selling first. Here, too, there are two instigating reasons: simple anxiety that if you don't sell, the profit that you have will be taken away from you, or when the action of a stock you hold may become disquieting, so that the anxiety at least has some external justification. You can't put your finger on anything dangerous, but you don't like what's been happening. The chart may be saying, "Not so good," yet still not be screaming "Awful." Is it temporary? Minor? The first warning clue? Should you ride it out? Flee now? Are you, in your gut, a longer-term investor or a short-term trader? There are a number of things to search for: studying the Moving Average; the current price level in relation to the long-term picture, support and resistance; a potential pattern; a useful trendline. Some will also resort to upside vs. downside volume; money flow statistics; stochastics, and the like, but we believe in keeping it simple. We're going to look for clues in the charts of A.E. Staley, covering most of 1974 and the start of 1975.

STA's rally at point A was a powerful move, signifying the start of an important uptrend. Note the confirming volume as the stock broke out above its prior high. If you had bought the stock around 33, in that little congestion area (point C) just before the breakout, you'd have been confident, with no thoughts of selling. But not long after A, at B, the stock inexplicably seemed to have run into trouble, like a rocket just off the launching pad that begins to wobble in clear view of the spectators. There was a gap on the downside as sellers poured in, and the slide carried alarmingly *below* the level of the previous short-term dip that had followed A. With the Dow Industrial Average at this time plunging toward a new bear-market low, confidence would have given way to fear. As the stock fell under 38, you might have concluded that the burst of strength had been some sort of bull trap and so rushed to grab the few dollars of profit remaining. Using hindsight, you can see that panic would have been terribly wrong, yet the short-term behavior certainly was alarming.

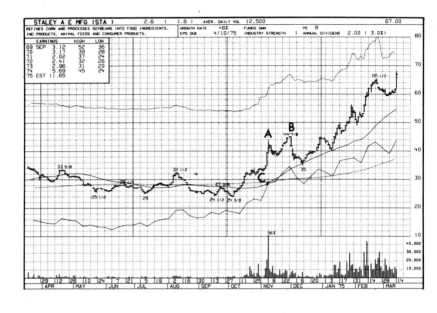

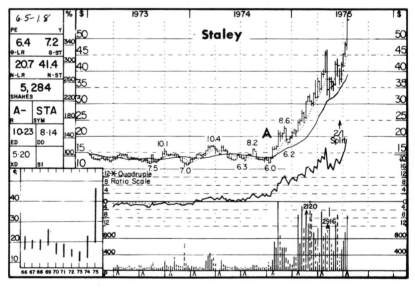

Hindsight isn't there to help at the moment, so let's see what the arguments against panic were. For instance, if you'd stepped back calmly, you would have taken solace in the pattern of volume. After the extraordinary burst of activity on the upside, you can see that daily volume shrank to next to nothing during the correction, denoting scant selling pressure as it kept on shrinking from the low level of the day of the gap to even lesser activity at the reaction low. Moreover, the unsettling decline did not take the stock all the way back down to the initial area of support between 32 and 34, with the dip stopping at 35, well above the long-term moving average line. (For what it's worth, it also stopped at the ten-week M.A. both then, and subsequently in January at 40. While this intermediate-degree M.A. is viable in this instance, we've never found it consistent enough to place sole faith in.) Last, and perhaps most important, is perspective: (1) all that upside volume argues for more than the minor rally to A and B; (2) the stock has been able to start upward even while the market climate was still bearish; and (3) recourse to the overview provided by Staley's weekly chart shows that the entire base from the left side of the chart—that is, throughout this bear market—to the point of the upside breakout at A was so extensive that just a few days of sloppy action shouldn't have scared anyone out. *A stock is entitled to, and almost always has, a sharp but short-lived pullback to the area of the upside breakout not long after that breakout.*

It is a helpful empirical fact that the breadth of a stock's base is related to the carrying power of its rally, the reason being that the more stock which has passed from weak into strong hands, and thus retired from an immediate return into the market, the less selling interference on the way up. Note that Staley's base on the weekly chart (which reflects a subsequent two-for-one split) was forming during a disastrous bear market. Although the stock did have its bouts of decline, the rally in 1974 carried above its 1973 high, and that was followed by a decline which held about the 1973 low—evidence of basing action *and* a great example of the term "relative strength." Someone wanted that stock badly enough to pay up for it even while the DJIA was tumbling. This perspective should have been sufficient reassurance during that short-term period of panic, especially since the stock really hadn't done anything officially wrong—its breakout level was holding, the uptrending moving averages were intact, and the long-term trend appeared likely to continue.

It is worth taking space here to note the nature and meaning of a base. By definition, it necessitates a prior substantial decline. The base forms as a battle commences between those who are willing to get out on any rally (usually folks who've been stuck in the stock and are now becoming convinced it is doomed) and those who want to buy on any further dip (usually those who are becoming convinced that the decline has brought the stock down to a "cheap" price level). Gradually, higher lows, even if only by an 1/8 or 1/4, indicate that buyers are willing to raise their bids to acquire more shares. The longer, and the livelier, a base that develops, the better the upside potential. Staley's chart action, backed by the infusion of immense *confirming* volume as the price rose up out of the base (breaking out above the prior 34 high), is a near-perfect example of how winners can appear right before your eyes if you are only willing to believe in them. And yet, some people who actually had bought such a winner got so nervous that they dumped at the first sign of a problem, settling for a point or two gain on the theory that "you can't go broke taking a profit." But, as STA illustrates, you can get left behind.

In contrast to this long-term positive base-building and breakout are stocks with small and inadequate bases, especially when compared to overhead resistance, as in the chart of Xerox covering much of the same time span as Staley. It is sheer folly to assume the stock will have sufficient underlying power to surpass such resistance.

We are all afraid of the unknown. The best cure for the anxiety over STA's brief misbehavior is to establish what you do know, and to assure yourself that what you don't know, while perhaps making you uneasy, can't be known, so there's no point in wasting energy worrying about it. Of course, you also don't want to smugly ignore warnings, either. The chart, while not perfect, is the most objective reading you can get—providing you evaluate it from perspective rather than emotion. If your decision turns out to be wrong, so be it; at least you'll have acted as clearheadedly as you could. It is the weight of the available evidence that would have kept a purchaser *in* Staley instead of letting him panic out too soon. And, we might add, there is nothing like a protective stop placed at a sensible level to let the holder feel he's not flying blind. In Staley's case, a stop placed: (1) under the long-term Moving Average line (heavy black line on the weekly chart); (2) under the congestion area of 32-34 (point C on the daily chart); and (3) under that round number of 30—at, say, 29 7/8—would have kept any potential loss to 10 to 15 percent. That's a risk worth taking in view of all the bullish action that occurred before that short-term dumping set in.

But we don't have only the evidence of the past upon us; there are also certain aspects of the future that can be determined. The overall market situation should be added to the evidence of Staley's substantial base, the verification of positive volume, and the fact that its long-term Moving Average line remained intact. To be sure, the DJIA was, at that time, frightening as it appeared to be heading downward once again. But certain indicators had already started to turn positive after a prolonged bear market. By that time, for example, specialist short selling was at minimal (buy signal) levels, and even as the Dow made one final minimally lower low in December, enough stocks like STA existed to cause fewer new lows for a positive divergence. These indicators, plus the doctrine of contrary opinion, plus the stock action itself, were all reasons to stick with the trend Staley had established on its upside breakout. Indeed, within a few months thereafter Staley rose to 120 for perhaps the best performance in the Street during the 1975 rally. Knowing "when to sell" includes also knowing when *not* to sell.

The Second Correction

*I*t will be recalled from our previous discussion that an intermediate-term bull move generally consists of three upwaves interrupted by two short-term corrections. The end of the first upleg and the coming of the first sell-off can be winked at—by long-term investors—as temporary misbehavior. But the second upwave and its inevitable fluctuation back down are not nearly so easily ignorable as the first. It is here that some of the weaker stocks will falter and depart from the pack, never to return for a third rally phase. Thus, it is at this point in the market cycle that you must really pay attention to how each of your individual stocks looks. One could be so far ahead of the game that its entire intermediate-term uptrend is concluded and a top formed while the market averages are still chugging upward. At other times you may find yourself holding a stock as it is about to resume some unfinished downside business, as with Xerox in the second quarter of '75.

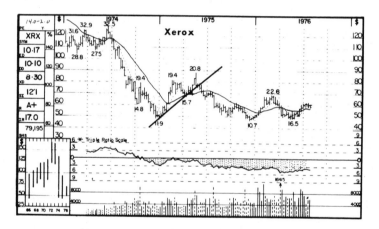

Studying this weekly chart, you can see that everything started off in reasonably good order—the overall market had turned upward, remember—except for the troublesome lack of any really sizable base for a sustainable upturn. Given a choice, you'd have bought Staley every time compared to Xerox, but the reality is that many brokers simply opt for the famous name and had never even heard of Staley in late 1974. As the averages soared up off the bear market bottom, XRX joined in, and its long-term Moving Average line turned upward and contained the first reaction. Since the ensuing rally went on to a new recovery high, all was well...up to that point.

But then something began to look wrong: the stock, instead of sustaining the upside, started sliding. Its M.A. was broken, as well as the uptrend line, and then additional pressure caused a break to a low below the previous reaction low. All of this was evidence that Xerox was not a stock to own any longer—even *before* news was released that the company was going out of the computer business at a huge loss. Obviously, several big holders found out in advance and/or analysts had dug out this kind of news. These "leaks"—not rumors or hot tips, but rather because those who are supposed to be paying attention do their jobs well—are what the chart of the stock can tell you. You don't need to know what they knew to realize you'd better be getting out, too. Depending on how quickly your chart alerted you, and how assertive you were able to be, (a) a protective stop just under the Moving Average line would have taken you out on the literal downside break; (b) if that break was what convinced you, then a sale into the rebound back up to the by-now heading downward Moving Average line (at around 70) would have made sense; (c) or at the least, this chart called for a stop loss order protective against further loss just under that prior low. You can see how the decline accelerated when *that* low was penetrated, so that even though it seems "late," it wasn't too late.

We want to add several more comments to this analysis. First, though the best—that is, ideal—time to sell is on the rally back up to resistance (and the Moving Average line) after there is clear cut evidence that the stock has failed, this is not as easy to do in the mid-nineties as it was twenty years earlier. Buyers willing to take the stock off your hands are not so plentiful on a stock's downside. Do *not* expect too much; do *not* convince yourself that just because the stock has begun to rally, that it will continue to do so.

This Xerox chart is also interesting beyond the point of getting out in time. Note that after the decline hit a sort of bottom (point Z), the ensuing rally failed at approximately the same level (B) the stock had broken down from before—that is, resistance around 70. The stock then declined again, held near Z, and bounced again, but this time failing at fresh and lower resistance (C) under the previous little area of trading. That succession of failures— lower highs demonstrating downward pressure against attempts to hold—leaves the stock looking precarious as the Dow was then about to head into a bear market. The entire period was one of worry and loss of capital easily avoided had one sold at the initial signs of failure.

Using Waves

*E*ach individual stock must be analyzed on its own. You can't rely on the market action itself to tell you what to do with all stocks, although knowing approximately where "the market" is in its own situation can certainly tip the balance when deciding what to do about individual stocks. Picture for yourself one of those head-and-shoulders tops. These form as the "natural" function of the way stocks trade. At first, strength begats strength; each normal consolidation/correction meets buyers, and the stock rises yet again. As the head is being made, nothing seems wrong; the stock has just made a new high, continuing the rising pattern, and still looks steadfastly bullish. It might seem perfectly normal for nothing more than another correction to arrive. But a few tremors of suspicion might creep in to those who are appropriately cynical and contrary—suppose this is the third wave up taking place, with volume and momentum lessening, while the press and other commentators have begun to enthuse about how marvelous everything is. You should be studying every stock you own for such signs of potential trouble. Remember the dangers of "good news" tops, when "heads" often materialize.

Strong stocks should have a mild second correction—perhaps more than the first but mild nevertheless—and then dash on ahead for a third upleg. They can be held so long as the stock does nothing wrong. Here's an example from the 1975 era: the DJIA itself, analyzed as an individual stock chart.

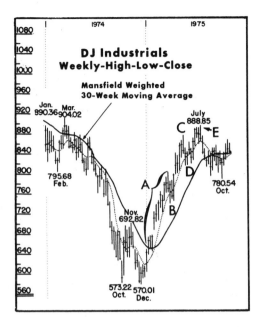

You can readily identify the three uplegs (A, C, and E) and the two intervening downlegs (B and D). Notice how each succeeding rise was less extensive than the previous one, with the first being the best, launched as it was with a gap. (This chart also illustrates the slightly lower low in Dec. 1974 which was accompanied by several positive divergences that identified the bottom of that major bear market.) To the upper left of the chart can be seen an area of resistance from early 1974, and you can see that this powerful rise was able to eat into some of that overhead problem, but was so late in its move that, like an aging human, it lacked the youthful vigor to press further upward with sufficient vigor. The third upleg ran into trouble precisely where it should have. The ensuing correction broke the uptrend line and the Moving Average line—individual stocks such as Xerox were, of course, doing the same. Rather than waiting for hindsight to announce that, yes, that was a standard end to the rally, it is better to acknowledge the lateness of the rise—the third leg up—coincident with the arrival at a major resistance area. Carrying a stock past E on its chart is an example of greed rather than objectivity.

This is an illustration of how a strong stock looks during an entire intermediate-term uptrend. But it is also a chart of the Dow, showing you that the action of this average, too, can be a guide to when to sell. The more aggressive would sell *into* leg E; those who need more convincing might perhaps have waited until the uptrend line literally broke. An intermediate-sized correction of more than 10 percent ensued—*and* as the Xerox chart shows, even when the market rise resumed temporarily in 1976, many stocks did not participate. Yet it was during this period that many analysts were becoming increasingly euphoric—recession ended, bull market confirmed, and even a correction/consolidation past. At the time to sell—third upwave ending at resistance—you don't know which stocks are going to do worse, which stocks may not come back up again, which stocks you don't own that might be worth owning for the next rise. What you do know is that it is an appropriate time to do some selling, and by getting into a liquid position you are not only safer during the slide, you have the capital to buy fresh ideas at the correction's end. Having flexibility as the overall market and individual stocks become suspect is always a sound policy.

Let us review this sequence. Early in a rise, there is a wall of worry, illustrated by talk that the rally is "just technical" or "only short-covering," and that the bear market is going to resume. The temptation is to snatch a quick profit before it gets taken away. Staley's chart shows the folly in that. You must take the risk of riding out the first correction, by accepting a pullback and relying on base support to hold the price at or above the stock's breakout point. Holding becomes more comfortable during the second leg up, but here again you must follow the rule that the stock must do something wrong before it becomes a sale, and thus far it shows no such failure. Both the trendline and Moving Average line remain intact. But on the third leg up market life changes: you are within a stone's throw of serious overhead resistance; volume is diminishing; too much bullish sentiment abounds; and so on. Market life is narrowing, and you may even begin to see problems develop in the various indicators discussed in previous chapters. You don't want to overstay your welcome. Even though the Dow Industrial Average may have additional intermediate-term uplegs ahead to flesh out its own entire primary bull market, *your particular holding* may never again see the highs it is making on this move. Xerox's chart should serve as that warning; even when it rallied with the market in January '76, it faltered 20 points lower than its 1975 high. And there are, of course, times when the market itself may be in its own third and final upleg of an entire bull market. Do not ever think/hope/dream that your stock has some magic quality to it, just because you own it, that will defy such an array of messages. Yes, there will be stocks that will top out after the averages, just as there will be stocks that have started downward ahead of the pack. Failures are what count, whenever and wherever they appear. And, we should add, the more serious the potential market top, the less likely will you find a sensible haven to switch to. Cash becomes better. Having the freedom and power to pick the market's potentially strongest stocks, instead of resigning yourself to potential survivors, is invariably the better policy. The return on your cash is not the miniscule yield, but the gains you make with that buying power during the next bull move.

Here are a few guidelines to keep in mind: (1) If a stock has reached its major overhead resistance area, sell without waiting any longer. After having already had a rise, the stock is highly unlikely to have the strength left to plow through an extensive area; it is more apt to be tired and in need of a substantial correction. Such a resistance area may appear as a prior cyclical top (such as the 880-900 range on the DJIA chart or as a sideways congestion area of trading during a stock's decline (as on the Xerox chart). Often, measurable targets (the size of a base added onto the breakout price level) will coincide with overhead resistance areas, thus confirming the "sell" target. (2) when the stock fails to make a new high and then makes a lower low, sell into the next rebound without hoping and praying that the uptrend will resume. (3) On a longer-term basis, you may want to wait for confirmation that the Moving Average line has stopped going up and is beginning to roll over. If the stock breaks below that Moving Average line, sell on the next bounce toward the line, considering it to have become major overhead resistance in itself. (4) Sell, if the stock has gone up long enough and far enough to have fulfilled a five-wave count, to have no nearby support any more, and when the market indicators themselves are producing negative divergences. (5) When those indicators are beginning to turn negative, indicating a market correction, sell any stock that has ceased participating during the latest rise in the averages. Inability to keep up is a loser in the market as in a marathon.

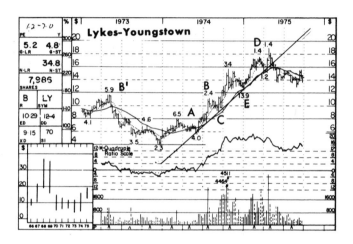

A now-deceased stock remains an astonishing example of how the market works. We showed the chart of Lykes-Youngstown in the first edition of *When To Sell* and want to point out, before we get into discussing the when-to-sell aspects of its chart, how it actually completed a decent-sized base in mid-1974 in defiance of the worst bear market since the '29 crash. Relative strength is where you find it—and is apt to be found in the least expected places: those stocks out of favor and considered undesirable— "hold your nose and buy" stocks—while relative weakness is apt to appear in beloved names whose longer-term weakness investors stubbornly refuse to recognize (IBM and Philip Morris in the early '90s are good examples).

At point A in LY's chart, the stock broke out on the upside from that good-looking base while the rest of the market was plunging. It then stalled at B as it ran up against the resistance from the prior 1973 rally peak (B1). A nervous trader—and who wouldn't have been during that market slide?—might well have been tempted to take his profit and run at this juncture, but the stock really hadn't done anything wrong yet. Selling would have been a mistake—easy to say in hindsight, but we think an investor should have noticed the reduced volume (B2) during the sideways action, plus the fact that the stock never came close to breaking its longer-term Moving Average line, while the major support of the base and the breakout level itself were nearby. A protective stop under the M.A. (point C) would have assuaged anxieties. Such an investor would still have been holding when the rise resumed on another breakout across 12. Note that the low at the "right shoulder" of the base and the correction low at C could be connected with an uptrend line which was confirmed when the stock pulled back at E in its second correction. At 16 an initial purchaser at the first breakout at 8 would have doubled his money by the time point D was reached...but, aha, that was the third wave up, and the stock was approaching a resistance area from many years before (see inset in the lower left hand corner of the chart) as if the stock had the memory of an elephant. The market, as we know from our previous charts, was by then in the midst of its first big rebound after its bear market bottom and yet Lykes was about to run into trouble.

Before we discuss that trouble, let us remind you of how useful the Moving Average was—never broke—remained heading upward—to keep a holder from panicking out of a stock that is acting well. The key is perspective. As a practical matter, when the M.A. is relatively far away, you can expect a correction and not a reversal. This usually holds true for such trendlines, too. The first test, the first attack, should hold, and the stock should bounce again. Whether it then goes on to a higher high or not should be watched closely: a rally failure, after bouncing up off an important line, is the precursor of all sorts of problems. Ultimately trendlines and Moving Average lines are made to be broken; the more times they confirm their validity by holding, the closer they are to the time when they will be violated. In this case, there is another lesson to be learned: never relax. It would have seemed, given this stock's strength even before the market itself was gathering its strength, that LY was destined to be a big winner in such a new bull market. The stop protection raised to just under E was to guarantee at least a 50 percent profit on the original purchase price, but as the stock charged ahead who would have believed it would be needed?

But something went wrong, as if sand had been tossed into the gas tank. LY lost its upward momentum, even though it did go on one last time to a marginally higher (and brief) new high. When it came down, it violated that uptrend line which by then connected four points, making it particularly valid. (Two points make a line; a third confirms its validity.) The ensuing weakness found some support at 14 but even as it did so, the M.A. had begun to roll over and now sat overhead as added resistance. An aggressive holder would have sold into the first bounce to that line, but even if one wanted more evidence it certainly appeared: further erosion made it possible to draw in a horizontal line connecting the low at point E with that subsequent low point, and when LY bounced back up to resistance at 16 a head & shoulders pattern could be identified. The stop order just under E still provided protection, and had become even more serious now that that top pattern would also be broken if E were penetrated—*so why wait?* If a broken uptrend line, and a rolling-over M.A. were not enough, this chart, at its moment of precarious survival shows, was toppy enough to sell without even waiting for that stop order to be set off. You don't need to wait until the boat actually sinks to know that when it springs a leak it's time to abandon ship.

Ten Rules

1. Smart selling has its roots in smart buying. Getting in on a stock as it breaks out of a substantial base is the path to gaining confidence: if you've bought too high, even a normal correction can give you a stressful loss. Remember that one of the best means to avoid this beforehand is to examine where you can place an intelligent stop. If you can put it within 10 to 15 percent of your purchase price, okay, but if the stop would be any further away, that should act as a brake on your buying. By the same token, make sure that the base is substantial enough to exceed overhead resistance and that the supply is sufficiently far away so that the stock has room to move before meeting serious sellers. And to ensure that you are not too too-early, the long-term Moving Average should not be still pointing like an arrow downward, but has already started to arc under.

2. Now that you've set yourself up for potential gain, let the stock have every chance to prove itself. So long as its longer-term Moving Average has turned upward and is trailing along underneath the current price, the stock should be held at least through its first short-term correction.

3. Keep in mind that any stock is *entitled* to a sell-off back toward its breakout point just above its base support, and that such a pullback is usually sharp and scary...but typically comes *early* in its uptrend.

4. Try not to be so nervous that you sell too soon. As long as the stock doesn't do anything wrong—hold on. ("Wrong" can mean not only such direct failures as violating a previous low, failing to make a new high, and the like, but also coming smack up to major overhead resistance and halting and/or reaching a measurable target.)

5. This "wrong" or "failure" message should be considered more seriously as the stock approaches a potential second correction. If at this juncture the stock has come to an important resistance level, you may be nearing the momentum peak, if not the literal high. An aggressive style would call for taking the gain.

6. An investor, however, should wait to see sufficient failures. The bigger the stock's run, the more significant its move (and the more important the stock), the more failures you are entitled to see before believing the rise is finished. Since you aren't going to get the high anyhow, you ought to wait for proof via failures. Give

a winner every chance—without becoming complacent or over-confident.

7. The basic exception to waiting to see failures is when there is a confluence of resistance, target reached, etc. *and* the market indicators themselves are giving off warning signs. Don't *hope* that your stock will stage one more rally if the market itself seems unlikely to.

8. Remember that failure to participate in a rally along with the rest of the market is as serious a message of failure as you can get; something is amiss. When a stock does not do what you expected it to do, odds are that it's you, and not the market, making the mistake. Hope is not a sufficient reason to continue to own such a stock. You are in the wrong place at the wrong time.

9. When you realize that a stock you hold has already failed, do not freeze. Stocks fluctuate. Note the two opportunities to sell into strength at resistance levels in the Xerox chart—in the first quarter of '76 at 70; in mid-'76 in the low 60's. Yes! down a lot, but if we showed you the subsequent continuing decline during the 1977-1978 bear market you'd realize how important it is to sell a stock that is clearly in a downtrend.

10. But, if you have bought into a strong stock...well, isn't that what you've been striving for? Once you already own a strong stock, you should not give it up and then have to search for another; sooner or later, you'll buy a fizzle. If these various factors—all definable as "failures"—are not present, wait patiently until an actual top forms. No stock climbs to the pot of gold at the end of the rainbow. Sometimes the best sell "signal" of all, and the one most likely to be nearest the end of that climb, is when you start boasting about your "winner."

Analyzing Tops

*I*n the preceding section we've shown you ways to avoid selling before the end of the rally. Anxiety that they (whoever "they" are) will steal your profit away can be offset by objectively viewing where your stock is in its trend. But it is equally important to avoid selling too late, after a stock's decline is well underway. This requires an understanding of how to spot a top as it is forming, of what to look for on the charts, and of how to react to what you see. Let's start with the ideal: the stock which has risen nicely and then started to form an important top. Such a top may be defined as a trading range in which, as an intermediate- or long-term upmove comes to an end, supply begins to meet demand and eventually overwhelms it. Sounds simple enough, and indeed it is, occasionally.

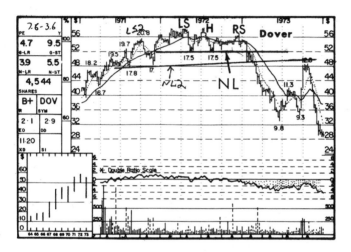

Here's an example of what we mean. After a major uptrend that began in 1970, Dover, at the outset of 1972, spent over an entire year carving out a near-perfect, highly visible top. More than half of that entire span, top-like as it appears in hindsight, was actually spent with gradually rising prices. The upside momentum had gone out of the rise, but the final new high (H) was not made until a year after the process had begun back in the summer of '71. No long-term investor need have sold so long as the sequence of higher lows remained intact. But once that failure occurred, and was followed by a failing rally to a lower high (RS) the degeneration was in process, and Dover then neatly gave up the ghost early in 1973, and did so with a vengeance.

The chart shows an awkward but valid "head-and-shoulders top," but even without making that sort of technical identification, evidence of a potential top forming could be discerned. For one thing, the long-term Moving Average had ceased to go up and during the period between LS and H was already moving sideways at best. The marginal new high (H) did little to alter that look. Second, volume had begun to diminish despite the higher prices. Third, the apparently simple sell-off after that high came down "too far"—that is, all the way back down to the prior low instead of maintaining the sequence of higher lows. Call these delicate warning signs, but then came the whopper message: even while the Dow Industrial Average was heading for record high ground, DOV failed to make a new high (RS), with the attempt occurring on even less volume. Dover's failure was a contributor to the unfavorable clues our market indicators in general were giving. It was time to sell.

An aggressive investor would have sold Dover as this deterioration was taking place, perhaps when the M.A. began delineating the end of the uptrend. But even a passive investor, were he reasonably alert, would have gotten out in plenty of time. He would merely have had to identify the head-and-shoulders top forming and to have drawn in the appropriate neckline, connecting the two dips. In its simplest form, what happens is that the stock, in an uptrend, experiences a normal correction, as it has along the way up, and then proceeds to another new high. But the next correction carries further down than it should, and then comes a rally which fails. In its failure, it manages to approximate the earlier rally peak, thus creating a matching shoulder, while the twin correction lows can be connected as what would be, on the human body, the neckline. On the Dover chart, a protective sell-stop order could have been, and should have been, entered just below that neckline at 51 7/8, so that even if the holder did nothing else, he would have been stopped out neatly when the stock completed its top by breaking down.

We would add a few additional comments upon re-viewing this chart years later. First, note how the stock, after its initial break, seemed to hold at some support—a price level that had stemmed little sell-offs way back in 1971. We've drawn in another horizontal line to depict this (NL2), and the very act of drawing in that line makes the top pattern much bigger (and hence much more significant) because now you can call the 1971 action a left shoulder (LS2), and combine the LS left shoulder and head together as one big double head. This is particularly important in telling us that even though the stock is already down 10 points from its high, it is still within the major top area—*not* too late to sell, even then. Also note that after the steep plunge that followed, DOV staged a tremendous, but *failing*, rebound all the way back up to that new neckline (NL2) and halted precisely, like a well-trained dog ordered to heel, where it was supposed to. A return to the bear trend then ensued.

By virtue .of its roots in reality, the head-and-shoulders formation gives the lie to those who conceive of technical analysis as something conjured up by mystics. The right shoulder is formed by a failure of demand; the stock might still be saved even then; sometimes the left shoulder, head, and right shoulder actually appear, but the neckline doesn't break, and the stock is able to stage one further rise, usually because the general market is still robust. But the breach of the neckline indicates that sellers now outnumber buyers and have a more aggressive motivation. Volume provides an important clue in this process: the healthier still-early rise that becomes the left shoulder (although you don't know it at the time) typically has the most volume; the head, even though it represents a new high, shows diminished activity; and the right shoulder lacks the volume needed to keep the stock rising—it fails in a sort of chicken-and-the-egg process of which comes first? the low volume that causes the failure, or the failure scaring buyers away. By placing a protective stop just below the neckline, you can be confident that you'll still be on board should the rise resume, but you'll also be sure that you won't be caught holding a stock that is starting to head down dramatically. The vividness of the right shoulder problem, and the magnitude of the entire top, may make it quite clear that the stock is going to break. So why wait for your stop to be elected? Our only cautionary rule is that when the market shows no problematic indicators, and the stock has had a great run, we ask for more than subtle failures; we demand more proof that the game is over. In such instances, make sure that the top is perceivable on the longer-term (weekly) chart as well as on the daily chart.

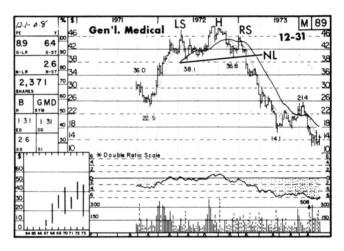

Another example of a head-and-shoulders formation is the accompanying one of General Medical Corporation. The top began to form while the Dow was still bullish, although overall market indicators were becoming more and more negative. Here, again, the head-and-shoulders pattern was readily discernible as it formed over an entire year. Watch out for tops as extensive as both DOV and GMD; the bigger the top, the bigger the subsequent fall is apt to be. We've labeled the various components of the General Medical top on the chart. In this instance, there was almost as much volume on the head as during the left shoulder phase, but far less on the right shoulder, and when the neckline was broken at 40, the price fell 10 percent rapidly. The traditional bounce back toward the neckline was so brief and modest that it can only be seen on a chart of the daily action rather than on this weekly chart—as if sellers became so anxious that they couldn't wait for a rebound to get out.

Perhaps this emergence of selling is an emotional aspect of relief, becoming anxious as the top increasingly forms but not acting until there is an overt message that the game is over. Look carefully at the prior action and you can see where an important sell signal had been given. While the stock price flirted with the Moving Average throughout the summer of 1972, the M.A. was rolling over during the period *between* the head and right shoulder and turned decisively downward not long after the right shoulder was in place—at about 44—thus verifying that the rally was already a failure. Thus, an alert holder had sufficient signal to sell into the right-shoulder rally or, at the latest, just after it formed, without needing to wait for the definite neckline break. Note how this major top and break (as well as the major top and break in DOV) served as indicators about the market itself—the presence of such tops belied the continued rise in the Dow Industrial Average; stocks "know" even if the average deceives. The more negative the overall climate—by which we mean, the more negative charts you see—the more aggressively one should act on any such signal. At the very least, of course, a stop-loss order placed just below the neckline (at, say, 39 7/8) would have been obligatory. GMD fell more than in half almost without interruption during the early phase of that major bear market. It then staged (as did the Dow itself) a contra-trend rebound back up to 26 before plummeting again. How does one know it is just a contra-trend fluctuation? (a) no base; (b) the long-term Moving Average is still pointing downward. GMD's eventual bottom for just that first year of the bear market was under 14.

The head-and-shoulder formation occurs with such frequency at market turns because it accurately represents the way a stock traverses its life: first, healthy; second, aging; third, unable to continue any further upward. Its reliability is highly pertinent to low-risk, short-selling techniques (see the next chapter) as well as getting you out in time. Even if you wait for the actual breakdown of the neckline, you will still be out well ahead of the crowd. Our third example is a definitive textbook case.

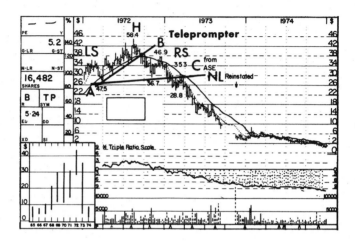

The unfolding of the major head-and-shoulders top in the weekly chart of Teleprompter took place during the same pre-bear market climate as General Medical's and Dover's. These are the salient features: the left shoulder forms while volume is still sharply rising, as the fresh rally stems from impressive bullishness. The rally ends, and a normal correction sets in which holds just above the still-rising Moving Average. The market, too, is still on its upward course, helping to boost TP to a new high on a series of brief but lively upswings. But the volume, on this apparently bullish move, is lower than before and diminished volume diverging from a higher price is never a favorable sign. Then comes a confluence of warning signals: the trend line (A-B) connecting several higher lows (the more points, the more valid the line) is decisively broken; next, the long-term Moving Average line is broken and starts to roll over, signifying that a change in trend is underway. The ensuing correction goes too far down, past all of those prior short-term lows—in effect, the pattern of rising lows has been destroyed—and we can now connect the end of that correction with the conspicuous prior low that helped delineate the left shoulder many months earlier. At that time we would only call this line a "potential" neckline because of the absence of a right shoulder, but the developing pattern clearly cries out for that missing right shoulder to appear on the next rally. That failing rally follows, forming the right shoulder, and does so on even less volume. How many signs does an investor need that it is now dangerous to continuing holding?

At the outset of 1973, even as the Dow Industrial Average was making what was then a new all-time record high, TP plunged below its neckline (at about 30), thus conclusively completing the huge top. After a few weeks of trading around 26, there comes a pullback rally, which stops, conveniently but to no surprise, right at the neckline (C) which now serves as overhead resistance. Notice how this "happens" to coincide with the level the Moving Average has slid to, so that *there is a clear rebound level at which to sell.* That juncture of resistance and the M.A. provides the ideal selling opportunity for those who have needed to be convinced that the stock is indeed breaking down in serious fashion. No one conversant with our theses should still be holding such a stock— but no one is perfect, either; such a pullback rally does provide a last "in the nick of time" chance to get out. It also serves as an ideal opportunity to sell the stock short (established weakness; a price level right at the resistance barrier, and a chance to act while there are still buyers helping you get the short sale off).

To review the sell signal sequence: the first chance comes when a valid (three points or more) uptrend line has been broken, confirmed by a break in the longer-term (150- or 200-day) Moving Average line. The second chance comes on a subsequent rally that forms a right shoulder (or visibly makes a lower high) on noticeably less volume. And if you've just returned from the wilds of Borneo to see such a chart, by all means sell on the pullback rally. Since TP ultimately went down below 5, it is clear that feeling locked-in, or that it was too late to sell because the stock was already down from 42 to 30, is an absurd idea useful only to avoid reality.

The kind of evolving failure that produces a head-and-shoulders top is not the only type. *The market is not going to oblige you by making its evidence simple and clear.* Other patterns can appear, although *all* patterns involve a trendline of one sort or another which will eventually break. One might even say that the rule is: *trendlines are made to be broken.* The accompanying chart of Eastman Kodak illustrates the process of living with an unfolding situation as it recurringly says "sell me." But it would have taken diligence to spot the trouble in one of the DJIA's key components under the euphoric headlines portraying the average itself as still racing ahead in a powerful upsurge.

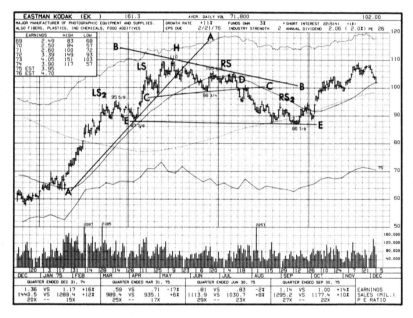

Nothing seemed to be wrong with Eastman Kodak as it registered successive new highs and higher lows, except that an important trend line (A) which touched at three points (remember: connecting two points makes a line, the third serves to confirm the validity of that line) was breached negatively in May 1975. The minor slide that ensued was arrested only slightly higher than the previous selloff low, but that apparent holding was deceptive. A chartist with a handy ruler would have connected those two lows to make line C, so that all that was missing to create a head-and-shoulders pattern was a right shoulder. It was no surprise then that the next rally failed (RS). Line B could be drawn in, connecting the high with the right shoulder's lower top, and you can see that this created a triangle: the slightly rising lows vs. the declining highs. In theory, a triangle represents indecision; you are not supposed to know the direction in which the stock is going to move next. The stock can, theoretically, break out either on the upside across line B, or on the downside through line C (and if you were short, you would have wanted to place your protective buy stop just above the RS rally high).

Triangles which form by themselves should be viewed neutrally. In recent years, a peculiar and deceptive result of triangular formations has been seen with frequency. We've dubbed this the Bermuda Triangle pattern. What happens is that the breakout is, more often than not, in *the wrong direction*. After the short-term break of the trendline, a more extensive, more real, move takes place in the opposite direction. But when such triangles arise within the larger context of a head-and shoulders pattern, as in EK's case, it adds weight to the evidence that the breakout will not only be down but also serious. Anyone holding this blue chip, and wanting to give it as much rope as possible to hang itself (due to the extremely bullish climate), should have protected that position with a sell-stop order placed just under line C. Failing that, the standard pullback which ensued (D) also provided a chance to get out virtually whole. (Note how that pullback bounce halted at the neckline which marked the point at which the breakdown began.) As you can see, the stock abruptly plunged another 12 points.

With the stock down under 90, such a seller would have felt delighted, especially since, by that time (August '75) the overall market was in a correction instead of a rally. But EK had held just about exactly where the March-April action had found support, so line E—at first experimental—could be drawn in. The stock also was holding at its long-term moving average line (this is a *Daily Graphs* chart, using a 200-day M.A.) Now the "feel" of the chart

began to change. A second left shoulder (LS2) and, on the rebound, a potential right shoulder (RS2) could be penciled in, etch-
ing out, in theory, a much larger head-and-shoulders pattern. Any
holder would at that time have become intensely anxious. Does he
sell on the (RS2) rally in case it turns out to be a big top? Or
should he take the chance that it may survive. Protection, of
course, would come from placing a stop-loss order under trendline
E, just in case. Or should he have estimated that the stock could
rebound as far as the major breakdown level at point C, and perhaps fail again as the first rebound did? Ah, hindsight is a wonder-
ful thing! The chart shows a gap as the stock exceeded the RS2
high. Gaps are evidence of more power than just an ordinary
move. The rally kept going, as did the rally in the overall market in
January 1976. EK gained nearly 25 percent (a typical *last* move
in a stock that forms a head and shoulders pattern that doesn't
break) but that was exhausting; by late 1976, Kodak was finally
down below line E and deep into a bear market. Anyone who held
because it was a blue-chip company would have been better off
fleeing when that first, relatively small, triangle and equally modest
head-and-shoulders pattern appeared and was broken. These
kinds of tops really are warnings.

The Triangle

*L*et's take a moment to discuss what the triangle is, other than a
variety of identifiable and related patterns (symmetrical, as-
cending, descending) carried over from mathematics. It is, as is the
head-and-shoulders formation, derived from the realities of stock
action. As we've said, not all stocks make their highs together. Nor
does an individual stock, except for the mathematically literal number, make its "high" all at once. In the head-and-shoulders pattern,
the left shoulder and right shoulder are also a part of the stock's
"high." In a triangle, the highest point comes first, and the failures
on rallies follow in succession, so that there is a sequence of lower
highs. Yet there is a form of success on dips, as each meets sup-

port at a successively higher level. The net result is that you can draw a down-slanting trend line across two or more peaks and an up-slanting trend line connecting two or more bottoms. (The highs and lows must alternate.) Since you have rising lows, implying continued demand, and falling tops, implying continued supply, you really don't know in which direction the stock is apt to break out. Such symmetrical triangles are, therefore, considered *indeterminate* patterns.

Some refinement can be applied to that broad statement: first, that a flatter line connecting lows—that is, a descending triangular look—is telling us that while support is holding, bidders are not willing to lift the price they are willing to pay. Such triangles usually break down, because that is the direction in which the pressure exists. Second, a rebound off a low that *fails* to go as far as the descending trend line overhead—sort of stops in mid-pattern and turns down again—is warning that it has gotten weaker and is likely to break down. (Conversely, a decline off the descending line that does not go all the way down to the rising line, but stops midway and turns back up, is suggesting that buying pressure is winning the battle, and such a pattern usually is completed with an upside break out.) Finally, and most confusingly, are the "false" breaks: triangular patterns which stage a sharp break that's only short-term; the stock typically completes the *minimal* measurement of the triangular pattern (the width of the triangle subtracted from the breakdown price gives you a target), and then reverses and stages what is often the longer-term move in the other direction. Why should the market make it *easy* for us?

When dealing with triangles, it can be fruitful to make reasonable deductions based on what is happening in the rest of the market. Perhaps the best illustration of this took place in the late spring and summer of 1970 when a large number of triangles appeared, along with many head-and-shoulders bottoms. Given those bottoms, and that those stocks with triangular patterns had also already endured a prolonged bear market, it took no great leap of faith to assume that those triangles were bottoming patterns, too, and that the breakouts were going to be on the upside. Similarly, triangles appearing in late 1972 and early 1973 were entitled to more than mere suspicion that they'd break down rather than up. Thirdly, and most dramatically, consider the post-crash climate in October '87. Many little triangles quickly appeared on the daily charts due to the enormous volatility—some investors were still spooked and sold bounces; others, sorry they'd missed the crash lows, sought bargains on dips. Initially, the sellers won; such triangles had downside breaks, but then came reversals because the market decline had exhausted itself, everyone who'd wanted to sell was by then out, leaving room on the upside for

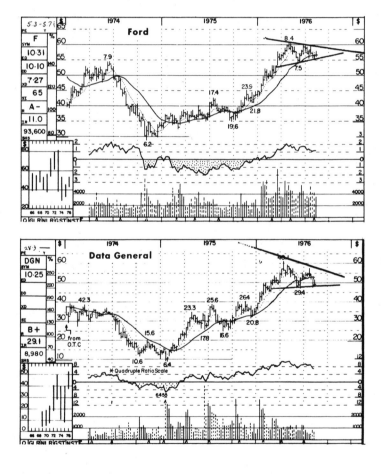

reversals. In large part, this explains the triangle complexity noted above: when the stock has already been in a prolonged down-trend, and a triangle appears, it can have one last shake-all-the-weak-holders-out breakdown, and *then* reverse to the upside to begin an entire new uptrend. After the stock has had a long rise, and a triangle forms, the bulls will be eager to do more buying as the stock breaks out on the upside; they rush in enthusiastically, *exhausting* their buying power in one spectacular last gasp, like an opera singer bellowing one more high note before expiring in a heap on the stage. Triangles have a large number of such "false" breakouts, but they aren't false at all, since they actually happen. The rule with triangles is, don't expect too much.

In more "normal" circumstances—if anything is ever normal in the stock market—when, after a big rise, the triangle line is broken on the downside, it is a sign that the forces of supply and demand, which hitherto had been battling to a standoff, have come to the end of the fight, with sellers finally winning. However, triangles often appear as consolidation patterns in the midst of a major trend; indeed, they depict the battle between bulls and bears very clearly, so that unless you have additional subtle evidence (as discussed above) you should (a) give some credence to the belief that "a trend in motion continues until it changes" and (b) to wait for evidence that the trend is changing via an actual breakdown. Here are two examples of triangles forming (in mid-1976) that we would wait for. (Examples of triangles at tops that could have been anticipated by aggressive investors will appear later—see Telephone and Monroe Auto.) These triangles, in both Ford and Data General, have incipient aspects of tops: the stocks have already risen a distance and their Moving Average lines, while still rising, are beginning to fade. The potential for trouble is certainly there, as is the possibility that after a consolidation the rise could resume. And there's no clue elsewhere: at the moment of these charts, there were few other toppy signals (neutral indicators, a prolonged sideways market). The stocks could emerge on the upside, and if so, such consolidations—a form of rest and rehabilitation—could produce good subsequent gains. You wouldn't want to have been scared out. But if the stocks were to break down, you can visualize how ghastly the charts would look. The Ford seems more symmetrical; the Data General chart more of a descending triangle, and hence more uncomfortable. In either case, the answer is to be ready, via protective stops, to sell if and when the break is to the downside.

There you have the essence of charting. It is not esoteric; it is not tea leaves or crystal balls; it is, literally, a graphic representation of the actual trading on the floor of the stock exchange, the picture of what everyone is doing in that particular stock, the collective wisdom of sophisticated and knowledgeable market players as well as dunces and novices...all there for you to see and study and tap into. There doesn't have to be a specific definable formation, as in Eastman Kodak, to spot trouble brewing; the item of practical importance is not hailing a descriptive name, but locating which price levels are vital. Trend lines, whether attached to head-and-shoulders or triangles or existing on their own, help to define those vital price levels. Although interpreting charts may be difficult and inexact, requiring practice and experience, so that one can begin to anticipate, a break is a break is a break—and acting upon a break will still be *earlier* than the crowd. Thus the charts do show what is happening in an objective fashion (as compared to a broker's, or the media's opinion) and can be used, at a glance, for that purpose.

There are two challenges. The first is to recognize important trend changes without getting bogged down in a labyrinth of pseudo-scientific refinements, or a maze of guesstimating alternative courses. Over the years technical analysis has fashioned a host of ingenious systems, but actually it is sufficient to pay attention to these objective factors: (1) trend lines; (2) head-and-shoulders and triangle formations, which consist, in their own ways, of those trend lines; (3) the long-term (150- or 200-day) Moving Average line; (4) whether volume serves to confirm the action—rising on breakouts, fading during consolidations; and (5) signs of failure—inability to make a higher high and/or to hold above a prior low. And the ultimate challenge? *believing in, and acting upon, what you do see.*

The Point-and-Figure Method

*W*e'll see other examples of these and some of the many other patterns stocks form in subsequent pages. But before we do, let's re-examine an entirely different method of charting, and discuss its merits and uses under identical circumstances with those of the previously featured high-low-close daily and weekly bar charts.

To many, a point-and-figure (P & F) chart, with its vertical columns of X's and O's, is even more a matter of tea leaves than bar charts. But the element that gives these charts their odd character is also their main virtue and chief defect: P & F charts have no time axis. Whereas bar charts get an entry for the range of each trading day (or week) regardless of what the stock did, P & F entries are made only according to price intervals, regardless of how long it takes to achieve that interval. If, for example, the price interval is the most common one point, an X would be entered whenever the price moved to the next whole dollar level from the previous X; that is, a rise from 19 to 19 7/8 would be meaningless, while to 20 would call for an entry directly above the previous X, in the same column. Were the stock then to continue advancing to 21, another X would be inserted above. A subsequent drop, however, back to 20 would require shifting to the next column and down one space for the entry of an O to signify a chance in direction downward. Thus both ticks at 20 would be side by side, one an X, one an O. Meanwhile, you could actually have a fluctuation as great as 1 3/4 points. For instance, if the last entry were made at 19, and over a period of several days, or even weeks, the price eased to 18 1/8 and then edged up to 19 7/8, and back and forth within that range, no entry would be added. The overall result is a compression of movement, which can be even more compact if you use an interval, say, of 3 or even 5 points rather than one for each entry. Two results flow from using such charts: (1) many years of history can be compressed in a relatively small space, and (2) activity within particular price ranges is more clearly delineated as support or resistance. That is, if the stock were to trade between 19 and 21, you'd have several entries in that area; if the stock were next to move above the 19-21 area, it could then be said to represent an identifiable area of support. If the stock were to break down below 19-21, the area would represent overhead resistance. A chart depicting a long period of trading would readily identify important clusters as support and resistance, and that's a convenience indeed—the main virtue of such charts.

The problems that we have, though, are multiple. The dependence of P & F on jogging up and down to create its formations eliminate nuances of price, and we have experienced many instances where fractional price levels prove to be meaningful. We prefer semi-logarithmic chart paper, so as to perceive the proportions of moves on a percentage basis no matter where they occur, and this can't be done with P & F charts. What's more, as the price level diminishes the inflexibility means that every X has equal value, whether at 8 or 10, and thus P & F chart activity diminishes, causing low-priced stocks to have less lively and extensive charts. (This is often dealt with by expanding the price axis to half-point intervals.) Finally, and perhaps most important, is that this form of charting is basically an abstraction of the rhythm of the actual trading; lacking a time frame prevents viewing how the stock has been acting in relation to the action of the market itself. Since we feel bar chart trend lines work within their own time frames, we have our suspicions about the virtues of P & F trend lines for timing specific moves. We've found, over the years, that bar charts frequently give identifiable breakouts *ahead of* the readings of P &

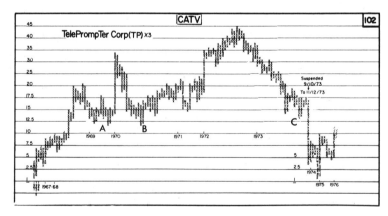

F charts. Lastly, of course, is the fact that it is much easier to maintain your own bar charts because the information is available in the daily newspaper, whereas a stock which has volatile and extreme intraday moves requires learning or observing all such swings to know how many X's and O's might have taken place.

That said, let's examine a chart of Teleprompter showing the same action as that revealed in the prior bar chart, so that you can see how clearly they pinpoint areas of supply and demand ("resistance" and "support"). You can see the support area created in 1969 between 12 1/2 and 15 (A). Compact and clear-cut, it served as the base for a powerful rally in 1970, and proved itself as support later that year on the subsequent sell-off (B). Far to the chart's right, the action in 1973 found that same area serving as support (C) for quite a while on the way down—that is, before all hell broke loose. Thereafter, with the price below it, what was formerly a support area now became a resistance zone, inasmuch as prior buyers in that 12 1/2-15 range now had losses and would emerge as likely sellers when and if the chance came to get out even. Indeed, TP rallied to about 11 in 1976, where it ran into a huge roadblock. Once you can identify key support and resistance areas, respect them.

Choosing Charts

Our own experience has been that a weekly bar chart is akin to the point-and-figure variety in that it presents more history at a single glance and clarifies resistance and support areas, but also adds that all-important sense of time while providing the same sort of valuable perspective over an entire trend. A weekly bar chart, with volume, is our choice for anyone who wants to keep (or purchase) only one style of chart but does not want to commit to keeping them every single day of trading. Since we do, we refer to the weekly charts for that longer-term perspective. Extra-long-term bar charts, such as those published by M.C. Horsey, also serve as valuable references for historic support and resistance areas. In that way, we get the benefit of the imminence that daily charts present in timing, with breakout points clear and often providing—with experience—the sixth sense of exactly when such important action is about to take place. Although it takes guts to act on what you are seeing on the charts (especially when it conflicts with what the crowd is saying), you'll be amazed at how practical the "feel" of such daily charts can be, even if it doesn't answer the question why. If you add to that "feel" the perspective of a weekly chart, you've got a viable combination. Here are a couple of examples.

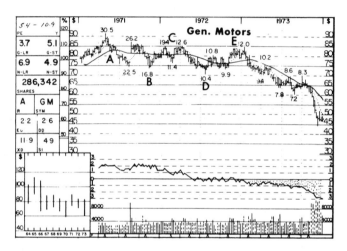

At first glance, General Motors seems to be moving so erratically that there is little pattern. Let's take the GM chart and break it down into those elements that tell us something. First, you can see that, at point A, the stock broke sharply below its long-term Moving Average. You can also see, if you peer a bit closer, that the break completed a head-and-shoulders top. Since this was a time when our indicators had already warned of an intermediate-term decline developing, no one, according to our prescriptions for selling, should have continued holding GM past that point in 1971 (approximately 82). This was given further emphasis when GM's literal breakdown occurred on a downside gap (that is, the opening was lower than the previous day's lowest price), and the stock never closed that gap all day. Such gaps across a specific breakdown point are superb confirmations of the legitimacy of the break. Thereafter, GM's price kept slipping. But nothing on Wall Street is so simple. Nixon's August economic game plan gave such a boost to the auto industry that GM opened on a huge upside gap, which, as we've already discussed in a previous chapter, was an excellent chance to sell if you hadn't already done so. Even lazy institutions were granted the chance to sell—note that the stock, even on that emotional enthusiasm, failed to exceed the previous high. What this chart of General Motors teaches is: *Never rationalize that you've been saved.*

Let's follow what the subsequent sequences say. Just look at B: GM was setting a lower low, while the succeeding rallies (C) were intimidated successfully by the resistance established during the August surge, a clue that a lot of sucked-in investors who had bought then were now trying to get out near the break-even point. Thus we already have a pattern of lower highs and a lower low, with the second of those rallies coming as the overall market was again emitting intermediate-term sell signals. The subsequent decline took GM to another lower low (D). Clearly, General Motors had become a stock to avoid. The small sideways action in the latter part of 1972 wasn't viable enough to overcome the substantial overhead resistance. Accordingly, while the DJIA was rallying to its then all-time high, this blue chip got stuck below its previous highs (E). The original sale price had proven sound during that entire period, despite the big big-cap bull-market rally. Indeed, one of the important negative signals of early 1973, unquantifiable but "feelable" on your own charts, was the abundance of such failures vs. the Dow Industrial Average itself.

This history of General Motors shows how resistance comes into being, and how it affects a stock's subsequent behavior. The many buyers along the way—August 1971 in particular—had no chance to sell at a profit any more than those who'd bought at the prior top did; getting out even became something to settle for. What's more, buyers who had come in at points B and D who did have gains could see the stock struggling, and if technically oriented would have noticed that the indicators were turning sour.

Resistance levels are born and grow this way, constituting an area where sizable selling can be expected to appear. By the time the year-end rally arrived, the prior failures had served to establish the importance of that overhead area which, in turn, generated even more selling on the way to point E. Only on rare occasions—very rare—do stocks barge through such formidable resistance levels: it takes a speculative market, a popular stock that has been heavily shorted, and a freakish spark of enthusiasm that causes the shorts to panic right at a marginal new high. (For an example, see Promus's new high in February 1994—trading in new high territory lasted about three hours, and the stock then fell virtually straight down some 20 points...without the shorts being on board for the drop they'd correctly foreseen.) A lot of basing work is required to overcome resistance—the rule being that the base should be at least as big as the top area in order to accomplish that.

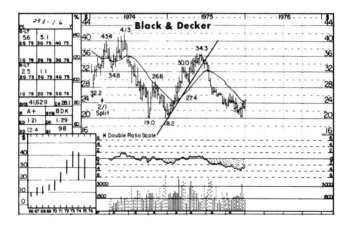

Often, by examining areas of upside resistance, you can get a good idea of just how high a rally will take a stock. Black & Decker's action in 1975 is an example of a stock that suddenly ran out of gas at the end of its second upleg and came all the way back to the beginning when it shouldn't have. Actually, the troubles could have been anticipated. Although the base is clearly a double bottom with a valid upside breakout across the M.A., it isn't a very big base compared with the overhead resistance running through the action of 1973 and the first half of 1974, centered in the 36-40 area. A stock fresh out of a substantial base area might have been able to assault this supply while it still had youthful vigor, but by the time the second upleg came along, with the market late in an intermediate uptrend. BDK had lost momentum and there were too many willing sellers on hand around 36 for BDK to climb any further. Thus an early buyer could have established a sensible upside target of 36 which would have been right on the money. Such charts literally tell you in advance where you must sell.

Even optimists who believed BDK could bull its way through the resistance overhead would have had a second chance to sell, when the major uptrend line we've drawn in was broken—a line that was too steep to trust. Yet another signal was given as the stock broke its M.A. at 32 and the M.A., in turn, slipped downward. Now the picture is one of a stock which has failed at resistance and is in a downtrend. That would have taken you out four points worse than if you had paid attention to the heavy resistance area, but still, 12 points better than the next significant low.

Case Histories

*T*o show how this selling approach can be applied in actual situations, let's review what happened in a number of stocks during the 1972-1973 top period. Bear in mind that, while we have selected pictures of situations that worked, the system we have presented is not perfect. Indeed, it is not a system at all but rather an approach to the stock market which is helpful in minimizing errors and maximizing profits. Many people were trapped at that top, and the cry of the so-called experts was, "How did we know it was coming?" How indeed!

The other day (April, 1994, but it's an eternal pattern of behavior), we were watching CNBC when an oil analyst was being interviewed. The chart for the June contract of crude oil had been rising, even though it had been widely expected that the price was going to go down. OPEC news had been extremely negative yet the price went up instead. How could that be? a simple refusal to go down any more on bad news is surely a positive thing to see. But this gent said, in succession, "How could any one know the price was going to rise?" and, a few minutes later, that he "never watched the market's action" because he was a fundamental analyst. But the market—we wanted to scream at the TV set—was telling him more than *he* knew, and precisely what he needed to know, and yet he wasn't interested in knowing it. That a man in a suit and tie, with a college education, could be so blind astounds us. To be sure, this is not a perfect solution, and so such "fundamentalists," when they perceive a mistake (even if it is not so much a mistake as a matter of the market producing new and different pieces of information), seize on that "evidence" as a reason to disparage.

That homily having been preached, let's return to our charts, starting with what was once the *grande dame* of Wall Street, American Telephone & Telegraph.

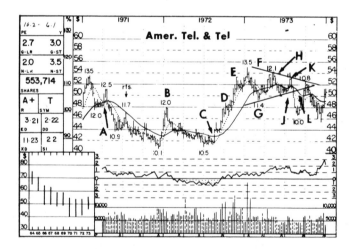

Let's assume you've been a buyer of Telephone near its low at the end of 1971 as it breaks out across the Moving Average line.

It rallies swiftly to 48 (B), where it runs headlong into the resistance formed earlier that year (A). You've made a few bucks. Telephone, at that time—it's speeded up nowadays—happened to be a relatively slow-moving "widows and orphans" stock, but its chart patterns work the same and merit the same consideration as if it were a rank speculation. Such a fast rise to resistance calls for taking the profit, especially when there is no evident base to justify expecting more (and when you can see on a longer-term chart— or even from the tiny insert—that there is plenty of historic supply over 50). The argument that the stock has been bought for safety or for its dependable dividend is naive. There's nothing safe about a stock up on a spike, leaving it capable of sliding right back down from 48 to 42, as Telephone did. Surely, selling at the higher price and buying back at the lower, which would have been a gain of 15 percent, is a lot better than the stock's dividend yield. Ah, that's hindsight, you may argue—how is one to become assured that the stock can be replaced at that low price again? Except for the inadequacies of base, and considerable resistance, there are indeed no assurances...but then, there are no guarantees in the stock market. We would reply that taking a $500 or $600 profit and simply putting the money away in the bank would yield more than T was going to yield for the next two or three years, with, we might add, *no* risk whatsoever. Missing opportunity has more cost on the sell side than missing a chance to buy a hot stock ever has.

Another homily having been blurted out, let's return to the chart assuming you've sold alertly, and do get back in at the next upside breakout (a lovely opportunity at C). You'd encounter the same sort of resistance at 48 as before, but this time there are two fresh factors to take into mental account: first, the entire 42-44 area has now assumed the characteristics of a base, thus holding out more upside potential than before, and second, the prior drive to 48 has already absorbed some of the resistance, so less supply can be expected on this trip. Besides, the Moving Average has swung upward more dynamically than on the (B) rally, and the Dow Industrial Average was also rallying, so you decide to ride it out through that first short-term correction (D).

The second short-term correction (E) coincides with the peak in early 1971, so it might be tempting to sell, using the strength at this juncture to get a good price. However, there's no top forming yet and, with the market increasingly looking euphoric at year-end we can understand someone continuing to hold. The high, in January 1973 (F), coincides with the Dow's all-time high, but of course no one knows that yet...although there are several factors now warning you to consider selling. Not the least of these is the euphoria, the very climate that may be making you complacent. Note the extraordinary volume accompanying that last rise, and the visible five-wave upward movement. Ultra-high volume so late in a move is often of the "blow-off" variety, when a spurt of late-comers, anxious to get in on the action, leaves a vacuum underneath, through which the stock can fall precipitously. Given the way other stocks were failing and then breaking down, we believe the aggressively alert holder would have sold Telephone at this time. But since there is still no top in evidence, some investors might want to stay around to see if higher prices might be forthcoming. (Remember to be consistent: if your style is to insist that a genuine top form before you sell, that's okay, so long as you maintain that approach in each instance.) Thereafter, we have a dip to G, a rally to H, a dip to J, a rally to K. By connecting the three tops and the two bottoms with trend lines, we have etched a triangle formation, while the volume shows gradually diminishing activity of the degree typical of triangles. Supply is battling demand, with each side coming closer and closer, so that the fight must be resolved shortly. Were Telephone to break out on the upside, the triangular action would be hailed as a consolidation. But with so many other stocks already breaking down, and with the market indicators in distress, this triangle could be presumed to be a top. The answer comes when Telephone smashes through the lower trend line (L) while the Moving Average is, by then, turning down.

Sell Telephone? sure! The lowest a seller would get in this instance is 49 7/8, based on a stop-loss order entered just under the lower triangle trend line and taking the round number 50 into account. At that juncture, a rough calculation, based on the width of the triangle at its widest of about 6 points (F-G), subtracted from the point of breakdown at L (50), suggests a drop to 44. Since the chart shows base support in the 42-44 area, you have a logical downside target, long before anyone knows just how bad the bear market is going to be. That "safe" and "conservative" holding is now less safe, and the more conservative thing to do is sell so as to conserve capital. Such selling, saving in capital nearly three years' worth of dividends, is certainly sensible, and would have seemed even more so when Telephone hit bottom at 40.

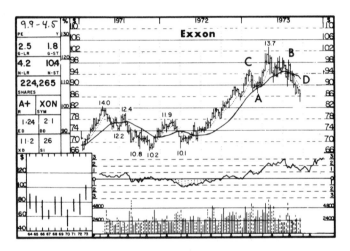

Exxon was a solid winner in 1972 as it broke out of a good base formed while the stock was ignoring the prior intermediate-term market upleg. The extent of the base, plus the room to move (see the absence of much overhead supply in the insert), made XON look like a viable long-term holding. The dip to A was alarming because by then the Dow Industrial Average had already topped. But Exxon managed to hold above its prior low point, and its long-term M.A. was still rising, so there wasn't enough of an individual top to warrant selling—yet. The warning didn't come until (B), when there were several successive failures to push upward, each halting at a lower price than the try before. By the third such failure, the M.A. had clearly reversed as well. It became more a question of time than direction, more a question of extent than whether. Compared to almost all other stocks at the time, this top was modest; a script-writing chart reader might have begun looking for a rebound (D) as a right shoulder to match the prospective left shoulder (C).

This is a crucial moment, however, and just because that scenario is a possible future development doesn't mean it should be counted on. A right shoulder provides time for holders to get out at relatively good prices, not far under the peak price. It is part of the distribution process, with strong sellers feeding stock to weak, and late, buyers. When it appears while the averages are still rising—often with similar problems appearing in other stocks—it is really representative of how a market top forms. But when the market is already visibly in trouble, as it was in 1973, the action may not permit such holders to get out; the stock tumbles before any right shoulder can form (or it has a stumpy abortive look about it), usually indicating a pell-mell rush to the exit. Often, then, the first slide is an extremely steep one, intensified by hasty dumping from those people perceptive enough to have wanted to sell, but a bit too greedily waiting for "one more rally" to get out on.

Although you can see at a glance the top on the American Airlines chart, and the breakdown, and the sensible time to sell, we've included this situation to illustrate a comment made by an NYSE specialist who, when asked how he'd survived the terrifying bear market onslaught of 1973-74, replied, "You had to believe in selling the stock all the way down." He went on to explain that, as a specialist, forced during the slide to buy for his own account when no one else wanted to buy, he couldn't afford to be mesmerized by the notion that, because the stock was already down by half, or more, it had become a bargain worth holding. During that entire decline, it was never too late for the specialist to sell (for AMR went even lower in 1974).

The same thesis holds true for a public owner of this stock. Notice that in late 1972 a chance arose for a sensible sale to be made, when AMR rallied from 24 to about 30 and ran smack up against its Moving Average line. The important point here is that you could not afford to rationalize: "Oh, well, I missed selling at

44, so now I might as well hold." How does one know the stock isn't going to hold? For one thing, the M.A. is still heading sharply down. For another, that's a bounce, not a base. In real bear markets, as compared to mere corrections, individual stocks often have intervening, contra-trend rebounds that look like this little pause in the AMR chart...and then the decline has a severe second leg down. A sale into that mid-way contra-trend rise would have netted a price about four times above AMR's 1974 low, after all those "could have" and "should have" excuses were erased.

Here's a neat and tidy, five-phase, intermediate-term rise with an equally tidy top. Monroe Auto progressed sideways through most of 1972, well before the Dow was finished. Where would you have sold? If not after the third upleg (fifth wave) at around 47 (C), which would have been a perfect sale, then still okay somewhere in the later stages of the prolonged horizontal spell that followed. At that point you would have been convinced that you didn't need a cyclical stock selling at 30 times earnings when it couldn't go up after three tries at its early spring high. And there was a last resort chance to sell at D upon the downside break, when a new low beneath that entire sideways movement, with its head-and-shoulders elements plus a now down-pointing M.A. made it emphatically clear that the major trend had changed

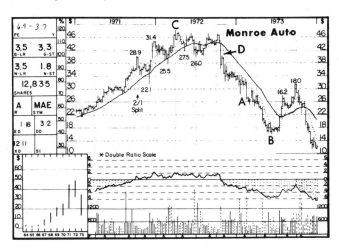

direction. Yet what is the typical response by an anxious holder? An initial sick-to-the-stomach reaction followed by the notion of getting out "on the next rally; a sell order may actually be placed around 42 back where the slide started. But this is a good chart to illustrate a great lesson because there was no such rally! You can see that the same thing was true in the AMR chart—for the sake of ego, or wanting to be made whole again, or reluctance to say the simple word "sell," most investors, seeing and sensing disaster, nevertheless put in their sell order above the market instead of "at the market."

After a considerable decline with virtually no rally to get out on, Monroe got oversold enough (B) to warrant a classic intervening contra-trend rebound. This one was greater in size and percentage upness, but the essential picture is the same as that in AMR. Such rallies typically make the long-suffering holder feel better, so he doesn't sell, although here comes the rally he's been praying for. Monroe's is particularly deceptive because it went far enough and lasted long enough to help its Moving Average start to turn up. But there is no base in sight but, rather, a sort of "V" bottom, which is typical of failing rallies. Note that the rise actually began to come to a halt where it was supposed to—at the resistance area at (A), while the second leg quickly reached, and reversed from a

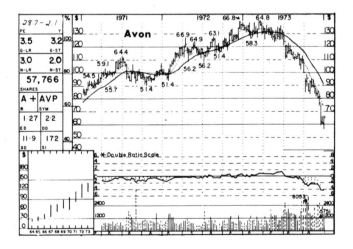

larger body of supply in the low 30s. A trader might have bought this stock for such an intervening rebound, and would have taken his profit as the stock neared what is so evidently a sensible target—so should stuck holders. And both would have been fortunate that they done so, for Monroe subsequently went down below 10.

Avon was a glamour stock that bit the dust along with the other high-fliers. But notice how long AVP's uptrend persisted before it finally got clawed by the bear—*and* that it actually peaked several weeks after the Dow did in early 1973, not really starting down until mid-year. We were premature in selling Avon, since a top appeared to be forming around 100 in the second half of 1971. The M.A. was beginning to arc over, and if you place your thumb over 1972, you can see how toppy the stock then looked. But as the market rose at the outset of 1972, the stock reversed, had a quick dip *which produced a higher low*, and then re-launched its rise to the final top. Often, such apparent tops that turn into this sort of reversal last another 25 percent or so upward; anyone who was short should have covered that position after realizing—via that higher low—that the stock simply didn't want to go down any more.

In 1973, however, clues to an even larger top became evident: upside failures and lower lows began to alternate. Then the Moving Average began rolling over much more convincingly than it had before; volume increased on the downside; and the stock staged an initial downside break at approximately 123. Notice how that plunge held for a while at the 110 level, matching a couple of 1972 selloff lows and creating a much larger top, which was completed when 110 was broken. Of course, when Avon hit 20 later on, it didn't matter much whether you'd gotten out prematurely in the 90s on the 1971 false top, or as it broke down successively in 1973. With a top so big and ominous, there is room for miscalculation as to when to sell, but absolutely none as to whether.

The time: February 1972. Bausch & Lomb had been one of the market's most popular glamours, shooting up fivefold. The Dow was still rising, and technical indicators had not yet signaled that trouble was coming. So there were plenty of excuses for

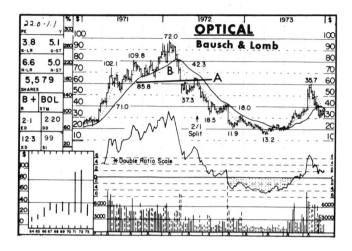

being overly relaxed about holding BOL. The plunge, when it came, arrived with devastating abruptness. Although that's the first reaction, you can't just sit back and say, "Oh, well, it was just some overdue profit-taking."

We gawked at this stock's chart action while it was happening, and we've looked at this chart many times since, but there really was no clue and no good time to sell before that break. An aggressive investor might have lifted his stop loss order to just under the reaction low at the onset of 1972 (under 78 at B) but much of that perception is hindsight—with the moral of the tale being that stop "loss" orders can be invaluable if they are continuously raised to protect profits after every positive (higher low) sell-off while the stock advances. After the break, a chartist might have anticipated the possibility of right-shoulder work to match the 60-80 range of 1971, but it never came. There was, finally, a small bounce back up to resistance—and the by-then steeply declining Moving Average line (A) to be seized upon. Better to sell into these rallies too soon then to wait for an extra point or two, risking not selling at all. Any holder who hoped for more, who dreamed of getting the old highs back like having a high school flame reappear, was doomed; the stock market does not offer so many second chances that any one can be ignored.

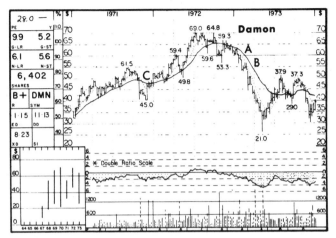

Damon is another example of a stock that topped out far ahead of the averages during this time frame. It, and many other stocks like it that did not participate in the late 1972 "Nifty Fifty" third upwave, helped to produce the divergences which signaled that major top—between the advance/decline line and the Dow Industrials and also between the high/low differential and the Dow. The deterioration in the indicators was a reflection of what was happening to so many individual stocks, such as Damon, beneath the surface of what the newspapers were extolling as a strong market.

While the Dow was rising to 1,050 in January 1973, Damon was already establishing a pattern of lower highs and lower lows. Volume had expanded on the downside and its long-term Moving Average had rounded over decisively. This rotten action called for a sale as soon as 60 was broken (A)—actually it simply called for a sale on the visual evidence that breaking 60 was a lock—or, at the latest, at the break below 55 (B). (Note that someone holding all the way down to that B level might have rationalized that the stock was due for a bounce, and held, and held, and held.) But you would have gotten no disagreement from us if you'd wanted to sell at year-end, when the top was forming. Why cling to last-ditch hopes when a stock is acting this way? It's not as if you can't buy it back if the climate changes. While some might prefer to wait for a top to be completed, others opt for "one failure and then good-bye." By December '72, and especially because it was collapsing vs. the Dow, that succession of lower highs and lower lows would've convinced us to sell.

Studying this chart, you might wonder if circumstances wouldn't have called for a sale at point C in late 1971, when there was a disruptive break, a rally to resistance, and an M.A. beginning to turn down. Yes, you could have done so—and switched into something else (for the bull market was still chugging along). Hindsight makes it look less reasonable than under the pressure of the problems at the time. But note that had you done so, you would have gotten about 48, which, in the long-run, wouldn't have been so very different than being late—selling at 60 (A) or 55 (B), especially since the stock continued on down to 5 before the tide was stemmed in '74.

It is also worth noting another rather typical bear-market performance along the way down: the rally that doubles a stock's price but is just part of the major downtrend, often coming *mid-way* in the overall decline. It is always only a rough measurement, rather than a pinpoint one, but most of the time if you perceive such a rally as the contra-trend rebound that it is, you measure the length of the first leg down (60 to 25, in this case), and subtract that from the point at which the intervening rebound begins to fail again (approximately 40-45), you get a target for the second leg down. What is tricky about DMN's move from 25 to 50 is that it is abrupt, having had no base formation beforehand. Unsupported rallies like this are the way bear market bounces look. They may be profitable to trade, but they require nimbleness and a willingness to admit that the bear market still prevails. As long as you relate your action to intermediate-term moves (and not the primary, or short-term, trends) you'll find yourself capable of taking advantage of these rallies and still getting out in time. As it turned out, the area around point C supplied the resistance that halted this rally, but drawing in a trendline that connected the spike low with the first dip, would, when broken, also have provided a clear message as to when to sell.

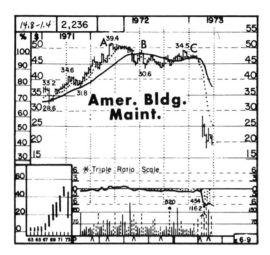

When a stock like American Building Maintenance has had an uninterrupted upward run, as defined by both a trend line and the long-term Moving Average, you know that the odds for a correction have increased; the risk begins to outweigh any further potential reward. Stop orders wouldn't have been much help, because the distance down to the previous important low was too far away, nor was there a message of a succession of failures at the high as in Damon's case. But once that Moving Average line had been broken so clearly—a line which had supported the entire previous rise—common sense might have dictated that selling into the rally (B) as it ran into resistance from the sideways dawdling that followed the high at A. Why not get out as soon as rallies begin to fail? oh, not early in a move, as a stock breaks out on the upside from a base, but much later, after the stock has had a grand run (and just when everyone begins to believe it's going to go up forever). Actually, ABM's action in 1972 mirrored the market's "sidewaysness," and then, after Halloween, stocks began to rise again. Anyone still holding had to decide: get out at point C—in case the stock failed again as it had at the roughly equivalent point B—or believe that everything was still marvelous and that the market rally was going to help carry this stock to the moon. Yet it did stop, the reality of the resistance proving more significant than the hopes of holders. If you hadn't gotten out by then, you literally didn't get another chance for 20 points.

This is as good an example as any to use for arguing against the technique of selling out only part of a position "in case" your original decision is wrong. There's merit to selling into strength (as in giving your broker a "not held" order), but when the signs point to selling because of evident weakness, as at points B and C, sell everything. The fear of being wrong causes the hesitation, but what happens is that one's mind changes—"Oh, I'm okay," the holder says, "I've already lightened up" and therefore doesn't worry about a deteriorating situation any more, with the result that one stays long too many shares too long into a decline.

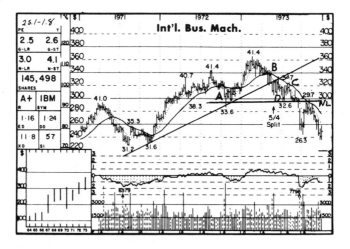

Because there is considerable emotional involvement with a company like International Business Machines, the personality of these stocks makes them perennially tough to be objective about. (Gold stocks, too, have this mythic quality that creates prejudices.) Analysis of what is actually happening to the ticker symbol—in this case, IBM—rather than the company, becomes paramount. Let's examine what IBM's chart was telling us two decades ago.

First, note that the Moving Average line meanders through the pattern, making it difficult to get a reliable long-term fix on the underlying trend. Yet, if you peer closely, the M.A. has validity for intermediate-term moves. There's an upside breakout at the end of 1971, and another at the end of 1972. Two downside breaks (A and B) signal the ends of those particular upswings. Selling at the time of either downside break seems valid; the problem is, as you've perhaps already muttered, that the A break was only temporary, the B break was the major message, and, of course, psychologically, anyone who saw the stock bounce back up after the A break would be less willing to sell when B occurs—to his terrible determent. It might be argued that since the stock price ultimately was cut in half, the price one would have gotten for selling at A is not so much less than at B to make a big percentage difference.

But here's a further test. What would you have advised your mother-in-law if she'd come to you at the time this chart was printed and asked what she should do with her IBM stock? That's the kind of advice that carries a big risk. The chart certainly looks like a huge top on the verge of breaking down. But it's IBM. In late 1972—even though the market indicators were giving negative signals—you might have hesitated. The uptrend line we've drawn in after the A break might have caused you to give the stock a chance, as long as that line were to hold. At B—this is your mother-in-law and it's IBM, so you can't afford to be wrong in your advice—the uptrend line is still intact even though the market itself is sliding. And when the line actually is broken, she snaps back at you that the stock is down so far already. But after a decline to point D, followed by a trivial rebound, which was aborted at the now descending Moving Average line (C), it becomes possible to draw in a more scary neckline-type line, saying the stock would officially break down if it fell through the 300 level.

Look at how awful, huge, and disintegrating that chart looks. Whether it is IBM or not—goodbye. Ah, but she didn't listen to you. One last "gift" opportunity to sell comes along; IBM has a standard pullback rebound that fails at the breakdown point (just under 300) exactly as it is supposed to. But it's IBM; now that it's rallied she mocks your advice, insisting that "now it's okay again." So you think, "well, this isn't a perfect game, why can't it be held until it comes all the way back?" But the ensuing bear market cut the stock price in half (and here we are two decades later *knowing* we would have been delighted to have sold at 300). Consider: although there were several opportunities to sell along the way, the major breakdown was *less than* ten percent lower than the best "objective" price you would have gotten by selling at any of those possible levels. It was clear. It was decisive. It even gave you a second opportunity on the pullback. And there was a psychic profit, too, for anyone who did sell: having one's capital tucked away under the mattress as the market careened downhill and everyone else was in hysteria.

Chapter Ten

Selling Short

*D*on't Sell America Short" is a slogan we've all grown up with. There is an enormous emotional resistance to selling short in the market; that is, to selling stock not yet owned by borrowing the certificates to deliver to the buyer, and hoping to return those borrowed certificates later with shares purchased at a lower price. The act seems to be expressing a lack of faith in the future, in the economy, in the country. The psychological discomfort is made worse by one's guilty glee if trouble does indeed arise. Further, there is a sense that "it's not nice" to sell something one doesn't own and a suspicion that short-sellers are at the mercy of stock market manipulators. None of these is true.

Unfortunately, emotional distortions are more prevalent in short selling than in any other market transaction. The fear typically occurs just as a market glows during its last gasp of strength before topping out and heading into a substantial decline, and is least apparent at the bottom, when short selling seems like a great idea precisely when such a notion should be dismissed. During any market cycle the concept of selling stocks short is wholly legal and above board, is a necessary element of the auction market (adding liquidity and free choice), has been scoured of any taint of manipulation, and, most important of all, can be a conservative approach to capital management during declines. That is, it can help in "conserving" capital when properly used to hedge long positions that an investor doesn't want to sell.

Some Elementary Notions of Short Selling

Specialists sell short as part of their obligation to help maintain an orderly market. Their shorting, as we noted earlier, is usually done out of necessity, when they are the only sellers available to supply stock to eager buyers. Without such shorting, price increments in market rallies would be abnormal and unmanageable. Similarly, the need to cover, or buy back, the shares that have been sold short, thus closing out the position, adds buyers to the marketplace, a particularly helpful factor during a retreat, since it supports stocks which otherwise might find no buyers. For that reason, it has become a cliche that a large short position is "bullish," but the enormous increase in arbitrage trading and hedging has turned the Short Interest Ratio, once useful, into a non-indicator. In the nineties, short covering tends to provide an emotional excess to oversold rallies, rather than to be an underlying support—still, there are times when any buyer helps.

To enable their public customers to sell short, stock brokers arrange for the needed stock certificates to be borrowed, so as to be delivered to the buyer, who, of course, is entitled to receive bona fide shares. This borrowed stock comes mainly from shares held by the brokerage firms for margin accounts, and left with the firm as collateral for the loan. The stock remains borrowed until such time as the transaction is completed by purchasing the equivalent number of shares in the marketplace. That may be days or years later. It doesn't matter, for the Internal Revenue Service treats all short-sale transactions as short-term gains or losses. The system works easily for active and popular stocks, but from time to time a thinly capitalized and/or closely held issue may prove difficult to unearth in margin accounts. This is how the "short squeeze" can develop: many overanxious short-sellers in a stock with few, if any, certificates around to be borrowed to deliver to the buyers. Naturally, if he is unable to make delivery to the buyer, the short-seller is obliged to rush back into the market to cover the sale himself; he has been, in effect, "squeezed." Accordingly, one blanket rule in selling short is not to get yourself in instant trouble by dealing in obscure issues where it may become impossible to borrow stock. Stick with broadly held issues, with relatively large floating supplies; and, if there is any doubt, *ask first*. If your broker comes back with word that it will be difficult to borrow, but (his reputation being at stake) he'll find certificates somewhere, tell him to forget it, you don't want to be anywhere near such a situation.

Not So Speculative

*I*n order to help dispel any of the emotional trepidations you may feel about going short, let's deal with some of those fears directly. It is important to recognize that short selling is not a radical act or a highly speculative deed, as it is often said to be, but is actually a sound tactic in its time. The stock market goes down as well as up, as you may have noticed, and not taking advantage of both directions is poor capital management. Selling short is, simply, the most efficient way to protect your money during a major bear market. What's more, even though the market goes up some two-thirds of the time and down only one-third (which may make it seem feasible to wait out the declining period), those down periods can be explosive. Consider one cycle: it took eighteen months through 1969-70 for the market to tumble from 1,000 in the Dow to 630; thirty months, nearly twice as long, to struggle back up a trifle higher, to 1,067; and then, in less than twenty-two months (1973-74) it was all wiped out on the plunge to 570. Since a lot more money can be made in brief stretches of time on the short side rather than on the long, it would be foolish to ignore this tool when playing the market.

In sum, you are protecting your capital when you use the short side during downward cycles, plus giving yourself a chance to actually make your capital grow while your neighbors are bemoaning their losses. But if shorting is so rewarding, and there are billions of shares available to sell short, why is it that the maximum number of shares held in short positions is so small? Despite what seem like record levels when reported each month, the literal percentage is only 5 percent or so of average daily volume, with most of that, as noted above, due to arbitrage and hedging positions. For most people it is evidently unthinkable to sell short; even institutions (the so-called professionals) are averse to the idea. As a matter of fact, most mutual funds—unless specifically set-up to be on both sides of the market—have bylaws prohibiting such a tactic, so as to pacify fearful customers, while almost every pension fund manager is charged by the client to be fully invested long. Without being short during a bear market, traders and investors alike can do no more than hope that their holdings will decline less than the averages, for there is no way they can profit. (In 1994, the market had become so volatile that hedge funds became socially acceptable, and several were offered to the public, to the extent that at least one such fund advertised regularly—a sign that the ads were working. Their popularity produced too much short selling; the result—as contrary opinion could have predicted—the market refused to go down.)

Cash itself, held aside to be able to buy stocks at the next bottom, is the only viable alternative.

The vaguest but perhaps the most pervasive emotional barrier is that a short position is unorthodox in the expected scheme of things. It is done backward—selling first and buying later—and that's hard to grasp. In addition, the seller has invested capital (must put up the required sum according to the margin rate then in effect, and is subject to margin calls should the trade go against him), but he owns nothing for his money. Further, he is responsible—to the buyer—for any and all dividends paid during the period he's short. Investors are also accustomed to the notion that if wrong on the long side, at least there are certificates of ownership to live with until the stock comes back. Owning nothing but having the potential to lose a lot is scary.

Theoretically, there is no limit to the amount of money you can lose if a short sale goes against you as the stock rises in price. Conversely, the most you can make is 100 percent if the shorted issue goes to zero, whereas you might double or triple your money on the upside if you hold the right stock. True enough, in the old days there was the outside chance of being caught in a corner, such as the infamous Northern Pacific corner of 1901 or the Piggly Wiggly maneuvers of 1922, but such a disastrous bear trap hasn't been successfully sprung on Wall Street in our lifetime (although the Hunts almost pulled a corner off in the silver market). Bringing off a corner (in which the perpetrators buy up all the available stock so that short-sellers must come to them to buy back at astronomical prices) is unlikely to ever happen again. You can avoid the occasional hysterical excess of more short-selling speculators than there are shares to borrow simply by refusing to play that game. Whatever losses may be involved in selling stock short can certainly be avoided by ordinary defenses—including *not* acting as if you are a sky-diver about to launch a death-defying leap by shorting a strong stock that is still going straight up.

The Practical Side

*B*efore getting into tactics, let's review the processes involved in short selling, since they differ from an ordinary long-side sale. When you order a stock sold short, your broker, adhering to the rules, must so specify on the sell order sent to the exchange floor. The floor broker must execute the order on an uptick, a price higher than the last different price. Since the coming of the SEC and reform legislating after the 1929 crash, a stock can no longer be forced down directly by orders to sell it short. Everyone—specialists, professional traders, and public alike—must sell short only on a rising price; someone else has to take the initiative to purchase the stock "up." Very rarely will there be a bid on the exchange floor entered at a higher price than the previous sale price, so usually the short sale is made by a buyer's stepping forward to take your offer. This can be nerve-wracking. The stock, since it is still in demand, is likely to go still higher, however briefly, against your short sale. This is a fact of market life that must be endured. Proper timing will keep it to a minimum, and the proper use of a "buy stop" order will protect you from fighting excessive additional strength.

Let's follow an example to see how it works. Suppose you spot a stock you think is likely to go down, and you enter an order to sell short at 70, the last price, down from 75 but up from the previous transaction of 69 7/8. Thus an execution at 70 would be on a zero-plus tick—higher than the last previous different price—and a short sale would be legitimate, so your shares are offered at 70. However, if the stock were next to sell at 69 3/4 instead, your order, being limited, would still require a buyer at 70; had it been a market order to sell short, the specialist would reduce your offer to 69 7/8 since this would be the best price at which it could be sold on an uptick following the trade down to 69 3/4. But imagine that it is sold at 70. The buyer must then pay $7,000 to your brokerage firm, for which he is entitled to a stock certificate signifying ownership. Your firm delivers such a certificate from among those it is holding "in street name" for its own margin customers.

The firm also gets money from you, at least enough to meet the margin requirements, so as to secure the trade from your side. Even if you put up the full amount of the transaction, it still goes into the margin-account ledger. Now the brokerage firm has extra money, yours plus the buyer's, from this trade, and thus should not charge you interest in your margin account. However, it does have the extra money, so that instead of needing to borrow from the bank to loan to the firm's margin accounts, that excess can be rented directly, so that the firm gains the full profit of the interest charged, an arrangement that has often made the difference between a firm's surviving or not. Then, when you decide to close out your short position, you simply buy the stock as you would any purchase, except that the order is designated "to cover short," and the certificates received by this purchase are used, via the brokerage firm's back office, to replace the previously borrowed certificates in a bookkeeping transaction.

This simple sequence can serve to assuage the fears created by one of the oldest bugaboos against short selling: that there is a potentially limitless loss. Obviously, in this manner, you can lose no more than the margin clerk, doing his duty, will permit you to lose. A margin call is a severe but practical limit on short-side losses, particularly since one of our inviolable rules of emotional restraint is: Never put up more money when you get a margin call. (Of course, you should never let yourself get even close to a situation where a margin call is imminent.) Thus the concern that possible short-side losses could be limitless is really just one more psychological hurdle, designed to keep you from employing this capital-protecting and enhancing tactic.

To be sure, if one could choose which side of the market to play, almost everyone would pick the bull side, except for those who recognize that their own psychology functions best when selling short. But the market rarely offers such a simple choice, and even when it does, it's not for long, and then, it occurs to us, seeming so clear that it has become dangerously close to the end of that particular move. Let's suppose you realize the market, as measured by the averages, and as "forecast" by the indicators, is heading south. What can you do about it? Sell, to be sure, as already advised, but with your now idle capital, would you shift to supposedly defensive issues? Why buy something that is "okay" because it is going to go down relatively less than the stocks you've sold? Buy golds? they don't perform against the trend with consistency. Buy paintings for protection? real estate? How would you get your money out when the time came to get back into stocks? What about bonds? Typically, interest rates rise with tighter money which, in turn, may be the impetus for, or part and parcel of, the bear—meaning that bond prices can decline, too. About the only alternatives are: a simple savings account, or cash under the mattress, or selling stocks short. If you'd been short from 1929 to 1932, or during the 1973-74 bear market, you'd have emerged with a lot more capital, and been able to buy a lot more shares at a lot lower prices. What's more, you'd be continuing to track stocks, using the same indicators and other tools as before, and thus you'd be much more alert to spotting the bottom than that neighbor of yours who, still long and long-suffering, has stopped looking at the stock pages months before. Cash, in one form or another, will get no argument from us as a positive holding during a bear market. The argument against cash—that it generates no yield—is silly stuff: we've seen "innocent" investors hold a stock for its dividend while giving back three years of return in capital loss. The return on cash comes not during the bear market but from the rises of those stocks you were able to buy at the next bottom. If you are still reluctant to sell short, "own" cash. If you do sell short, you get the added benefit of remaining in constant touch with what is going on.

In any event, in *any market* climate, pick the stocks with the most potential to move the greatest distance, be it up or down. There'll be periods of transition when some stocks are still positive, others are becoming negative. Later in such a transition, when you don't like the "market" generally, but do want to hold onto certain stocks that are still healthy—"haven't done anything wrong"—and that you expect have further upness to go, selling weak stocks short can be a vital hedge against the market's onslaughts and vagaries.

Selecting, and Timing, the Short Sale

*I*f selling short is essentially the antithesis of buying long, does it follow that your tactics can be the reverse of the way you buy? No, the market does not make things that easy. There are several important differences in viewing the indicators and in actual tactics. But there is one element in terms of stock selection that is exactly the opposite and therefore exactly the same.

The goal in stock selection is to find the *strong* stock to buy. We are not believers in guessing at a bottom, but in letting the stock's own action prove to us that it is a strong stock. Our objective then is to try to identify such strength, and to buy, as close to bottoming support as we can. To that end, we frequently will buy in a "right shoulder" area (of a head-and-shoulder bottom), anticipating that the stock is going to break out to the upside; at other times, we recognize the power of such a breakout, and want to buy the first dip back toward the "neckline." (We're using "head-and-shoulder" terms here as symbolic of what we have in mind regardless of the actual chart pattern.)

Just as we want to own a strong stock, we want to be short a *weak* stock. All too many traders try to short stocks that have soared—"it's up so high already," they think, guessing at a top. Let the stock *prove* that it is weak—lower highs, lower lows, a toppy pattern such as a head-and-shoulders, a rally that fails at overhead resistance...*that's* what we want to be short.

Second, there is a tendency—enforced by the IRS—to accept short side trades as just that: trades. And that's fine during a volatile market that's swinging between overbought and oversold levels. But once you get your teeth into a real bear market (whether in the individual stock or the averages), what's the point of taking a quick profit in a *proven* weak stock? We call such long-term short positions by the same phrase as long-term long positions: *investments*. Yes, you've got to pay attention, so as to identify the ultimate bottom when it appears, but we recommend riding out intervening short-term swings when you've got a short position in a truly deteriorating stock.

Third, there are certain rules as to when to head for the short side. We've already examined a number of useful indicators based on short-selling statistics that reveal the emotional states of mind so that, based on their activities, we can know when, and when not, to act on the short side with relatively little risk. Most of all, we don't want to get caught up emotionally ourselves, and short *late* in a slide; short-covering rallies can be panic-inducing. Having shorted near intermediate-term tops, we'll want to cover as the next bottom approaches. Unfortunately, as discussed in a previous chapter, one of the best guides for that—heavy odd-lot short selling—no longer "works." So we've had to change our rules from the first edition.

1. Rule 1 is to sell short only when the ten-day oscillator (our advance/decline ratio) is on the verge of getting maximum overbought. The reading should be above the zero line, and we would also prefer that a downside crossing of the ten-day down through the thirty-day occur above the zero line—that mitigates against potential whipsaws. *Never* sell short when the oscillator is already well down into oversold territory.

2. As replacements for the demise of odd-lot short selling, you can use the put/call ratios. These percentages—both for the CBOE and, separately, the OEX—should be low: the former down in the 50s being a sign of excess optimism, the latter under 80 being an extremely low reading, too. High numbers—more puts bought than calls—serve as a warning that you're part of a consensus trying to sell short too late in the game.

3. Specialist short selling levels should be in the upper 40s. No shorting when their readings are, say, below 37 percent.

omit Chart of member shorting on p. 221

4. Your own potential choices of which stocks to "do" must be a guide. It takes many weeks, sometimes months, even a year, for a top to form; distribution ahead of a bear market can last six quarters before the stock breaks down to a lower low. So there's no hurry, nor any need to aim for the top 1/8, no need to get frustrated if the stock is already going down—*that's* evidence of weakness, to be admired, not to scare you away. Runaway stocks that you own may make you such a nervous holder that you can start to cash in on a big long-side profit via a "scale up" order. But it is never a viable idea to sell short for no other reason than that the stock has already been run up so much that it appears due for a correction, or because it has begun to look overpriced. *Stocks always go to an excess beyond what you or anyone else thinks conceivable.* You don't have to try to short a parabolic at the top 1/8; once it's done, it'll retrace for quite a distance and quite a while. It is one thing to protect an already-established position by locking in some profits, but entirely another to commit fresh capital to a new position until the chart action has become convincing evidence not only of the failures overhead, but of the room to go down.

Selling long closes out a position; your choice is not one of selection but of timing. When buying, the ability to time a bottom is (within reason) pinpointable. But tops take a long time to form, and selling short requires not only the same sort of careful stock selection scrutiny that you must use when buying, but patience as well. Just as it is sheer luck to buy close to the ultimate bottom when bargain hunting, it is also mere accident if you happen—

once in your career—to get off a short sale close to the all-time peak of a high-flying stock. *Wait until the stock has proven itself:* strong stocks prove themselves by going up, weak stocks by completing sizable tops. The conservative short-seller avoids the still-rising target and waits until there is decisive evidence that his candidate has become tired, has established resistance overhead, has shown some failures already as proof that it has reversed direction. Inevitably, there'll be some mistakes (that's the challenge of the marketplace), but usually the stock can be caught near the best price available, after the top has formed, and as it is about to fall apart. Patience is rewarded as the risk is reduced.

The Inevitability of Being Early

*T*he problem of patience becomes complicated by the requirement that short sales be executed only on upticks. Many people understandably fear that if they wait for the stock to start sliding, their short sales—although accurately picked—may never be executed. Accordingly, they toss in "at the market" short sale orders as the stock starts to tumble, with this result: on each sale at a lower price, their offer to sell short becomes the best offer in the marketplace, 1/8 above the last sale price in order to be an uptick; after the price falls a whopping degree, the market's customary fluctuation comes into play; buyers arrive at the specialist's post; the short is executed at the first uptick, several points lower than when the order was entered, and the short-seller is bagged at the outset of a rebound, often causing him to panic to cover the "mistaken" short during the bounce. This, naturally, can be abetted by floor traders who know that orders to sell short have piled up in the specialist's hand, since they can see the loose orders tucked into his book (such orders can't be recorded since they keep changing price as the stock falls). If you see on the tape a sudden string of sales up 1/8 of a point, you'll know that the professional traders are grabbing all those "at the market" short-sale orders as they try to "give the stock a goose."

This mistaken attempt to get the execution too late—after the decline you wanted to be short for has taken place—is a cousin of the mistaken attempt to short a stock too soon (simply because it has run up a huge amount). To avoid the frustration of watching the stock you'd wanted to short tumble steadily, while your short order remains unexecuted (until it gets that execution at a dangerously down price), the discreet short seller will use limits on his orders—permitting some leeway to try to catch an uptick, but not much. At least you've learned that you're on the right track in having identified a weak stock—good for your ego if not your wallet. But by being patient you can reduce the risk of this sort of trading trap; there *will* be a fluctuation back up, so you can adjust your price accordingly. Too many short-sellers get emotional—excited, out of control—when they see their pick proving profitable without them, so they wind up with a loss and blame the notion of shorting instead of their own emotions. In a suitable "down" climate, there should be plenty of other shortable charts—if there aren't, it isn't such a shortable climate. (Note that we are talking specifically about making short sales. It must be repeated that when selling out a long position, where no uptick restriction is involved, while your capital surely is, a market sell order does the job promptly and properly.)

The inevitability of being early—but not *too* early—helps avoid the tribulations of chasing a stock down. But we must also discuss the problem created by the very nature of the market itself. Even after a top has developed over an extensive period of time, and it appears that enough is enough, there may be a bit more, a last gasp, a final convulsive shudder upward. Consider 1972 and the many tops which had formed along with the advance/decline peak and subsequent negative market action. Along came that last upward "Nifty Fifty" dash over 1,000. Many stocks which had already clearly formed tops had rallies which—in hindsight—could be seen as part of the entire top formation, but which at that time would have been nerve-shattering for the holder of a short position. That December (and in early January '73), a few popular stocks carried to new highs, compelling shorts to cover—yet that action proved to be nothing more than the head of an even huger head-and-shoulders top. Such decisions are tough: you know you're "right" about the top, the vulnerable market, etc. and yet there's the rally staring you in the face on the ticker tape, looking as though you'd better run for cover. And even if a new high doesn't arrive, the rally may carry above what looked like the first line of resistance, so a close stop used as protection gets set off.

It is as if the market is by its very nature out to get you. Those who had sold out long positions were tempted to start buying again—"one more rally" has caused many investors to give back their bull-market profits in precisely this act of suckering. It's even more difficult if you're short, for you haven't had the bear market yet to prove you're on the right track; the optimistic news, the optimistic brokerage comments, the optimistic-reading tape, are all against you. Let 'em rally? it's easier if your shorts are so well-chosen that they aren't part of what is essentially, so the indicators will remind you, a narrow rise. Many stocks, as they did in January 1973, simply got back to their major resistance levels. "Early" means you have to have patience to ensure such irritating rallies, so long as the overall indicators continue to suggest that the market really is topping out. And remember, just because you may have been early is no reason to be discouraged from renewed shorting, as the decline unfolds. It certainly wasn't "too late" in February 1973!

Here's what you should look for as a check on whether you might have been wrong:

(1) Is the long-term (30- or 40-week) Moving Average still rising? It should already be arcing over. If it is still heading upward, you really were premature.

(2) Is this rally a classic "one last fling" or can a case be made for the previous market drop having been just an orderly correction within an on-going bull market? Have the key indicators actually reached signal levels or were you trying to anticipate them? Has anything in the market's action heralded a violation of the uptrend, such as a lower low in the Dow or S & P 500 on a dip, a divergence in the high/low differential, an important trend line broken? Is market volume on this scary rally noticeably less than

on previous rallies? are other stocks failing, even if your short isn't?

(3) Is the individual top you spotted still there, or has a higher low, followed by a higher high, started to appear?

(4) How's the volume in that particular stock? Does it rise on substantial trading activity or on far less than seen earlier? Are there any signs of churning: heavy volume and little price change?

(5) What are other stocks in the same industry doing?

(6) Is the "market" awaiting some "good" news that might end the entire rally? Don't be faked out by good news. Remember that bullish news items are the fool's gold of market tops.

If you've made a mistake, or so it seems, by all means get your house in order. There's no point to be gained by being stubborn; the market'll be there tomorrow, and the next week, and the next month; this isn't your only chance ever. It's best to have already established a sensible place for a protective buy-stop order so as to deal with the intense emotional pressure that arises at such moments. (See our previous discussion of how to place "stop-loss" orders—in this case, just above a descending trendline, just above a previous rally high, etc.) Let the "objective" stop take you out of a worrisome position, proving that you were wrong at least for that particular period.

Eventually, you'll learn to accept being early when selling short, simply because it is as built into the system as taxes. The distinction you'll have to make is when. You may notice, upon reviewing such checkpoints, that you were premature (which is a bit different than being early). In that kind of situation, a close stop may be best, taking you out quickly at a minimal loss if the stock still has more to it. However, as the top gets bigger, as the Moving Average finally starts to round over and then aims downward, as the indicators flash signal after signal, give the stock more leeway so you don't get stopped out on a freakish "final" rally. You may be early, but you are unlikely to be wrong, so if the stock has more rallying within the overall top area, let it wear itself out by placing your protective stop sufficiently above the pattern so that it will be set off only if you are proved emphatically wrong. We've heard many anecdotes about selling a stock too soon that ultimately soared, but they're acceptable because the teller of the tale has other suc-cess stories; but anecdotes about how "I was short that blankedy-blank and got scared out just before it plunged" always have a tone of frustration and anger about them—because those shorts were chances to be victorious during a market decline. Don't let that happen to you.

Shorting at Primary Tops

Given these parameters, let's take a look at some actual exam-ples where selling short is applied. A chart's a chart, so to speak, so we're going to discuss the examples given in the first edition, although with an extra insight or two along the way. Obvi-ously, some of the disasters discussed previously would have been profitable shorts as well, but the point of view is different, so let's begin fresh with one of the stocks already discussed, Teleprompter. You'll recall that in January, 1973 the DJIA had just reached an all-time peak, accompanied by a batch of negative signals which the eternal and preponderant optimists were blind to (chiefly because the two dozen or so stocks that were up were

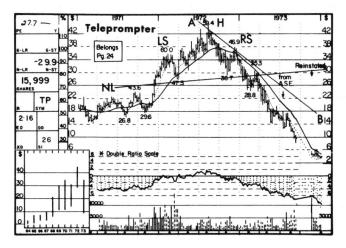

their big cap darlings). There was no way to tell in advance how extensive and precipitous the drop would be; all one could do at the time was determine which stocks should be sold, and of those, which looked like the best short candidates for an intermediate-term downleg. With hindsight, of course, one can see many more stocks that could have been shorted with impunity, but when you are right in the middle of the fluctuations, trying to minimize risk as you proceed, it's a lot tougher to plunge ahead.

Now let's take another look at that Teleprompter chart:

Here you can see the major head-and-shoulders top as it formed in late 1972. We asked, in Chapter 9, how many signals a holder needed to become convinced TP had to be sold. There was the lower volume as the head and then the right shoulder formed, the break of the uptrend line off those successively higher bottoms during the rise, the long-term Moving Average rolling over and turning downward, and the warning formation of the right shoulder itself. A reasonably alert sale of a long position would have been around 34 in the week or two *after* that right shoulder had clearly formed. That's not top dollar—the high being well over 40—but it is a sound sale price and not far off the 38 or so that an aggressive seller would have gotten by selling the moment the Moving Average and the uptrend line were broken.

So much for reviewing the long sale. What about shorting this baby? With a price/earnings ratio of 35-45, it certainly was an attractive (i.e., overvalued) fundamental candidate as the top was formed. The lack of quality, the observation that other stocks in the CATV group were also struggling, and the satisfactory pattern of trading all added to the appeal. But singling out TP as a short-sale candidate is one thing; the stock still has to provide a low-risk entry point. At the time the right shoulder formed, the DJIA was still in the midst of what proved to be its last suck-in rally—but rally it was—and that might well have been too uncomfortable a situation to try to buck on the short side. You are now interested in initiating a position, and that's different from having to close out a dangerous and vulnerable one.

The key point to remember is that you are looking for a low-risk place to put your capital in the hope that you can make it grow. Forget how far down the stock has already dropped. Some of the best shorts can be the weakest stocks on their way to the graveyard. (Think of the percentage profit to have been made by being short a stock like Wang at, say, 10, and simply having the patience to maintain the position until it went out of business.) Although TP has already dropped from the low 40s, it becomes confirmed as shortable when the head-and-shoulders top is completed, via breaking the neckline. The interested short-seller should have, so to speak, a shopping list, and could then spot TP on this list as being worth watching closely due to that completion of the top pattern. With the stock having plunged under 26, the next thing to watch for is a chance to short the stock on any pullback rally. Such moves are a normal expectation and typically retrace to the area of the now-broken neckline. At this juncture, the potential short-seller cannot be deterred by the fact that the stock is now rallying, and he can't permit himself to be frightened away by all those upticks, because he needs one to get his short sale off. But where? Note that there is now heavy resistance in the low to mid-30s, plus the neckline, plus the now established long-term downtrend line (A-B), plus the now descending Moving Average line. (All of that provides a chance to place a protective stop overhead; in this instance a likely level would be 35 1/8.) Given these facts, we'd have entered an order to sell short at 29 7/8, feeling that the round number at 30 might be the maximum extent of the pullback. As it happened, TP managed to edge a mite higher than that, but such a price, however momentarily early, would have proved terrific in the end. And, as the stock began to decline in earnest, the holder of that short position could feel more comfortable knowing that TP, a popular speculative favorite of that day, was now scaring out holders as it fell. Because the stock was actively traded, the pressure remained high. One might also suggest that a short-seller could even add to positions such as this as they prove themselves; for example, shorting more the next time a downside break was made, in the 25-26 area. As a general rule, why look for a different situation when you already know one that is working out?

Such a seller might have wondered where to cover the by-now successful short, especially when noting the degree of support evident on the left side of the chart picture in the 18-22 range. However, a measurement of the head-and-shoulders top (from about 44 to the point the neckline was broken near 30) amounts to 14 points downward, or 30 minus 14, for a target in the neighborhood of 16. With the overall market decidedly bearish, our tactic would have been to place the buy stop, now protecting a profit, just above the Moving Average line, at, say, 20 1/8 at first and then lowering it to 18 1/8 after those two little attempts to get across 18 failed. Now, if you'll take a quick look back at the P & F chart of Teleprompter (Chapter 9), you'll see that substantial support exists starting at 15. Given that prior support, an entirely acceptable alternative to the use of a stop order would be to cash in the profit in that neighborhood. Perhaps, having seen the stock bounce off 14, one would then seek to cover on the next dip. However, hindsight says it would have been better to use the stop method, since it would never have been set off and you could have stayed short all the way to under 5. When you have a remarkably clear point at which to place the stop (18 1/8 being just above two failed rally peaks, as well as a Moving Average line that has flawlessly marked the downtrend thus far), it makes sense to stick with those aspects. Now that you've achieved your goal of finding a truly weak stock to be short of, let it turn into an investment.

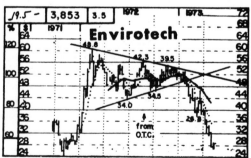

We've drawn in on its chart the obvious triangle formation which developed in Envirotech. A triangle, second in reliability to the head-and-shoulders formation, requires at least two points of lower highs and two of lower lows for a sort-of symmetrical formation. A descending triangle would have a flat bottom line where two or more dips were holding at about the same level, to go along with the successively lower highs. In theory, triangles can produce breakouts in either direction, requiring patience to wait to see which it will be. But after a prolonged run up, and when head-and-shoulders tops abound elsewhere, it can reasonably be expected that the breakout will be to the downside, as it proved to be here. (Note that if you make such an anticipatory bet, the descending trend line provides a super-sound level just above which to place a protective buy stop.)

EVT didn't give much time to get a short off once the breakdown took place. When you see such a formation, you can alert yourself to the price at which the downside break would be an accomplished fact, so as to be prepared to try to catch a quick intraday pullback to the trend line. Thereafter, you can mark the stock down as a genuinely bearish situation, with plenty of resistance overhead, plus a weak industry group popular enough to bring out a ton of stock for sale once the slide begins in earnest. Some patience, therefore, would have spotted that subsequent pullback to near 48, where the long-term Moving Average line also served as resistance, not a bad price to sell short, in view of the ultimate drop to 15.

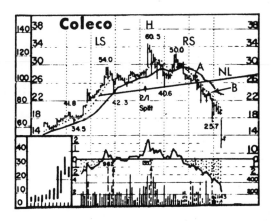

While we're picking your shorts from visible and traditional charting formation, let's take a look at another of those major head-and-shoulders tops that marked the big 1972-73 top, this one in Coleco. Here was one of those little-known institutional pets of that era, with an absurd price/earnings ratio of over 50. Note that it wasn't necessary to catch the top 1/8 in order to turn a hefty profit in this stock on the short side. Indeed, Coleco eventually fell to around $2 per share.

But while there was no rush, that sideways movement for several weeks at about point A was a pretty good tip-off to anyone posting the chart that the neckline was inevitably going to break. So here you might have ventured a trifle more daringly by going short, with, of course, a protective buy stop placed above the right shoulder's rally peak. Be careful when placing your initial stop; you want the protection, but you also don't want to be so close that a last-gasp rally attempt takes you out just before the stock becomes a big winner on the downside. (That can happen not because the stock market is out to get you, although it may sometimes seem that way, but because we are not talking about pinpoint accuracy or perfection, only likelihoods and probabilities.)

Often, when a stock hangs just above the breakdown point, as Coleco did just above the neckline for several weeks, it is building for a more rapid plunge once the dam lets loose—buyers are being used up. In this case, the stock fell apart so rapidly that the typical pullback rally was not even in sight, although during the trading after the break there was a brief return for anyone alert enough to notice. We want to warn you, in such cases, not to toss that order to sell short in at the market. To avoid giving back half your trading profit before the order is even executed, always place a downside limit on the order at the next lower round number, and no lower.

Once you have your short order executed, and the stock starts behaving badly (meaning profits for you), be alert for the chance to lower your protective stop so that a move which reverses the trend will take you out of your position but minor bounces will not. In the Coleco chart, the clear long-term Moving Average provides a good guide. For example, once the neckline was broken, the stop could be lowered to just above both point A and the M.A., to about 28 5/8, and then, after the plunge below 22, the stop could be lowered again to just above point B and the M.A., which is about 23 5/8 on the chart. That would put the stop order just above an area of some resistance that no minor rally should be able to penetrate.

Automatic Data Processing was also among the many stocks that had no sensible business selling so high (about 90 times earnings). Just a glance at the chart reveals how sound a short sale AUD was, but when should you have taken that step? It looked tempting in the vicinity of point A, but the needed components for a low-risk short were not yet in place. For one thing, this was near the start of the market's final rally, so that the overall market indicators were not then so one-sidedly bearish. Shortable stocks were developing, but AUD was less ripe than they were. For example, although the long-term Moving Average was fading, it had not yet definitively rolled over. If you put your thumb over the right-hand half of the chart, leaving only point A visible, you'll get a "feeling" of an incomplete picture, one that is bothersome but has more work to do. Although in the long run you'd have been right to go short at that price, when the rally arrived that price would have

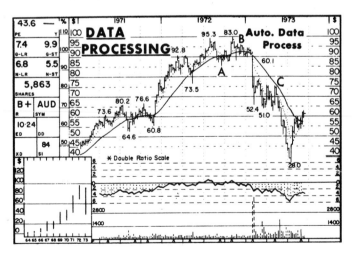

included some sleepless nights. Patience would have been preferable. As you can see, too close a protective stop order would have
taken you out on the rally back up toward 100, where the double
top finally formed. There's nothing like being stopped out to get
the message of having been too early. But you can't let that aggra-
vation cause you to back away from starting over again when further evidence develops.

It is not unusual for the evidence of a stock breaking down to finally become clear when the overall market indicators are also
clearer and more precise. The savvy market observer could well
say, "I know AUD is a great short up here at 90," and "I know
this rally is no good and I want to sell short into it." That'll make
him early every time, and this time too early. Little will be lost as
long as the trader is alert. By point B a "double top" had been
etched out, and a marvelous little trend line connecting three
higher lows could be drawn in as momentum was waning. Several
weeks of sideways movement, similar to that noted in Coleco, developed. Sideways is best for the potential short-seller because it
puts the stock in shape for his purpose. If AUD had slid quickly
from point B, it could have gotten temporarily oversold as it
reached the breakdown level, and thus such a move might fizzle.
Sideways work helps it rest before the real move down. With the
M.A. now having had the added time to round over, the stock is
itchy to break 90—the uptrend line; the previous low—on the
downside, but because you need an uptick, jumping the gun by a
little bit is certainly feasible. Now, a stop placed above the double
top, at, say, 100 1/8, gains the added benefit of being just above
a major round number, and would have been a mere 10-12 percent above the shorting price, not a bad degree of protection for a
high-priced stock.

The next thing to note is that after the initial plunge another
short-selling situation developed. As yet, there was no reason to
cover a proven success; we want to let such winners run. You
would, of course, have lowered your protective stop to 80 1/8,
just above the initial bounce and above the M.A. It wouldn't have
been touched off, and by point C on the chart, you'd already have
seen three successively lower rally highs, plus a matching set of

lower lows. All that adds up to a picture of continuing weakness within the context of a major bear market. The investor who saw this, but was inhibited from acting because he'd "missed it at 90" was depriving himself of a good profit.

Having added to that initial short position, or taken a new one at that juncture, the stop could now be dropped to just above point C, at 75 1/8, to relish the next decline. But now what? The stock is collapsing, but you know that no stock goes straight down forever. Rallies always intervene. Do you cover? In the summer of 1973, a number of indicators began to improve and to give some favorable signals. You may not have believed the bear market was over, but as the stock fell, the wise course was to at least review where the next important level of support could be expected. Reference to a point-and-figure chart book, which would have had much of the past history compressed, or, alternatively, Horsey's *The Stock Picture* chart book, which goes back more years than the Mansfield charts, is needed. Here you would have seen that AUD developed considerable support around 35 as it made its 1970 bottom. Furthermore, note the useful application of a simple measuring device: from 90 to 65, the initial plunge amounted to 25 points. Subtract this from the 65 level, where AUD broke down again after its period of consolidation, and you get a downside target of approximately 40. In combination, therefore, you had the basis for targeting the downside at 35-40, at a time when the overall market was shifting to at least a contratrend rally climate. It takes a strong will to cover a successful short, the same kind of decision-making decisiveness we want you to get in the habit of doing when selling a successful long. But, given that the market is imprecise, you can't ask for better objective reasons to cover for a huge profit than two different approaches producing the same target area. If a third reason is needed, note the power reversal week: the stock is down, but it reverses to close the week sharply higher. That action says you're in for more than just a brief bounce. For our money, therefore, we'd have covered that short near 40 on the decline, or at around 45 on the rebound. However, if we had not, and were still short as the rally continued, there is a point at which we'd have stuck the position out until it resumed the downtrend. Heavy resistance overhead, starting around 65, plus the fact that no base of any sort had formed, indicated at the least that a test of the low was required; it would have been wise not to cover late in the rally. Why, then, would it not have been better to simply stick with the short all the way? The answer is that there would be no way to know whether the subsequent test of the low would be successful or not, putting pressure on you down around the 45 level as to whether to cover or not. By covering, and garnering your profit promptly when the target area is reached the first time, you free your money and avoid that potentially difficult decision, except to make the easier one of going short again as the stock got up over 60.

On the Way Down

*T*he market is an ever-changing phenomenon, and you can never recapture the brilliant trades of yesteryear. So when the bear market takes hold, it is no use crying over lost profits and all those "I could have shorted AUD at the top" excuses. Today's picture is all that counts. Fluctuations, rally attempts, oversold bounces, always come along to change the picture. We are back to the importance of perspective once again, with the added note of emphasis that what you see right now is the reality, not the vision of what might someday take place if you hope hard enough.

Because there are such pullbacks, as well as, from time to time, a genuine intervening intermediate-term contra-trend rally; because in a bear market an enormous amount of premature bargain-hunting causes frequent bounces; and because the IRS deems shorting a short-term capital gain no matter how long the position is kept open…trading the short side as opposed to investing in it is not such a bad idea. To be sure, sticking steadfastly to a successful short like Teleprompter or Coleco can ultimately prove triumphant; a case can be made for not giving up positions in such long-term weak situations because you may cover blithely but have your back turned when it bounces, and thus never get back in on

the short side again. That's a telling argument, when you've dis-
covered a stock that's ultimately going to disappear (Wang, for instance). However, it isn't easy to stay around that long, and it
takes a substantial bear market to wreak such damage. Since we
know that stocks fall rapidly in short bursts, with ensuing rallies
often giving you a chance to get back in, thinking of yourself as a
trader during such periods—and thus paying attention—will produce the properly aggressive approach.

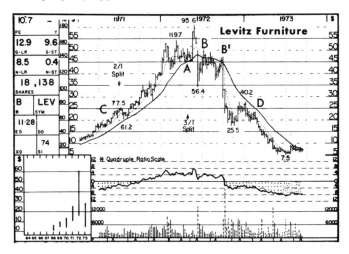

Here's another example of what we mean. Levitz sprinted from
10 to 50 in a year, and then started to move sideways as 1972 arrived, well ahead of the coming bear market. At point A it looked
as if a downside break were imminent, and many seasoned pros
went short at this juncture, figuring that LEV was unthinkably
overpriced and about to get its dumping. But Levitz, like many bull
market runaways, was not so cooperative. There's always that rise
to an excessive extreme to cap the move. The stock shot up in a
burst of frighteningly fresh energy; the shorts felt squeezed, and
their covering added buying impetus to the fling. As you can see,
the stock actually went to a new high.

To be sure, an apparent top had formed, but the stock had not
broken 45 and the Moving Average line was still rising. If you

were long, the rarefied air, in conjunction with the potential for serious trouble if LEV dropped below 45, might very well have led
you to sell out, or, at the least, to raise your protective stop to 44
7/8. But it was still too early to sell short. In this case, it wasn't
even possible to get off a perfect short at 60, for, although the
chart doesn't show it, that was when the SEC suspended trading.
But by our line of reasoning, the perfect time to short is the least
risky time, and that came later, when the 45 level was finally
breached and the Moving Average line had rolled over and headed
downward. Now that we know we're officially in a downtrend, we
look for precisely what did appear—a pullback rally to the M.A.
(B); that bounce failed when Levitz met resistance in that range of
the upper 40s, and a second similar opportunity came a few
weeks later, at point B1, when the weakness was even more evident. (Note how the volume had dried up by then.) Even if you felt
uncomfortable being short such a swinging stock, a stop just above
point B would have afforded close protection and never would
have been touched off.

A rip-roaring slide ensued and the short-seller, thinking like a
trader, could well have reasoned that a fall of 20 points, virtually in
a straight line, meant that LEV was getting due for a technical rebound. Over to the left, at point C, you can see a small area of
support. And you might also, in search of a measurable target,
take a swing measurement of the bounce from 35 back up to
point B (15 points) and subtract that from 35 when the stock
broke down again to a new low. That equals 20, which confirms
the support area, so that a reasonable target might be assumed in
the 20-25 range. That the stock smashed deep into that support
area, actually penetrating 20 for a while before bouncing, was a
solid clue that the stock was still extraordinarily weak. There would
be nothing to prevent you, as a trader, from adding to or establishing a new short position when, at point D, Levitz was failing
smack at its still descending Moving Average line (and the market,
too, as you know, was then warning of a major plunge to come).
A short sale anywhere down to the 20 level would not have been
amiss, even without the benefit of hindsight. Indeed, this is a good
example of a floor trader's truism: each trade is a new trade. Just

because that might have been the price you covered at doesn't mean it can't be a good price to re-establish a short position. As soon as 20 broke, whoosh...again.

The Jones Boys' Philosophy

*M*any years ago we learned a valuable lesson from contact with a hedge fund (a privately organized fund which is set up so that its managers can both buy and sell short) then being managed by the Jones boys, the nickname for a group of money managers led by Mr. A.W. Jones, who was considered the father of the hedge concept of trying to be long the strongest stocks and short the weakest. (Many of the hedge fund managers of the 1990s have lost track of, or never understood, that basic grounding, but have treated hedging as a license to do whatever seemed like a "hot" idea of the moment.) Late in the 1962 decline, we met someone who had access to their portfolio activities, and we asked what the Jones boys were then selling short. The answer was surprising: Brunswick Corporation. The stock was already down from 77 to 14, which seemed to us sufficient, so why were they selling it short at this low level?

The answer is twofold: first, on a simple mathematical basis, if the stock were to drop from 14 to 7, as indeed it soon did in the last stage of that bear market, wasn't that a sizable profit in and of itself, regardless of the larger decline that had already taken place? You can't go back and play that game at your convenience, but you can analyze the current situation and determine that BC at 14 looks like a good short. Second, since the stock had already fallen in that manner, it had already proven itself to be weak. Instead of trying to be brilliant by catching a strong stock just as it begins to break down, this hedge fund's tactic was to take less risk by shorting an obviously already-ravished stock. Perhaps in part this extreme attitude reflects some nervousness when dealing on the short side, therefore being more defensive than aggressive, but regardless of motivation, it works. (There is also the useful fundamental factor that once a stock becomes weak, negative news becomes more overt and available.) Stunned issues such as this are capable of producing abundant and relatively safe profits, even if close to the so-called bottom. Weak stocks become even weaker with far more consistency than they reverse and rally; weak stocks can remain weak even when the market itself reverses and rallies.

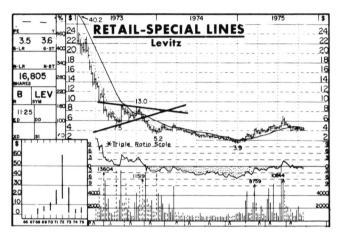

Let's go back and take another look at Levitz with this in mind. It would have been easy to apply the Jones boys' philosophy to LEV at point D, for the stock had already proven weak, was still overpriced fundamentally, had trapped a lot of now-frightened institutions at twice the price, had a still steeply descending long-term Moving Average line, had formed a small head-and-shoulders consolidation pattern above 20, and was in this precarious position at the outset of 1973, just when bear signals were being given for the entire market. Whether you had previously covered or not, this was an entirely new situation, and one well worth taking advantage of.

The chart below shows you what rewards would have been reaped had you followed that attitude in 1973 without regard for prior events. A new consolidation area emerged as a triangle between 6 and 9; you can see how, if you applied this "short the head and dying stocks" attitude, a short sale made when the stock broke out on the downside, for a price of about 6, would have reaped 2 points on a relatively fast drop to 4 (not a bad percentage play) and ultimately, if no sensible stop-loss order was touched off, to 2. By that time, the rest of the market was perking up and there were plenty of indicators that shorting was no longer suitable.

When assaying short sales during a bear decline, and looking for already weak stocks, it may be important to check the monthly reports of outstanding short positions. As discussed previously, this used to be much more significant than it now is; the stock may be of interest to arbitragers, hedgers, program traders, and whatever. What you are looking for that once was a message from overly large short positions—that is, an excess of bearishness that you don't want to be part of—is now best dealt with by being aware of media and brokerage comments. Just remember that hostility is a trait of bottoms, and while a short seller might be glad to have company so as to bolster any anxiety, the market works in just the opposite way—if everyone's bearish, everyone's *already* sold and shorted. Since you are dealing with stocks that have been severely eroded, the primary emotional aspect to be wary of is the reaction—both yours and the stock's—to bad news. Prejudiced by already being short, your instinct may be to cheer at news of another earnings deficit or a huge write-off, but if the stock fails to react to the news by falling further (it may even hold steady or actually rise instead), you are being told that the bottom has been reached and you should close out your short position.

Another Warning

*D*o not confuse what we have just described with a situation similar on the surface but entirely different in reality. We've been taking you through a bear market, a genuine primary downtrend, when you want to be short, not long (recall 1973-74). Accordingly, while you may function like a trader, covering when a rebound is due, don't chase the long side the way others do in search of bargains. Rather, let the bear-market rally come. Sit on the edge of your chair and wait for clues that it is fading, and then, only then, go short again.

During a bull market, the game is much different. Here you are, flushed with success from shorting during the previous bear, and with added profits from buying stocks as the turn upward unfolded. But now the indicators have told you that the first full-scale, intermediate-term correction of the bull market is due to arrive. The temptation is great to sell short; after all, you feel like a whiz at the game, there are stocks with evident tops appearing and/or getting stuck at resistance, plus, you remember how low they were not so very long ago. Do you act as a trader and aim for a few of those vulnerable stocks?

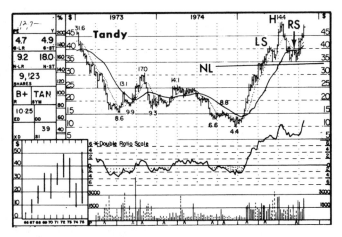

Our vote is no, not during the bull market's first correction, and probably not even when the second one arrives. Only a very short-term-oriented trader can catch fast moves in stocks as they tumble and be quick enough to cover before the whole profit vanishes on the next rebound. For the rest of us, it is simply not sensible to trade against the primary trend (and that goes, of course, for buying stocks during a primary bear market). It's the "Gerry Ford" syndrome: you can't buy and sell at the same time, so stick to trading with the underlying major trend; don't try to defy it.

The chart of Tandy is an example of what we mean. If you stick your thumb over the rally, you'll see that Tandy had formed what looks like a nearly perfect head-and-shoulders top, with the neckline at 35. Indeed, the right shoulder seemed to be unable to rally any higher, because the Moving Average line was resisting and beginning to level off. Wouldn't you be able to make a huge profit by shorting TAN, especially since (1) the market was flashing correction signals, and (2) the stock, being up fivefold, looked particularly vulnerable? Any fool can see, with the wisdom of hindsight, that such short-selling ideas ought to have waited for definitive proof via breaking the neckline at 35; people who tried to anticipate this break got badly burned. With TAN an ideal-looking situation at a correction time, you can see why it isn't safe to sell short against the major trend, especially so early in the bull market. Often, it can be the best, the strongest, stocks that develop such huge patterns; they prove to be prolonged consolidations, rather than tops; and these periods of digestion typically come midway in an entire bull move—so, worse, you may be shorting into a very strong rather than vulnerable stock.

Yes, but ...

*T*he "but" stems from those periods when you'd like to have your cake and eat it, too. That is, you see a potential correction coming, but you own certain stocks that you don't want to give up—maybe they'll be relatively untouched, maybe your long-term dreams should be respected. What's more, suppose there isn't a correction, or it is milder than expected. Why sell something that could be a big winner down the road? Well, you might be hurt if you're wrong by not selling, that's why. What's the solution?

Our answer in the original edition was to hark back to Mr. Jones: a hedge fund of your own. By going short to balance the long positions you want to keep, you are in some degree protecting yourself in the event the decline turns into something more than you expected. This notion of turning your own portfolio into a mini hedge fund is even more useful the further into an uptrend you are (as in the fall of 1972). It is also viable during those periods when the major trend is blurred, or when it looks as if a sideways course, perhaps via a wildly volatile roller-coaster ride, is in order. You'll have some longs you want to keep, and you'll want to protect those positions. In such circumstances, the short side can be effectively used to provide balance, safety, and the chance of added profits. If an investor uses hedging, holding both longs and shorts, a much more conservative portfolio can be attained than if he foolishly assumes he is being conservative simply because he is sticking with well-known blue-chip issues through hell, high water, and market declines.

In hedging's simplest style, you'll have picked longs from among the market's strongest sectors and shorts from among the weakest. In theory, if the market does rally, your longs should rise more than your shorts go against you. And if the market slides, the shorts should come to the fore profitably, while the longs rest. With a little luck, and considerable practice, you ought to have occasional triumphs when your longs go up *and* your shorts go down. But keep in mind that you want to sell short those stocks that are already under duress, and that you want to be long only those stocks that are still strong—don't ever—that's *ever*—hold stocks going into a correction because you can't bear to take a loss; that's sort of like remaining long the kind of weak stock you should be considering as short side candidates.

The advent of derivative products has changed the manner in which such a hedged portfolio can be constructed. "True" proportionate representation is not so necessary, if you use a market put option (such as the OEX), or sale of a futures contract, to hedge those stocks you want to continue to hold long. Some investors should consider selling calls against those remaining long positions. But buying a put in such a stock is too much like betting against yourself. The flaw, of course, when dealing with such derivatives, is that time works against you. These are useful "imminent" tools.

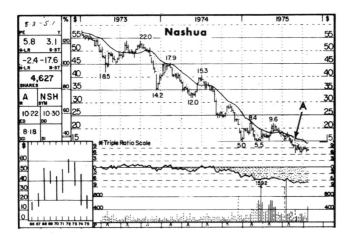

Remember: what you are basically in search of, whether long or short, is to have your money in the best possible stocks. That means those with the least risk, and the most profit potential, regardless of direction. "Best" has nothing to do with "proper" or "dignified;" it has to do only with their potential to move up or down.

The Nashua chart is an example from the same period as the previously shown Tandy chart. The market was ensnared in correction time, but because it seemed to be still early in an ongoing upward primary trend, there were bullish stocks worth holding. Indeed, after the correction had lasted several weeks, some stocks actually looked buyable while others still looked dangerous. But rather than shorting Tandy, note how much safer it would have been to short Nashua at point A. While the basic thesis is not to sell short during a primary bull market, and particularly to ignore the market's first intervening correction, as a hedged approach to portfolio management, this sort of stock would have been both safe and, as it turned out, satisfactory. The downside profit potential is nowhere near as great as an apparent top such as Tandy's would have been had TAN broken down, but the percentage play was certainly fine, from 15 down to under 11 with little risk.

The primary uptrend did indeed resume with a bang in January 1976. That was a time to be 100 percent long, but subsequently the market became very tricky, with the averages whipsawing back and forth. A number of stocks were well worth continuing to hold long, but at the same time, sound analysis said that the bull market was a year older and a lot more tired. This produced some noticeable negative group action—a bear market arrived less than a year later—so that it was possible to uncover shortable stocks with group confirmation to use as a hedge against those stocks still being held long, so that the portfolio itself was capable of rolling with the punches at all times, whether the market was whipsawing up or down.

Time and time again, the basis for playing the short side of market is weakness. On some occasions that means the completion of a major top; on others, a stock that has already proven itself in trouble over a prolonged period, especially as it fails to rally when the market does. Such failures denote more than the obvious aspect of fundamentals going sour. By the time such news becomes public knowledge, it is usually too late. Therefore, technical evidence, with its objectivity and easy availability, is the basic tool for determining when a stock's trend has changed and can continue to guide you thereafter as to whether the stock has suffered enough or is to continue in distress. Dividends may seem invitingly high, or price/earnings ratios may appear remarkably low, but the market knows best.

In 1974, Bowmar Instruments, a major player in the then red-hot pocket-calculator field, sold at 1 times earnings. That's right: 1! The price of a share was equal to its year's per-share earnings. How much lower could Bowmar possibly drop? Those who bought the issue on this premise got the answer a few weeks later when Bowmar went into bankruptcy and was delisted. Rather than being the upside speculation it seemed to be, it was the perfect short. Weakness is as weakness does, technically; believe what the market is telling you above all else.

A Brief Summary

1. Be patient. Wait for the top to be completed before taking action. Better to go short at a lower price, and know that the stock has already broken down, than to try to anticipate that it is "sure" to fall. Try to avoid being caught in a last-gasp, nerve-shattering rally.

2. The least risky time to sell short is on a pullback rally following the breakdown. Be alert for such a pullback both immediately thereafter and a few weeks later, looking for a chance to get your short off just under a rounding-over Moving Average as well as just under a resistance area.

3. Assume, because you need to sell short on an uptick, that the stock will probably go against you a bit after your order is executed.

4. Never use an "at the market" order to sell short when the stock is declining on the tape.

5. Make sure that there is a sensible place overhead to enter a protective stop order. If you sell short when the stop level is too far away, you can expect to get bagged by a bounce.

6. Don't try to be brilliant. Avoid strong stocks that look as if they're "too high." Instead, search out proven weak stocks, those whose strength is in the past, based on a clear-cut trend reversal, lower highs, and a downside break of an important level We repeat: having patience until the long-term Moving Average rolls over and starts downward is vital.

7. Do not ignore stocks just because they've fallen a lot already. There are times—corrections, hedging, a mixed trend—when stocks that are very weak are the safest shorts. They do not readily rally and still may produce sizable percentage gains on the downside.

8. Pay attention to volume on rallies. Heavy volume on the upside is a warning that the stock may be reviving in strength. Also, heavy trading on the downside, followed by an abrupt reversal upward, is often a sign that the decline is climaxing (although time is then needed for a base to form).

9. When it comes to covering your short position:

a. Always start with a protective buy stop, so that you can be taken out objectively if the market tells you you are wrong.

b. Be alert for bad news; your first reaction is "oh, isn't this terrific, boy am I going to get rich on this short," but such news usually comes near a bottom. If the bad news comes and the stock shrugs, it is telling you that all the sellers are gone and it is time for you, too, to depart.

c. Cover shorts if the market indicators reach favorable levels. No need to milk the last 1/8 from the short any more than to hang on to a stock for the last upside 1/8. A bird in the hand...

d. If a rally catches you, as it might, and reveals signs of more power than you expected, do not panic. Instead, remember that there will customarily be a test of the low. Such tests are necessary to help form a new base, and they provide you with a quieter chance to cover your short. Always assume that the test of the low will be successful. You aren't going to get the great price you could've gotten before you knew enough to cover; now that you "know" that the stock has gone down far enough, act accordingly.

e. Cover if there is a trading delay or delayed opening with more sellers than buyers. That can be a climactic occurrence.

f. Remember that you can always cover and live to go short again on the next rally. It is just as destructive to be a stubborn short as a hopeful long.

Shorting is a more difficult activity than buying stocks because, especially for the novice, the subconscious desire to be punished, to lose, to be wrong, has added to it the implication that the negative side of the market is not nice. But once your head is clear, you'll find that selling short has a nifty bonus to it: your ability to sell long is greatly enhanced. Erased will be the perennial optimism, the culturally demanded unrealistic notion of up, up, up. You'll be more on your toes. Looking for a profitable position in either direction, without prejudice, will help you spot tops in time. You'll be far more willing to step forward and sell out your long positions, and you'll constantly track the indicator clues so that your timing will be sharpened as well. And, as you take profits down near bottoms, you'll have a lot more capital to buy stocks with for the next rise.

Chapter Eleven

Self-Reliance

*I*n the period since the original edition of "When To Sell" was published, we've become more "sophisticated" about the brokerage business itself. Our market advisory letters have had institutional clients as their main audience, as compared to what is rather uncomfortably identified as "retail" clientele—by which is meant the public customer. Individuals may indeed pay "retail" commission dollars rather than "wholesale," but in reality, discounts are now the norm everywhere. So-called "discount" brokers essentially do "retail" business, and "retail" brokers even for large firms have the leeway to give preferred customers a discounted commission rate. In recent years, we've talked to an increasing number of "retail" brokers and, in fact, have reached the ultimate accommodation by marrying a "financial consultant." As a result, we have to mind our language here.

Nevertheless, we have our prejudices and, generally, view the brokerage profession with a jaundiced eye. It is true that *if* you do *all* of your own investment-digging and decision-making, you only need an order-executing relationship with a broker. Since we've been advocating the advantages of market "at the opening" orders, it logically follows that such a broker needs only minimal skills to get your orders executed properly. It is also true that there are far too many duds, lunkheads, and churners handling people's life savings. The regulatory bodies worry about those few brokers who've been cited for misbehavior and malfeasance;*we* worry about the quality of managerial supervision over brokers who mishandle accounts, *primarily via inappropriate recommendations.*

Accordingly, it is equally true that you should search out, and reward, any broker who gives you fresh, fruitful, and forward-looking
ideas, that are suitable to you, personally. Such a broker should
provide the kind of service that you need in all respects: advice,
overview planning, forthright dealing with market-generated problems. We think it would be unusual indeed if a *good* "full-service"
broker wouldn't be well worth the commission paid to have someone watching your portfolio while you're on vacation, phoning immediately about a stock you're interested or involved in, and also,
yes, holding your hand when the market's in trouble and you
didn't sell enough. You pay for someone not only to properly execute an order, but to be there for you, providing service even during times when you aren't actually doing business. Do you call
your doctor when you aren't feeling well? Or do you believe you
have to wait until you're really sick? That's the kind of relationship
you want to have with your broker.

That speech having been made, it is clear that finding such
"brokers" is not easy—it is harder than finding an appropriately
dependable doctor or lawyer. (Referrals from people you know
who have found such a broker is usually the best way. If you are in
search, you can also call the office manager of nearby firms, describe the kind of broker you feel you personally would relate to
well, and interview their recommendations.) Brokers are not the
savants their television commercials would have you believe, nor
are they as foresighted as the number of times they are quoted in
the newspapers would suggest. You deal with a particular firm not
for its overall name recognition but (a) because that's where you've
found a good broker; (b) the firm's research (including technician
and strategist) works for you; and (c) that firm's back-office makes
few if any aggravating record-keeping mistakes. Some brokers are
particularly skillful at trading, others quite capable of digging up
special situations, still others at helping structure a client's financial
assets into a long-range investment plan, but it's hard for any one
individual to be all things to all people. Over the past decade, the
typical broker has gradually handed over the stock-picking/deci-
sion-making process to mutual fund managers, recommending a
selection of funds in the name of that cop-out word diversification,

or by hawking the brokerage firm's stock-of-the-week kind of conventional idea, always on the buy side of course. In the nineties that has resulted in too many brokers who know next to nothing about individual stocks any more; too many, in fact, know nothing about how the market fluctuates, or have ever experienced a genuine gut-wrenching bear market. But a broker's ignorance or youthful inexperience is not the most discouraging aspect of the broker-customer relationship. There are many good brokers out there. It is the nature of the business itself that can truly hurt.

Brokerage firms are merchandisers, like any storekeepers who have to turn over inventory to make a profit. They market their products with the best of intentions (most of the time), reflecting the conventional wisdom of the day before (when you've learned that the market anticipates), and "only" get greedy near the end of major moves (when the burn rate will prove to be the greatest). An individual broker doesn't have those goods on the shelf the way a grocer does, for his income is based on commissions; but he doesn't get a commission unless the goods move. It's against SEC regulations for a broker or mutual fund manager to charge fees pegged to a percentage of generated market profits (this is not true, by the way, for managers of commodity portfolios or private hedge funds), and no firm pays a regular salary to its sales force unless it is commensurate with the degree of commission business being written. A broker may have it in his heart to do right, but he also has to feed his family. A broker swears he'll be forthright with his customers, but when a client calls up and wants to buy General Motors, can he tell him it's not the right time when, in a tricky game like Wall Street, the customer might prove to be correct? Or, should he call up that client and, fearing worse, advise taking a loss when the vagaries of the marketplace might cause that stock to rally the very next day? How can he afford to tell his clients, "This market is weak, sell everything," when, first, they'll be taking losses in stocks he put them in, and, second, if they sit on the sidelines, perhaps for months, there won't be any income, no matter how right he may be, and they might then leave him to go with a broker who promises more action, who swears he can beat the bear. Even the best of brokers tend to be affected by a need to find the exceptions to buy, while the great mass of brokers can become stubborn, panicked, prayerful, over-exuberant or paralyzed, all with your money.

It's not easy. It is stressful. And then, of course, employers demand production. Although there is just as big a commission dollar involved, brokerage firms seem never to issue genuine selling advice...unless, that is, it comes after the stock has already tumbled so badly they finally have become frightened. All of this is too bland, too careful, as if the broker is Casper Milquetoast of historic cartoon fame. This is where you and your broker have to do some work together—better by far, if the broker is any good, than trying to do it in isolation just to save a few bucks in commissions. Keep in mind that fundamental analysts and the stock market do not have a direct link. Brokers' consciences are soothed by semantic salves. If you learn to read between the lines, you'll realize that the words "fully valued" really mean that if the firm's analyst had it in his own account, he'd sell. Ratings become a statistical recourse—downgrading from "buy" to "above average" contains a message that something's not so right any more—caveat emptor, hidden within a "don't worry, we're still positive" appearance. And besides, they say that although the stock is expected to go down "over the short term," it's still a great buy for the long pull—a form of eating one's cake, and having it, too. Even though admitting that there will be a built-in loss at first, the brokerage firm wants you to buy now, instead of waiting for the bottom, because that commission is needed now, or, perhaps, because they fear missing the bottom when it comes. A lawyer can tell you what the law is, and stand by that advice; a doctor can analyze your symptoms and be specific about what ails you. Either might be wrong, of course, but they have limited alternatives, and direct experience to rely on. But a broker has a much greater and often much more blurred playing field to consider—choices of what to do and when to do it and for how long. This is an "ongoing auction market" for which, compared to the years of education for other professionals, he is much less trained or experienced. Even a guru can run into a period of market behavior that is stressful and difficult and unclear; at such times training and education—of great resource to doctors or lawyers—may do no good whatsoever on Wall Street...only street smarts may help. The best of brokers try to overcome such problems, and know whereof they speak, but many others, although having the appearance of "professionals," really are just salespersons, and do what the firm itself wants them to do.

We could carry on at great length about the tragicomic aspects of expert advice from the brokerage community, but no doubt you've experienced just about all of it at one time or another. There is no simple solution, no broker with a Midas touch. If you are doing business with a big firm, you do want to beware of being pitched to buy the firm's idea of the week, or new issues of mutual or closed-end funds sponsored by the firm itself, or a secondary offering "at no commission"—anything that smacks of an inside promotion being peddled rather than being a recommendation particularly suited to you as an individual. The best brokers at such firms don't treat such products as automatic sales pitches, are often on the outs with the sales manager, but know enough, and do enough business to be tolerated; if you can find such a broker, you then get all of the many resources that are positive about doing business with such firms. We've also found that the big producers at such firms—the so-called "million-dollar" producers—are too busy and too conceited to qualify as anyone we'd give an order to; they don't have time to be sensitive to what the market is doing, and the money-success has made them so egotistical that they think they know something...usually superficial catch phrases from glancing at Business Week while watching the Sunday football game. Brokers often join smaller firms so as to get some independence from a big firm's product-pressure, but then they must be "good" stock pickers on their own.

The customer's man (a quaint old "title" that encompasses both men and women nowadays) you must find, and settle in with, is not a genius who will be dead wrong during the next market cycle, or a hot shot who will blow sky high as soon as the market turns, but a broker who fully understands your particular investment philosophy, has other accounts with similar interests (so you won't be an odd client), and certainly needs to have experienced both bull and bear markets so that he, or she, knows the difference. (Investors should avoid a broker with active trading accounts; traders, however, need someone capable of perspective.) Such a broker needs to be able to stir up the courage to phone you with bad news, so it can be dealt with promptly rather than swept under the rug, and he should, from time to time, actually phone to comment on the health of your portfolio or even to ask about your health, without asking for an order. Let him know you, what you want to do, how you want to exist, and the kinds of moments when your instincts are apt to be right (or wrong). A broker who understands you as a customer can truly be the "financial consultant" that title proclaims him, or her, to be, both in the broad planning sense and in looking out for your interests while sitting there watching the game play out directly in front of him on the tape and desktop machine. How do you then profit in the stock market? Well, the rest is up to you.

Patience, Perspective, Failure

The more we learn, and live through, in the stock market, the more we are convinced that success can be summed up in three words: patience, perspective, and, unfortunately for alliteration, failure.

First, patience. The market, it can be said, acts more slowly than any person believes it will, and takes its own time getting to where it wants to go even though along the way each day may seem so volatile that it "feels" speeded up. How many times do we wake up thinking, "Today's the day," when hope alone is involved? Cycles last longer, trends last longer, even short-term rallies and selloffs last longer than expected because humans are so impatient. Our impatience is tied to our dreams and our fears. The net result is that investors tend to think a decline is over much before it really is, and they buy too soon. Similarly, so worried are they about any gains they may have, they think a rise is over before it really is, and they sell too soon. This is especially true when recent performances have made the investor impatient for what he has become familiar with; a bear market gets him in tune with selling and selling short, so when the bull comes along he is still thinking too bearishly and is anxious to jump on the sell side— much too soon.

Later, of course, the painful past is forgotten, and lethargy sets in. Everything has turned out okay; you've survived; the market is rising again. Patience evolves past complacency into paralysis. The investor becomes akin to a bureaucrat: when first taking the job the civil servant is eager to get things done and acts too quickly. Learning that lesson, he determines to wait patiently, trying to fulfill his job slowly but surely, until finally, with little to show for the years put in, the bureaucrat decides that perhaps it is better to do nothing at all. The proper moment has already gone by.

Can these twin foes of impatience and paralysis be combated? In our opinion, no one (except the professional trader) should be playing an in-and-out game. It is easy to be right for 1/8s and 1/4s, but impossible to profit thereby over any stretch of time. One loss tends to wipe out three or four small gains, so you are constantly forced to start all over again, until you have a portfolio full of those losers, and none of the gainers. Any reader of this book should be aiming for the bigger swings of intermediate-term trends. That, of course, requires the patience to sit through intervening shorter-term fluctuations. The only way to do that is to make sure you accept in advance that you are going to have to endure days when your stock will go down and that once in a while you'll wind up with a loss that wasn't a loss earlier in the move. Sometimes such losses will stem from your own mistakes, at other times from the vagaries of the market; in any event, they will, we believe, be offset considerably by the much greater profits made by letting other stronger stocks run their course. Then, when you finally do begin to see, and not merely anticipate seeing, tops form and trend lines break, you must act so that paralysis doesn't take over. The most dangerous cry is: "Let's watch it one more day."

Two tools will help: first, give priority to weekly charts rather than to daily ones (which should be used more for timing exactly when to act); perhaps that should be phrased as "believe the weekly chart rather than the daily when they differ; act when they agree." Second, attend to the longer-term Moving Averages. We've found no consistent reliability for ten-week (or less) M.A.'s, which tend to feed impatience, but there are considerable virtues to the thirty-week or forty-week (200-day) Moving Average lines, especially in keeping you from acting too soon, but forcing you to act before it is too late. All the machines on all of those broker and money manager desks and all of the readings available to them have tended to turn frustrations into a shorter and shorter-term attitude as if in-and-out trading is the answer to dealing with the problems of a difficult market. But they are, in a sense, playing with the pieces at the beginning of a chess game, when all sorts of moves seem sensible, and the dangers two or three moves later unforeseen. Use the daily charts for timing, but frame them within the readings that require patience, such as the weekly charts, the longer-term moving averages, indicator and price extremes. These tools, as you have probably already noticed, lead right into our second key word: perspective.

Obviously, longer-term charts, with related longer-term Moving Averages can provide visual pictures of great help in terms of perspective. You'll see, for example, how far a stock has fallen, if it has held in that area before, how big a base it has built, how much it has already bounced, how long that rise has gone without a correction, and if the move has had the scope to pull the Moving Average along with it or has been against the M.A.'s definition of the underlying trend. A glance at such a chart, therefore, can answer the simplest yet most important question of all: Where, in its cycle, is the stock at that very moment?

You also need to gain the perspective that the various indicators provide. Sure, the stocks tell it all, but it is too easy to look at them through subjective eyes; indicators have unassailable statistics that will provide a check—answering such unasked questions as, should I really be complacent about this particular stock when the market is so overbought? As we've shown, you don't need a million different indicators. You do need to spend a little time every week to follow those that have good historical track records, because they will show you what is reasonable to expect and what is sheer hope. If several important indicators have readings in their warning zones, you have the perspective to combat what will then be widespread optimism. Conversely, there will be times when a ton of bearish sentiment isn't matched by the readings of the indicators (the days just before Desert Storm in early January 1991 being a great example), so you'll grasp that it is not a good time to sell—which is, after all, as important as knowing when to sell.

In addition to charts and indicators, there is a third aspect to perspective. It is vital to remember that selling is not the reverse of buying. That is the basic error fundamentalists make. They often reason that, having analyzed a company and ascertained that there are satisfactory fundamental reasons for owning that stock, they will also be able to apply the same approach to spotting when to sell. But stocks are often—quite often, indeed—screaming buys based on valuations, especially near the bottom of a bear market, when no one wants to ever buy a stock again, so hysterically bearish have they become. Only the technician, seeing the indicators begin to turn, and the individual stock charts begin to improve, can overcome emotion and buy. Thereafter, the fundamentalist, after the stock has started to re-rise and there is evidence that the company, the industry, the economy, is doing better, no longer fears to put his money on the line, but gets increasingly bullish as the upward path continues, and therefore over-confidently believes that when something begins to go wrong he'll see it. He might—but no more will he believe it than he believed in the valuation case at the bottom. A great example recently occurred as we were rewriting these very pages, when Cheyenne Software was cut in half (16 to 8) overnight on news that analysts already knew! There was a well-known, and totally tolerated, back-up in inventory at the distributor level, but this sign of slowing business was excused because "Cheyenne was a growth stock." But the chart knew what the fundamentalists refused to admit to: that the market didn't like such a lack of growth!

There are also—as part of the way the market works at tops— times to sell that come for reasons that at least on the surface have little directly to do with corporate fundamentals: "All the good news is out" is fundamental stuff, but it is also an opinion that motivates sellers; or perhaps everyone who wants to buy has already bought; or those with great profits are simply waiting for the next "blow-out" earnings report as the opportunity to take their profits in a big block while there are still plenty of buyers around; or when it is perceived that the industry is fading from fashion; or when the rest of the market has become so toppy, and bearish, it pulls even good stocks down with it. But underneath all of this is the perception on the part of holders—no matter where or how that perception is derived—that the fundamentals are shifting. That doesn't mean they become bad, but only that, perhaps, the rate of growth has ebbed for simple mathematical reasons, or a product is delayed in introduction, or a competitor has announced something new. A few insiders may know, but the brokerage firm's fundamental analyst may not spot the shift quickly or may dismiss it as merely temporary—not understanding, perhaps not even considering, how buyers and sellers might react. Time and time again, the stock is clearly forming a top and the "neckline" is broken, with the price collapsing, when bad news is announced. So who was doing all that selling to make the top, and what did they know, and when did they know it, and how did they know it? You can base your buying on a combination of fundamentals and technicals. The fundamentals may help you make a choice between candidates, but *you must sell when the technicals say so, regardless of the "known" fundamentals.* That's where perspective comes in.

But what are we talking about when we say you must sell? Our third key word is, you'll recall, failure. The more we toil in the marketplace, the more convinced we are that, of all systems, the only guide that works consistently is the notion of failure. It won't—obviously, it can't—catch the top 1/8, but it will be close enough and it is clear enough so as never to be missed. Believing it is the problem, not seeing it.

You may recall the Sherlock Holmes story about the dog that didn't bark, when the dog might reasonably have been expected to. Wall Street's equivalent is the hitherto strong stock that fails to make a new high when it ought to have done so. Is that all? Is life so simple? Of course not. You have no perspective, in terms of time, when a stock fails to make a new high in the course of its uptrend. Suppose it is merely resting? Suppose, after you become bothered, it goes on to make a new high a week or two later? Myriads of investors cling to stocks long after they should have been sold precisely because of such supposes. The failure doesn't come from that single aspect; more is required, but the first failure is the "acorn" from which mighty tops can grow. Suppose after failing to make a new high, the stock also fails on the downside by dropping below the level which had previously held, thus making a lower low after having made a lower high. *That's failure.*

The longer a trend has been in existence, the more significant any failure is. The first failure will seem trivial, no big deal, but may eventually prove the equivalent of "The Princess and the Pea." By having a clear sense of where you are in a cycle (perspective), you will be able to judge small failures more objectively. Knowing that a stock has been rising for a prolonged period, small failures become an important alert that the stock's uptrend may be beginning to end. Once the stock has ceased doing what was expected of it, hope is being replaced by the reality of failure.

A Last Word

*T*he one thing we can guarantee is that none of this is easy. Just try to walk that fine line between not selling too soon and not procrastinating one day too long! Any time any one of us, from professional trader to odd-lotter, can boast of taking a profit, we have done something right. Luck is a mere bonus. What was right, simply put, was that a stock was bought cheap and sold dear. But don't let anyone claim that the two halves of the act are equally easy. Only someone who has never played the market game would believe that.

We've maintained throughout that it is only after a stock is bought that the hard-core intrigue, subtlety, and treachery of the market come into play. All you have to do is take a loss once in a stock that otherwise looked flawless, made perfect sense, and perhaps even went shooting up temporarily after you bought it, to know how infinitely difficult the market can be. As in any challenging game, the contestant has to be prepared to answer both to the mood of the market and to his own personal capabilities.

More than anything else, it is this inner struggle that distinguishes the act of selling. For, as our partnership with a stock, selected from among thousands and bought in the bloom of innocence, grows older, a parade of complications—guilt, greed, potency, paranoia, anxiety—start marching across the tape of the mind. Investment in the stock market is also an investment in the ego. Turning money into inner work is an old trick of psychiatry: if the price of treatment is high enough, the patient will waste no time in coming to the point. In the stock market, however, the participant is not sent a bill for his mental travail. That day of reckoning comes only when shares are sold and converted back into money, more of it or less of it than when the contract was entered into. No wonder many people don't face their losses until it is too late! How much more pleasant life would be if we never had to face an ego loss.

But the market as a mirror of life shows us such crises to our faces. It has its ups and downs, a suspect past and an uncertain future; it reminds us, every day, what the latest price measurement is, pumps up our hopes that the next day will be saving or rewarding. Thus the agenda on every page of this text has been how to make the selling decision as objectively as possible.

Can it be done at all? There are those who believe it's all random, unforeseeable—"who knows what the market is going to do?" How come we, and those we consider our peers, have been doing it, not perfectly, but well enough often enough? The naysayers want us to be perfect, or it doesn't count, when all we can strive for is a high enough batting average. There are indicators that tell us when the general run of emotions has gotten beyond reasonable limits, which mean we should count ourselves out. There are indicators that remind us of our own emotions so we can check them against the facts. We have emphasized the special mental conditions wherein hope can be modified by practicality, dreams can be superseded by reality, and fear can be translated into action. And short of being able to wire yourself to a listener who would make more objective judgments, we've detailed the basic methods whereby you can handle your stock ownership in an objective, and thereby ultimately profitable, manner. Anyone who repeatedly uses the market as an arena for an emotional contest is destined to lose, because that is the definition of neurosis itself: a means of repeating failure in a socially acceptable way. Loss in the stock market is, please note, explainable to one's peers, a white collar means of gambling, a place where ego can play the game and shrug if defeated—"Who knows what the market's dice are going to roll?"

No matter how we may try to relate to it, the stock market is a "thing" and things do not listen. But if it will not be a party to our desires, as a thing it can be measured, weighed, and analyzed. As a game, it has odds and strategies. As mass psychology, it can be tabulated. All these are significant ways of keeping emotion at bay, and thus, creating some sort of order out of what seems to others chaos.

Yet emotional shackles are not readily broken. Our minds do not come equipped with doors to lock out hopes and dreams, even if we identify them as such and have charts and graphs to help us. So we must make allowance for their presence. For most, the hardest mental conditioning will come in admitting to losses. "What won't go up must come down" is a sensible market variation on the law of gravity, so learning to recognize positions which show little prospect for gain must be accompanied by the ability to dispose of such positions with the least amount of fuss. Hand in hand with this goes the discipline of not berating oneself for honest mistakes, for doing what seemed objectively sensible at the time, even if the future's inputs changed the appearance into something different, requiring a fresh decision.

Interestingly, we play the stock market because, although other games may have close to even odds, in the stock market risk and reward ratios heavily favorable to the player are often available. If/when they are not, the bets can be modest, hedged, or sidestepped. And if the bet turns sour, the bulk of it can be retrieved.

(Try that at the track or blackjack table!) And the stock market is capable of huge variation. If we don't like, or are baffled by, today's game, we can come back next week or next month when the picture is different. Also, bets can be placed at any given time, even on a "horse" that has already proven itself far ahead of the field. And whatever the players know can be observed, because they must buy and sell to profit on what they know, so that everyone's cards are always on the table. It's sometimes dull, but never boring; and even when it's dull, we're learning something. This paean could go on, but let's interrupt it with these words once again: All these attributes will do you no good unless you know when and how to close out your position.

The buying is easy, and there are plenty of people willing to help you. But when it comes to selling, you are on your own. No excuses, no apologies, no injuries or "bad luck" or house odds against you. The decision, including the decision to do nothing, is entirely up to you. Tomorrow's game will start where yesterday's left off, and it will be the solitary burden of the seller to call his own shots.

Appendix

As an addenda to this edition, we'd like to present some real
time chart analysis of both IBM and Philip Morris to illustrate
what has been described in this book. The following discussions
are reproduced directly from our weekly advisory Letters. (A few
irrelevant asides, pertinent to that moment but not to the analysis,
have been 'whited out' where we felt the references might confuse
and distract.) Our first long analysis of International Business Machines, written on June 23, 1991, evidently referred to something
the then IBM Chairman Akers did or said or both. (You may remember, but we can't, and it isn't important enough to look up.)
Chapter Nine shows a chart of IBM as part of our discussion of
identifying individual stock tops; big Blue's peak of 360 at that
time is the same peak (split adjusted) of 90 identified with the first
wave number 5 in January 1973. Also note our squeamish forecast that "before this century is over, IBM will sell in the 60s..."
Hah!

June 23, 1991

WHAT DID THEY KNOW?
and
WHEN DID THEY KNOW IT?

One of the mysteries of how the market works is that no one
seems to know anything, and yet a top forms. Someone had to be
selling, but only the chart "knows." No one had an inkling about
Columbia Gas—except that the stock had been in bad shape for
weeks, often being blamed for, and used to excuse, the DJU's

leading-indicator warnings, and then it fell sharply for several days in succession (from 40 to 34 1/4). Someone knew. If an analyst found out, by dint of doing his or her job well, it's the SEC's fault that investors weren't warned at 40 instead of after the gap; their 'Ray Dirks' rules lead to more, not less, "inside" information being spread, so that someone trying to get in a mother-in-law's good graces by tipping her off may get caught while those who obviously did know bad news was coming are revealed only on the chart.

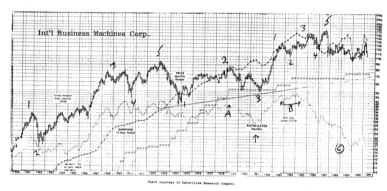

Chart courtesy of Securities Research Company.

And when, we wonder, did Mr. Akers learn? Who gave him some "inside" information? Was he let in on the IBM news-to-come while the stock was at 139 as the *Wall Street Journal* printed its now famous effusive praise about "the king is back"—or was it later, as the stock gave advance warning that something was wrong, as it tried to hold around 128 for several days? And what is there about Wall Street's persona that it doesn't want to know, even after it is told, and wants to buy even now, as Mr. Akers himself makes public what someone(s) knew 30-40 points higher: "some of our people do not understand that they have a deeply personal stake in *declining market share, revenue and profits.*" Has any analyst ever put it better *after the stock is already down 35 percent*?

Wall Street's a funny place. Everyone wants to know in advance...but there's a reluctance to believe until there's some pain. How many times have investors, like battered wives, accepted apologies and believed in promises of future good behavior from Caterpillar and Raychem? Prices of stocks that are topping out after having had great runs are viewed as "cheap" when they sell off...but emerging stocks are considered "over-valued" as they start up out of bases. Unowned stocks might as well be from alien races, but stocks in one's portfolio are like relatives—even if they are overweight and wheezing, they're thought of fondly.

As a result, a down IBM becomes a popular recommendation. "After all," goes the cliché, "it's a chance to buy IBM at a 5 percent yield." Why IBM? If one wants to invest for yield, would the broker recommend an electric utility with the same deteriorating earnings? Ah, it's a "growth" stock with a yield...a description that resembles a mermaid out of water. The last time analysts were recommending that odd combination was Burroughs around 35. This is not funny; to bolster the stock price, the newspaper reports that IBM is considering raising the dividend. How many stocks do you continue to own when a rising yield gets out of line with declining earnings?

What about the argument that "it's still IBM, so when they get their act together"—which is why Chairman A. sent his sure-to-be-publicized memo around *before* the conference call with analysts—"it'll resume its growth." This is analysis by reputation, sort of like voting for Reggie Jackson for the all-star game. Among the 117 analysts who follow IBM, is there one who could make a case that the long-term prospects for IBM are better now than the case that was made the last time little Big Blue traded under par?

Most importantly, what about the chart? Is that a quadruple bottom forming? How about a chart version of the "three steps and stumble" rule? The super-long-term chart shows the days when IBM *was* indeed super. The stock price climbed from under $4 (adjusted) in the mid-1950s to leadership of the "Nifty Fifty" top in January 1973. The '73-'74 bear market produced a severe decline and—as with the Dow itself—IBM went sideways for years thereafter, took a tumble (but successfully held above the '74 low) during the 1981-82 bear market until it burst out to another new high in conjunction with the extraordinary bull market that followed. This history can be summarized in two phases: phase one was the remarkable growth era as IBM took over market leadership (from Du Pont) and never needed to be sold (that's hindsight, of course) despite several bear markets along the way. The second phase began at the January '73 high; for the next fourteen years—until the '87 Crash—IBM may have seemed to be the leader, but in actuality it led, like a politician, by joining the crowd; its action mirrored the DJIA's.

If phase one is youthful vigor, and phase two a well-behaved white-shirted middle age, then it is easy to dub the current phase three as old age, replete with ailments and aches that take longer and longer to heal. IBM's price peak came in the last vain moments before the Crash of '87. As is invariably the case, subsequent chart action then makes prior action look like part of the same top, so that on this super-long-term chart we can see the super head-and-shoulders pattern vividly—with the left shoulder starting at the technology rally peak in mid-83, and post-crash action proving to be the right shoulder. Viewed this way, a hypothetical neckline was broken last year on the plunge under par, was followed by a pullback rally, and now by this renewal of the downtrend. *Pattern aside, the entire period from 1983 to today begins as loss of momentum, becomes a top, and then turns into a very clear downtrend.* These are standard sequences: old age, and weakening, come to all.

Added evidence of this long-term sequence of phases comes from a calculation of *relative strength*—IBM's price vs. that of the DJIA itself, as calculated in the *SRC "Green" book* by what they call a "Ratio-cator (arrow)." In this form, IBM leads the DJIA to a momentum peak in 1979 (A), followed by *a final peak as the left shoulder* (and not the crash head) is being made (B). Its subsequent under performance (C) is dramatically steep—and yet the stock is still over-owned!

Note that there is no worthwhile support until one gets back into the trading range area of the 1970s. We've drawn in a trendline connecting the two previous major lows and it intersects around 68. Measuring the entire head-and-shoulders pattern yields a Data General target. But if one measures the recent toppy action—that is, from the peak at 139 to the 100 level, which approximates the (theoretical) neckline—and then subtracts those 39 points from 100, the target becomes 61. Such specific numbers are not as important as knowing that *IBM's downside target is somewhere in the neighborhood of the trendline confirmed by also being where the next, and major, support is.* We'll bet that before this century is over, IBM will sell in the 60s the way it is now dipping into the 90s. If IBM, as this long-term analysis insists, has lost its connection with market leadership, then such a decline on its own, no matter what the DJIA does, would be but a variation on the Wang and Burroughs life spans.

Why can't it hold above 96 as it has held before? Any "chart" argument that it is okay to buy IBM down here because it has held three times already (at 93 in December '89, and 96 in both August and October of '90), must resort to the daily chart, because on the long-term chart that kind of holding looks like no more than a couple of pimples. (Compare those dips with the genuine holdings of 1974 and 1982.) An attempt to start holding, and a bargain-hunting bounce toward 108 has been followed by this fizzle, leaving overhead a minor downtrend line *and* an intermediate-sized line from the top both of which would interfere with any rebound at around the 104-105 level. *But there isn't much more to say.* Maybe it'll hold for a while. Can IBM survive above 96 during the kind of modest 10 percent market correction the consensus is willing to accept? Perhaps if we felt less grumpy about the entire market climate we wouldn't sound so stark. But we've seen

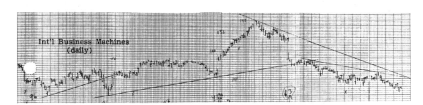

charts like this before, in less symbolic names, and lows such as those three we've already seen, plus the current attempt, eventually do not hold...all the more so when there are plenty of sellers overhead. *Buyable lows come on bad news when all the sellers are scared out.* See Travellers at 11, for example.) Wire house analysts finally cut their ratings to "3 or 4," giving up at a low instead of trying to find something good to say about the company. Even more realistic earnings forecasts of $5 to $7.50 per share draw squeamish conclusions—after all, it's IBM and apple pie. But potential sellers have not been scared out—they own too many shares *to get out.* IBM still has an enormous outstanding investment position that holders can't sell all at once—even a single holder would have trouble—so that scaling out into rebounds will become the rule, "watch out be low" will become the anxiety, and "who needs to be overweighted in this XqhrZyt?" will become the slogan.

At the outset of 1993, our first *Mamis Letter* for Hancock Institutional Equity Services (dated Jan. 3, 1993) included a follow-up commentary about IBM. Unfortunately, it doesn't reproduce as clearly as a machine-made chart would, but that's our own daily chart in the Letter, posted on semi-log paper with a sharp pencil and a ruler kept handy.

The worst of such bargain-hunting is in what superficially gets called "buying good stocks that are down"—otherwise known as the "how can you go wrong with IBM" syndrome. We see a number of charts that remind us, uncomfortably, of how IBM was trading several months ago. You may remember—we'll never forget, although the *Wall Street Journal* probably has—their marvelous headline about "The King Is Back" which top-ticked IBM at its recovery high of 140.

Having tumbled from its all-time high to just under par during the Kuwaiti bear market, that grand rush back up seemed like a bargain-hunter's dream. *Warning #1 of the IBM syndrome,* therefore, is the way it peaked amidst such headlined genuflecting—no top formation, no distribution...just a failing rally. IBM's demise was easily identified as the stock broke down and proceed to plunge through support. Don't tolerate such behavior: *good stocks*

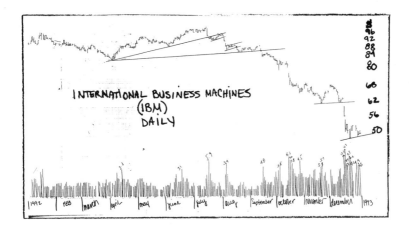

don't collapse on a tick; those that do prove to be only fluff-filled contra-trend retracements.

Warning #2 comes from the "lovely" head-and-shoulders base IBM appeared to be making in the fall of '91. Notice how IBM started up across the putative neckline—and died. We've seen a lot of such "breakouts" lately; the stock kind of oozes up, on no increase in volume, and by its own action denies that it was a real breakout. This is when volume, or lack of volume, is vital to track. But the apparent price rise breeds complacency, so you draw in another line, and say "it's still okay"—until it isn't.

After that failure just over par, IBM drifted down again, with bargain hunters eager to buy—and to recommend to the public—what had become a "yield" stock. "How can you go wrong with IBM when it yields more than T-Bills?" For all of the pleading, IBM didn't get sufficiently oversold until it got to 82 last April, when it did then actually begin, to bounce: the chart shows a series of higher highs and higher lows. Indeed, on the way back up it actually "broke out" across its intermediate-term downtrend line. But there isn't much more to this story. The chart look is that of an untextbook-like upward (bearish) flag—elongated (as a flag pattern is not), extended over time (as a flag pattern is not), but nevertheless looking like a flag as IBM recovered against the underlying trend. *Flags come from bargain-hunting*, from wanting to own a stock by name rather than from "knowing" fundamental change or value, and so there is little life to the formation, and less chance of success, but up the stock goes for a while nevertheless. And then when it dips, bulls point out "all that support" that seems to exist underneath. Smaller, more properly textbook-looking, flags appear, but the stock collapses: uptrend lines break, with "high volume on down days"—to quote a fax on IBM we sent out on August 6.

Thus *Warning #3 of the IBM syndrome is the confusion of a fluctuation back up with a long-term change in trend.*

A few months later, we wrote in detail about Philip Morris as an example of aging gigolos capable of seducing investors.

May 3, 1993

AGING GIGOLOS

The morals of Philip Morris: Section A (as marked off on this weekly *Mansfield* chart) is simple stuff—the 1991 rise, beginning with the "right shoulder" end of the Kuwaiti bear market. Each consolidation/correction along the way was followed by a higher high; each pullback made a higher low. The third in this sequence (B) followed the January '92 new high, culminating five months later in a more severe roll-over and decline to 70. This first "warning" break created a sense of loss of momentum, and MO coulda/shoulda failed on the next rebound, but that, of course, would have been too easy and too obvious. Objectively speaking, its long-term Moving Average line was still heading upward; the sequence of higher lows was intact, and so Phillip Morris proceeded to blow through to yet another all-time high (C).

This seemingly easy rise often happens near an end, when investors have become "assured" that the stock will *always* come back up after profit-taking bouts, and therefore decide to hold or even buy more. With that over-confidence in place, the second whack (D) became easy to tolerate. The "market" was blamed (that's the October 5th low), with MO backing down only to about 74, so that the pattern of higher lows remained intact.

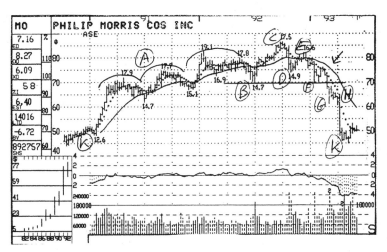

Ah... But... The next rally (E) was, finally, feeble, breaking the pattern by failing to make a new high. "Oh, that's okay," those who bought the dip reassure themselves; at worst they may have to tolerate yet another sideways consolidation before the advance resumes. How does anyone know it won't? there's only that first is-that-really-lipstick-on-his-collar? failure—but nothing convincing enough to give up on such a beloved stock...until the unsettling second failure (F)—a lower low to go with the lower high as MO slides through 74 to 70. Since MO held at that "support" level before, and even though the Marlboro problem was already in the newspapers, the bulls use a Mary Jo-style denial, insisting that the stock "hasn't really done anything wrong."

And it hasn't. The bears can only grunt: "Now we can draw in a *potential* neckline across 70." *But:* The long-term moving average line has rolled over and is finally heading downward. "Sell on a rally..." (which is what we wrote then) becomes a glib remark about a stock that has begun to show feeble rebounds and increasing vulnerability. It took six quarters to get to the high at 87; it took 'only' four months to get to this point of visible deterioration. *This is how the new high, and the process of getting there, ultimately lulls investors just as the stock finally begins to fail and roll over. The "feel" has changed, and the deception becomes the briefness and recentness, and ultimately, the abruptness, of the failures compared to the big uptrend.*

"Curses, foiled again." MO impolitely breaks without even waiting around for more than a minimal right shoulder to form. [*Note:* the consequence (arrow) of the now downtrending M. A. line and the feeble rally to overhead resistance marked the ideal "When to Sell" point.] The top is officially completed when the neckline at 70 breaks (G). A measurement of what has become a major top—the 17 points of 87 to 70, subtracted from the breakdown level of 70—yields a target of 53, which turned out to be the approximate level at which the specialist was finally able to open Philip Morris on its "surprise" news. The stock had become so weak that it couldn't even muster (H) a standard rebound back toward the breakdown point—few buyers, easily renewed weakness; was the news such a surprise? And then, of course, MO caved in again, all the way back down—amazing!—to the same mid-40s price it reached at the Kuwaiti bottom (K).

The morals of this tale: 1. Don't be lulled by a new high. 2. Failure is the key word in all chart analysis. 3. The purpose of charts is to point out such failures, not to be perfect. 4. In contrast to the conventional wisdom of "I can't afford to let them go up without me," this kind of action shows that you can, and ought to, because the portfolio costs of "all going down together" are too great. In the long run, preservation of capital *always* makes for out-performance. The portfolio manager and/or grumpy technician who berated himself for selling too soon, or making a fuss too early, is ultimately vindicated many more times than not. 5. A combination of over-owned and big profits can be deadly once a stock becomes a sale. 6. All rises are finite. (All declines are not, unless you include Wang-like ends as comparable to MO-like tops.) 7. All tops may be different, one from another, but in the end they all consist of three elements: (a) the positive rise that *gradually* loses momentum; (b) the high area that seems to maintain the uptrend but is actually distribution; and (c) the speeded-up process of failing that begins as yet another 'buy the dip' decline.

This theme of "aging gigolos" continued with a further discussion of IBM. You'll note that at this time IBM had come down to what looked like a holding, and perhaps even a base forming. We were, however, premature; it was only part of a base that actually required much more time and work.

Our Old Friend IBM: *another leading seducer.* Its top was long ago discussed in great detail. Now the stock wants to go higher, so the question has become, *what kind of base has IBM formed?* The bullish case, beyond a summer romance, begins with recalling the huge and panicky volume that developed on the initial plunge under 50. Such high volume dumping (as happened to the market on August 23, 1990) is typical of a left shoulder of a head-and-shoulders bottom, and in turn is customarily followed (because so much selling has already been done) by a bigger than expected but ultimately failing rebound.

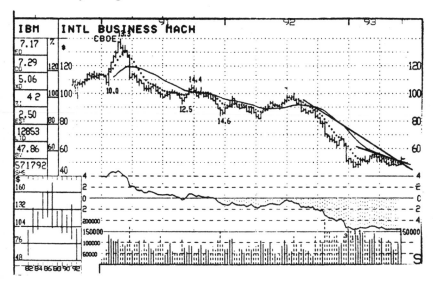

IBM has subsequently spent considerable trading time in this area (a lot more than MO has), and is now, as we write, "breaking out" across a couple of decent downtrend lines *and* its longer-term M.A. line, too. There's a nearby target of 55 (the good-bye-Akers rally) and a slew of resistance overhead in the same area as MOs—the low 60s. That looks like a reasonable objective, and would, as MO would, serve as a means of seducing sideliners back into the market. Only Scrooge would want to scowl at a DJIA rise led by IBM and Phillip Morris.

But MO has no base, and can do little more than a relatively impotent rise. Lots of people would like to buy, even if only to average down, which is—isn't it?—like a couple getting back together one last time before the divorce. Nor can IBM be in the forefront of anything more than just a rally, although bigger and better than MOs. Its days of being in, or beginning again, a long-term uptrend are as over as Data General's, Tandem's, Unisys's, DEC's, Amdhl's (remember that one?), et. al., but it sure does look like a good trade!

It may be that we are pipe-dreaming…that MO and IBM can only manage to do 55 or 56. Sometime we think the rally is going to be better than expected; at other times, worse. But whenever and wherever they've accomplished their seductions, it will show in the sentiment statistics. The old leadership, the old darlings, will "lead" only by making the market, and the Dow itself, look romantically better. Plastic surgeons will understand.

So where are we now? Well, in the stock market "now" is an ever-changing situation—it's a "continuous auction market" (to quote the exchange). IBM continued to do more basing work, and MO seemed to. Both have been subject to the desire to buy such fallen angels (or "aging gigolos") at what looked like low prices. Here are our updated chart readings *as of July 4, 1994.* You'll have the benefit of hindsight, and can identify our imperfections, but read these comments not to judge but to gain experience in chart analysis and forecasting:

IBM: What had looked like a base instead turned into a symmetrical triangle pattern from which—in the summer of '93—the stock actually broke down! There was all sorts of talk about IBM cutting its dividend again, and a price of 35, the downside measurement of that triangle, was also talked about by fundamentalists as a "reasonable" valuation level. But that was all the selling there was to be. It proved to be one of those triangles that break in one direction, shake the last remnants of weak holders out, and then reverse into the direction it really wanted to go. IBM moved rather easily back up all the way to 60.

The Mansfield chart makes that entire area look like a base, a much bigger one than before. A twin pullback to base support at 52 scared nervous holders, but the stock held right where it was supposed to, and then, on big volume, shot upward again into the 60s where everyone got (too) comfortable...precisely as IBM neared an area of some resistance.

Can the stock go higher? It should, although, as we write this IBM has begun to trade sloppily back down "too" far, too far meaning it should have held better than it seems to be doing. (These are the "Princess and the Pea" nuances that become so important as they accrue.) We'd use a protective "stop" at 51 1/2.

If it survives this particular flop, there is little further identifiable resistance until we get all the way back up to IBM's major breakdown level in the low- to mid-80s. We want to call your attention to our snide remarks about other computer stocks in the above reprinted Letters; stocks can and do have big *intervening* rises within major downtrends. Memorex doubled from 50 to 100 before disappearing, while Digital Equipment from 50 to 80, and then from 30 to 50, is only the most recent example. It takes a long time for great institutions to die (see the British Empire and the New York Stock Exchange). We believe that *if* IBM is able to rise to the 80s, *that's all it is capable of accomplishing,* and that kind of rise would be *nothing more than a classic "half-way" back rebound within an on-going bear trend.*

That makes us a seller in the mid-80s and a nervous holder as we write this, because IBM has become a highly speculative stock.

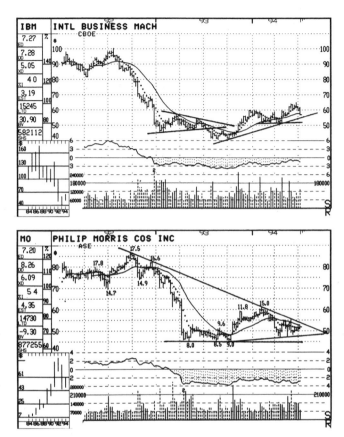

Philip Morris: Here's a difficult chart to "read"—the lack of good stocks to buy during the spring of '94; the desire to catch a well-known stock near its lows *if* it is going to be okay again; the guessing game as to whether the sum of tobacco and food companies, if eventually split asunder, would add up to more than the way the company is viewed now, have all made MO a turbulent situation. Keep in mind that the big gap breakdown in the spring of 1993 came from the low 60s—the low at that time was 60 1/2—so that area represents considerable resistance, confirmed when it repelled two assaults on that level. Following that failure,

MO came all the way back down (twice) to under 48 before buyers showed up. Trying to anticipate corporate rumors proved fruitless.

The result of all of this superficial buying interest has produced a longer-term weekly chart with a heavy, burdensome feel. After that failure at 60, the long-term Moving Average line has been rolling over again and is heading downward. This chart shows a lot of resistance sitting right on top of MO's attempt to stabilize. Who needs such a stock? How often does a long marriage, a messy divorce, and a trying to get back together again really work out? But that's essentially what rooting for Philip Morris to be a long-term buy-hold is, and explains why the action has become so ambivalent. A new low—that is, breaking 45—may seem unlikely intellectually, but quite feasible in terms of this chart. Alternatively, a move across 55—crossing that major downtrend line, and exceeding the previous rally high—would improve this shaky chart. Such either/or charts are often not worth the worry. We'd rather be somewhere else with our money, looking for a new love, so to speak—trying to make our money back in a better, stronger, more trustworthy stock.

About the Author

*J*ustin Mamis currently writes his weekly *Mamis Letter* for Hancock Institutional Equity Services—a joint venture of Sutro & Co. and Tucker Anthony. Quotes from the Mamis Letter appear frequently in *Barron's* and the Wall Street Journal, and his often heretical and usually grumpy comments can be heard from time to time on CNBC.

After serving as Assistant Director of the NYSE Floor Department, Justin Mamis founded and edited the *Professional Tape Reader* in 1972, selling it in 1977 to its current editor with thoughts of retirement. Instead, he spent several years as an "upstairs" Member-Trader for Phelan, Silver, a NYSE specialist firm, and subsequently settled into his role as market advisory letter writer, forecaster, and philosopher on behalf of Wertheim & Co., Cowen & Co., and then Gordon Capital. He is now Senior Vice President and Chief Market Technician at Hancock—"chief" meaning he has an assistant. Since 1988, he has been voted each year to the *Institutional Investor* "All-Star Team" in the categories of Market Timing and Market Technician.

In addition to the original edition of *When to Sell* (1977), Justin Mamis has written *How to Buy* (Farrar, Straus, & Giroux, 1981) and *The Nature of Risk - Stock Market Survival & the Meaning of Life* (Addison-Wesley, 1992).